STICKY FINGERS

MANAGING THE GLOBAL RISK OF ECONOMIC ESPIONAGE

STEVEN FINK

Dearborn™
Trade Publishing
A **Kaplan Professional** Company

Vice President and Publisher: Cynthia A. Zigmund
Editorial Director: Donald J. Hull
Senior Acquisitions Editor: Jean Iversen
Senior Project Editor: Trey Thoelcke
Interior Design: Lucy Jenkins
Cover Design: Design Alliance, Inc.
Typesetting: Elizabeth Pitts

Library of Congress Cataloging-in-Publication Data

Fink, Steven.
    Sticky fingers : managing the global risk of economic espionage / Steven Fink.
        p. cm.
    Includes index.
    ISBN 0-7931-4827-8
    1. Business intelligence—United States. 2. Trade secrets—United States. I. Title.
    HD38.7 .F56 2002
    658.4'72—dc21

                                                          2001005330

DEDICATION

For Harriet and Amanda

Two accomplished thieves
who have stolen all the trade secrets of my heart.
With love.

"Economic espionage and trade secret theft threaten our nation's national security and economic well being."

President Bill Clinton
Upon signing the Economic Espionage Act
October 11, 1996

"Economic espionage is the greatest threat to our national security since the Cold War."

FBI Director Louis Freeh
Two-and-a-half years later

CONTENTS

SECTION ONE Uncle Sam Needs You!
Globalization and the Economic Espionage Crisis

1. STICKY FINGERS—The Beginning of the End 3

Proof positive that a spy was in Avery Dennison's midst. How the lengthy crime spree—the nation's largest economic espionage case ever—began to unfold.

2. A Nation at War 7

The staggering cost of economic espionage to American businesses.

The steps the United States is taking to combat this threat to national security.

How globalization puts every company at higher risk.

3. STICKY FINGERS—Anatomy of a Spy 19

What motivates a trusted employee to betray an employer's trust and commit economic espionage? Victor Lee's story, and the lucky fluke that ultimately exposed him.

4. National Security versus Foreign Policy 35

If economic espionage is the biggest threat to national security since the Cold War, why isn't the United States doing more to protect American businesses from the threat of economic espionage from abroad? Three major obstacles.

Everyone spies—even our most trusted allies. A list of countries that spy.

Does the United States commit economic espionage? The Echelon controversy.

SECTION TWO Loose Lips Sink Ships!
Fighting Economic Espionage on the Home Front

28. Reducing Economic Espionage Risks 283

Too many companies spend too much money protecting the wrong things.

Economic espionage committed by insiders.

What companies are—and are not—doing to reduce risks.

Lessons for you and your company.

29. STICKY FINGERS—The Verdicts 287

Was justice actually served?

Afterword   EEA: Bear Trap or Mouse Trap? 293

Has the EEA succeeded? Has it been the bear trap the FBI promised, or has it been little more than a mouse trap?

Some final thoughts.

AUTHOR'S NOTE

As this book was being prepared for publication, terrorists struck the United States when four commercial airliners were hijacked on September 11, 2001. Two planes were flown into New York's World Trade Center towers, one into the Pentagon, and one crashed in rural Pennsylvania when a handful of passengers apparently thwarted a fourth terrorist attack on a site in Washington, D.C.

In response to these heinous attacks, an unprecedented outpouring of sympathy toward the United States came from people and nations around the world. And, in a crisis-prompted reversal of its previous tilt toward unilateralism, the Bush administration immediately began putting together a multilateral coalition of nations to fight the war on terrorism.

This book—originally written some six months before the tragedy—contains a chapter called "Fear and Loathing in the Workplace, Fear and Loathing in the World." The chapter takes President George W. Bush to task for being an isolationist in an era of globalization, for putting America's interests first, and for turning his back on some of the world's proposed solutions to global problems, such as the Kyoto accord. One of my contentions is that such actions— along with other causes detailed in that chapter and elsewhere throughout the book—have created an atmosphere of fear and loathing among many nations and businesses of the world toward America. These negative attitudes have led, and continue to lead, to widespread economic espionage against U.S. businesses.

To be sure, the terrorist attacks that were so pointedly directed at our nation's business, economic, and military symbols were themselves expressions of that fear and loathing, but carried to unimaginable and despicable extremes. Despite those attacks, our banner yet waves, and our businesses—repositories of the world's most coveted trade secrets—still flourish.

To that very point, when President Bush addressed a joint session of Congress—and the world—on September 20, 2001, he said, "Terrorists attacked a symbol of American prosperity. They did not touch its source. America is successful because of the hard work and creativity and enterprise of our people. These were the true strengths of our economy before September 11 and they are our strengths today."

I firmly believe that because those economic strengths still thrive, the fear and loathing I originally identified as contributing causes of economic espionage against American businesses remain so. This is true notwithstanding the recent outpouring of world concern and compassion toward America. We may have the support of the community of nations today to fight a war on terrorism, but economic espionage is a different type of ongoing global conflict. It is a scourge that will not be derailed by a contemporaneous battle against terrorism, no matter how many countries are behind us in *that* fight. As illustrated in the book, some of our staunchest, longtime allies are also the perpetrators of economic espionage against U.S. businesses.

Finally, I ask the reader to bear in mind that strong quotations in the book—such as former FBI Director Louis Freeh's calling "Economic espionage . . . the greatest threat to our national security since the Cold War"—were uttered prior to the terrorist attacks and should be considered in that context. The question, though, is not whether Mr. Freeh would use the same words today; but rather, whether economic espionage remains as much an attack on our national security, our economic well-being and our way of life even in the face of the terrorism that befell us on September 11. The answer is a resolute "Yes"—and perhaps even more so.

As I write this message a scant 10 days after the terrorist attacks on America, no one knows what the future holds and whether more terrorism is in store for us or for others. I pray that torment never happens again.

Steven Fink
Los Angeles, California
September 21, 2001

INTRODUCTION

The only thing necessary for economic espionage to flourish is a business with at least one employee, or at least one competitor.

Either can put a company at serious risk for economic espionage and possible ruin. One lone, nefarious employee can steal your trade secrets today and go into business against you tomorrow; a single competitor can steal the fruits of your expensive research and development efforts and undercut you in the marketplace.

Huge Risks for Companies of All Sizes

Virtually *no* company is immune to the risk of economic espionage. If you think economic espionage happens only to the *Fortune* 500 giants who have huge secrets to steal and operate on a global basis, think again; while *all* companies are at risk, the biggest victims of economic espionage are typically smaller businesses. Why? Because these companies have the largest number of competitors, which translates into the largest number of possible spies. You also need to know that globalization has raised your profile significantly. This may very well put you squarely in the crosshairs of someone's espionage scope. Economic espionage, without question, is the single largest crisis facing American businesses today, and globalization has only compounded it.

The question is: Can anything be done to stop economic espionage? Stop it, no; stem it, yes.

And I think it's important that you know that up front. In fact, I think it's important that we define our terms early so we both know what we can expect of each other.

Coming to Terms with Economic Espionage

The first term to define is *economic espionage* itself. A lengthy congressional definition of the term comes later in the book, and we'll yawn our way through it just to be thorough, but it really doesn't get much more complicated than this: If your company has confidential "secret" information—legally referred to as a *trade secret,* which is one type of intellectual property—that has independent economic value, which you have made a reasonable effort to keep secret, and someone (such as one of your competitors) illegally gets a copy of it, you have been victimized by economic espionage.

It doesn't matter whether we're talking about chemical formulas, patent applications, marketing plans, business expansion plans, customer lists, pricing information, new product launch information, production schedules, new technology drawings, new customer prospect lists, old customer lists, and on and on. If the information fits the description in the preceding paragraph and somebody steals it from you, you are a victim of economic espionage.

Since the passage of the Economic Espionage Act in 1996 (EEA), the FBI splits hairs because of its own internal bureaucracy. The Bureau defines *economic espionage* as that which is carried out by foreign *governments* against U.S. businesses, and *industrial espionage* as theft of trade secrets carried out by foreign or domestic *companies* against other businesses. The reason for the hairsplitting has to do with which of two FBI divisions investigates the crimes: the National Security Division or the Criminal Investigative Division. Although, even within the FBI, divisional crossovers occur.

But let's be crystal clear: For our purposes, the term for both activities, which fall unmistakably under the EEA, is *economic espionage.*

In contrast, *corporate espionage,* sometimes referred to as competitive intelligence gathering, can be carried out to gain knowledge— from open source documents for instance—and is not considered economic espionage or any sort of crime. In fact, companies engage in corporate espionage and other competitive intelligence gathering all the time without breaking any laws. Increasingly, though, recipients of valuable business information attempt to delude law enforcement authorities and themselves that the information in their possession is merely the fruits of "competitive intelligence," when, in truth, the harvest has crossed the line deep into economic espionage territory.

While some corporate espionage and competitive intelligence can be harmful to companies, economic espionage is far more serious and certainly more costly. Former FBI Director Louis Freeh called economic espionage the biggest threat to our national security since the Cold War.[1] It is so common—and so costly—it is frightening. In fact, economic espionage should be likened to a war—a war that we must win at all costs.

Using military slogans and rallying cries, I have divided this book into two main sections: In much the same way that the United States rallied Americans' sense of patriotism during World War II, Section One, "Uncle Sam Needs You!: Globalization and the Economic Espionage Crisis," is a broad, macro view of economic espionage. It demonstrates how globalization has made all businesses—especially U.S. businesses—more vulnerable to economic espionage.

Section Two, "Loose Lips Sink Ships!" a WWII message reminding U.S. workers to maintain security by being careful what they said and to whom, is about fighting economic espionage on the home front in the United States, where the largest threats loom. This section covers a wide range of plans and strategies all companies can employ to protect their trade secrets from economic espionage.

You or your business may already have been victimized and not even know it. Unlike a bullet wound that causes instant pain and external bleeding, economic espionage is more like a cancer that causes delayed pain and internal bleeding. It often takes a long time for a victimized company to even know it's hemorrhaging, because it doesn't see the "blood."

This book will show you how to manage the relentless global risk you face every day from economic espionage. I did not design the book to show you how to commit economic espionage, and if you get any ideas on your own from reading this book, consider that an unintended consequence. Frankly, it is not possible to discuss economic espionage candidly and not reveal how crimes were committed, and I won't shirk from that commentary.

Economic espionage, as you'll see, is a business crisis and should be treated as such. My primary consulting business is helping client companies manage crisis situations. In most cases, my crisis management clients come to me already victimized by someone or some company who has figured out how to commit the economic espionage. They seek my services to help manage their crises reactively and all of the many risks associated with those crises. And, with economic espionage on a steady rise, they frequently hire me to train them and to help them figure out how to reduce their risk of potential economic espionage *before* it happens.

Sticky Fingers covers both the before and after aspects of economic espionage. The "after" is extremely important and is often overlooked, because even after the espionage has been committed and discovered, there are still enormous risks for the victimized company. "What do we do *now?*" "Is it better for us to go public, report it to the FBI, or just sweep it under the carpet?" In many cases, some of the most serious risks to a company occur *after* the espionage has been discovered, and we'll examine why.

In trying to stem the risk of economic espionage, we will look at what individual companies can do, and also what governments around the world are doing. The United States passed the EEA at the strong urging of the FBI as a way to fight against economic espionage from home and abroad. Was it necessary? Has it been successful so far? We'll look at the EEA, warts and all, and draw some conclusions that will be helpful if you ever have to weigh the risks and consequences of reporting an act of economic espionage to the FBI—an action that many say actually increases a company's risk.

The Landmark Avery Dennison/Four Pillars Spy Case

Interwoven throughout both sections of the book, I will give you an up-close look at the largest economic espionage case to date, the Avery Dennison/Four Pillars spy case. I was intimately involved from beginning to end in this truly landmark case, which was the nation's first to go to trial under the EEA. One important reason to read the details of the groundbreaking Avery Dennison case is to learn how easy it is to be betrayed by a trusted employee, and how treacherous, costly, and wholly unexpected—and undetected—acts of economic espionage can occur right under management's nose. In fact, as you will learn in this book, most economic espionage crimes are committed by company insiders, sometimes involving foreign interests. In an age of globalization, there are more buyers in the world for ill-gotten trade secrets. Plus, certain economic events are happening right now in the world that are putting all businesses at even greater risk, and we'll examine a few.

Before getting started, a word is in order about the style and convention used throughout the Avery Dennison/Four Pillars story and the book as a whole, and the important Constitutional right that an accused is considered innocent unless and until proven guilty. When you read about the recipients of Avery Dennison's trade secrets, know that at the time this book is being written, the Four Pillars company and its executives have been tried and convicted in a criminal trial and found liable in a civil trial. Their main accuser has pled guilty to his own crimes and testified against them and their complicity at two separate trials. Nevertheless, keep in mind that our criminal justice system allows for appeals. The same holds true for other individuals and companies mentioned in other cases, some of which were breaking as this book was being prepared for publication. It is my intention to provide any relevant updates on economic espionage cases that I could not include in this book on my company's Web sites, <www.crisismanagement.com> and <www.economicespionage.com>.

With these caveats, in reading about the Avery Dennison/Four Pillars case, you will, I hope, come away with a better understanding, appreciation, and respect of economic espionage from the perspectives of the spy, the spy's "masters," the victimized company, the FBI, and the Justice Department prosecutors. The Avery Dennison spy case, perhaps more than any other, can show companies the perils and profits of managing the global risk of economic espionage—before, during, and after the crisis.

My premise is simply this: Companies are under attack and at enormous risk every day from the global threat of economic espionage, but that risk can and should be lowered and managed. Here's how.

Uncle Sam Needs You!

GLOBALIZATION AND THE ECONOMIC ESPIONAGE CRISIS

"Economic espionage is so pervasive that it cuts across national boundaries. Its impact undermines U.S. national security and our very way of life."

–National Counterintelligence Center

CHAPTER 1

STICKY FINGERS
The Beginning of the End

Victor silently entered his boss's office. Cautiously, he looked around to make sure he was alone, glanced out the window, closed the blinds, then slipped on heavy, black, winter gloves. Slowly, he made his way over to the file cabinet where he very quietly opened one of the drawers and furtively peered inside. The document he sought was still there. But then, he quickly closed the drawer and fled the room.

Did he hear something that made him withdraw so suddenly? Did he have a change of heart concerning what he was about to do? Whatever caused him to retreat so abruptly, it did not deter him from his ultimate mission.

He returned in a short while, again wearing gloves, and locked the door. He opened the file cabinet and withdrew the highly sensitive strategic business plan outlining his employer's top secret expansion plans in the Far East. Victor inspected the document more closely. It was marked CONFIDENTIAL *and* For Internal Eyes Only. *It would be well received by another company–a company that was paying him to steal. It was, he thought, gold.*

He left his boss's office with the document carefully tucked under his arm to review or copy the plan. Then, he returned the original document to the file cabinet and casually went home to his wife and daughter on a cold, wintry Ohio evening in January 1997. Another job well done, he thought.

Except for three details of which he was unaware.

First, his employer was already suspicious that Victor was stealing company trade secrets. Little did they suspect at that time, however, what and how much Victor had actually stolen and over what an extraordinary length of time.

Second, the document he stole that afternoon was created specifically for him as bait and planted as part of a government-led sting operation under the then-new Economic Espionage Act of 1996.

And third, a hidden FBI surveillance camera was silently videotaping Victor's every move. The document Victor stole was not gold; it was dynamite that was about to blow up in his face and send shockwaves through corporate boardrooms and businesses around the world.

Victor is Tenhong "Victor" Lee, Ph.D., a Taiwan-born, U.S.-educated chemical engineer.[1] At the time, he worked as a Senior Research Engineer at Avery Dennison, a $3.9 billion *Fortune* 500 company initially best known for its ubiquitous self-adhesive products, such as "Hello, My Name Is" labels, and now considered the world's largest office products company. Dr. Lee was one of the world's foremost and respected authorities in the highly technical, arcane specialty of rheology—the measurement and science of how well labels stick to, and peel off of, a wide variety of surfaces. He had been a highly valued and trusted employee at Avery Dennison's Concord, Ohio, research facility for 11 years . . . and he had been picking the company's pockets clean for eight.

During those eight years—from approximately 1989 to 1997—Dr. Lee actually served another "master," Four Pillars Enterprise Co., Ltd., of Taipei, Taiwan, and its aging founder and CEO, Pin Yen "P.Y." Yang.[2] Four Pillars became one of Avery Dennison's leading competitors in the Asian market. And, dangerously, Four Pillars' owners and management apparently did not hesitate to steal from its rival, according to criminal and civil trials that unfolded in this case.

In certain ever growing global circles, stealing trade secrets from a competitor is viewed as simply more cost efficient than spending one's own time and money on actual research and development. And when you consider that during just the last three to four years of Dr. Lee's disloyal activities, Avery Dennison had spent some $200 million on research and development—as compared to Four Pillars' eight annual payments to Dr. Lee totaling a paltry $160,000—there is much to be said for the *balance sheet* side of that argument, ethics and the law aside.

In fact economic espionage—for an ever growing immoral universe in an ever shrinking world of globalization—seems to make sound business sense to those to whom ethics and legalities have no meaning.

CHAPTER 2

A Nation at War

"It's where the money is."

—Willie Sutton's legendary response when asked why he robbed banks

From computer chips to potato chips, record labels to sticky labels, optical lasers to safety razors, and everything in between, intellectual property—some might say American ingenuity itself—is widely recognized as *the* driving force behind America's individual and collective success stories in the last century.

But people—*spies*—companies, and even countries are after *your company's* property.

Economic espionage cost U.S. businesses anywhere from $45 billion to as much as $250 billion annually, according to recent survey statistics.[1] In the 1980s alone, the total cost of economic espionage to U.S. businesses was the mind-numbing sum of $1.2 *trillion,* according to the American Society for Industrial Security and federal government sources. The figures for the last decade of the 20th century are estimated to be even higher. The reason for the stunning rise in economic espionage and its colossal cost to businesses is simple: mountainous accumulations of tempting trade secrets that constitute the vast intellectual property achievements of U.S. companies.

More than 56 percent of the *Fortune* 1000 admit to having been victimized,[2] and more than likely, a considerable portion of the other 44 percent are either too reticent to admit it or simply haven't yet discovered that they, too, have been targeted and/or victimized by corporate spies and thieves.

America's nationwide economic espionage crisis is unique in several respects. It represents the first time a crisis of such mammoth proportions has been acknowledged to affect *every* company in *every* industry group without exception and *at the same time.*

Without question, economic espionage is a gargantuan growth industry and one of the biggest crises to hit U.S. businesses *en masse* in history. And in an age of globalization, economic espionage gets bigger and easier to commit every day.

When, in 1999, then FBI Director Louis Freeh called economic espionage the most severe threat to our nation's security since the Cold War, he went on to claim that U.S. companies are under constant economic attack from foreign countries, stating that in the mid-1990s, FBI investigations uncovered "23 countries engaged in economic espionage activities against the United States."[3]

But former U.S. Congressman Dave McCurdy, who served as chair of the House Intelligence Committee, thinks Freeh grossly understated the problem and that the 23 include only industrialized countries. McCurdy believes 100 of the world's 173 nations are actively waging economic espionage against U.S. businesses. "The question is not who steals," McCurdy said. "It's who doesn't steal."[4]

Stealing Trade Secrets Is Not New

Trade secrets and attempts to protect them are as old as trade itself. Chinese emperors thousands of years ago sought to protect the secrets of China's lucrative and monopolistic silk production from the outside world, going so far as to impose the sentence of death by torture to any who would try to pilfer the secret production methods. Eventually, the secret made it beyond the Chinese Wall, when a royal princess married a prince from another country and shared the secrets of silk production and fiber weaving as part of her dowry. When silk production started up in other parts of Asia and the Middle East, and vast fortunes followed, China's monopoly on its trade secret ended.

Even in the United States, concern over economic espionage is longstanding. Our Founding Fathers considered the protection of trade secrets and all forms of intellectual property so important to our national well-being that Article I, Section 8 of the U.S. Constitution empowers Congress to make laws to protect inventors and their discoveries and other forms of intellectual property.

Two aspects to this section are noteworthy: first, that it even exists in a document that was originally written more than 200 years ago (even though it took that long to pass a specific trade secrets protection law), and second, that it is placed so high up in the Constitution that it is even ahead of the duties of the President.

Why? According to Professor James Chandler, president of the National Intellectual Property Law Institute, "Without protection of its intellectual property, a nation will die."[5]

But that doesn't mean that the United States has clean hands. One of the nation's earliest documented cases of economic espionage involved the American Francis Cabot Lowell who, in 1811, traveled to Scotland and England to steal the secret plans for the famed Cartwright loom, an ingenious and superproductive water-powered loom that, according to writer John J. Fialka, was "the crown jewel of the British textile industry."[6] This ingenious weaving device was capable of turning out wholesale quantities of high-quality finished wool and cotton, and it meant to the British what silk meant to the Chinese thousands of years earlier. It had, in effect, helped launch the Industrial Age and generated enormous wealth for the people of rural Britain. So important was the economic advantage of these water-driven looms—which replaced the slow, traditional, hand-manipulated looms—that in the late 1780s, England passed legislation preventing the export of such technology from its shores. This was an antieconomic espionage act, by intent if not by name. And, while it stopped short of China's death by torture threat, it was a strong deterrent.

But not strong enough for Lowell, who somehow successfully managed to either pilfer or memorize the plans, and to duplicate the technology upon his return to New England. How significant was this lone act of economic espionage? It did nothing less than help start the Industrial Revolution in the United States, which directly fueled the previously inert economic engine of the North. This prosperity ultimately helped defeat the South in the Civil War a half century later. Lowell's espionage further advanced America's ability to compete head-to-head with Britain in the all-important burgeoning textile industry, forcing England to lower its formerly monopolistic textile prices. Without any regrets or apologies, Lowell stole what Fialka called "England's most valuable secret" at that time.[7]

Let's not mince words: The town of Lowell, Massachusetts, is named for a spy and a thief.

Knickers Deep in Espionage

Why did Lowell commit economic espionage? He was a wealthy man from a wealthy family. He didn't need British technology to make a living, let alone survive. He wasn't destitute. Why did he steal? What motivates an individual or a company to commit economic espionage?

By being able to produce massive quantities of high-quality cotton goods faster and at cheaper prices than any other country in the world, England controlled the global textile industry. Every other country was at the mercy of the Crown.

Maybe, with the American Revolution still fresh in Lowell's mind, he did not want to resubmit himself or his country to a new yoke of tyranny or dominance of any kind by his former Colonists. Lowell, by the way, was not the only American at that time knickers-deep in economic espionage. Such textbook luminaries as Alexander Hamilton and Thomas Jefferson, when the latter was ambassador to France, were also known to have engaged in various covert acts designed to bring British trade secrets to America.[8] In those cases, one could possibly argue that patriotism was the motivating force, but if any drop of red, white, or blue blood courses through your veins as a way of turning a blind, patriotic eye in favor of the perpetrators, hold that thought when we look at other countries—yes, countries!—

that engage in or sponsor wholesale economic espionage against Uncle Sam.

When Lowell went strolling in the British countryside to see what information he could pick up, he had to scale some walls, literally and figuratively. In addition to the charming stone walls that line the lanes of the Cotswolds in rural England, Lowell had to scale the "walls" that England, like most countries over the years, had put up at its borders to protect itself, its ideologies, and its trade secrets. In fact, until recently, most countries had walls, and in one way or another, these barriers were designed to keep certain aspects of each country somewhat isolated. But in 1989, everything changed.

As Thomas Friedman explains in *The Lexus and the Olive Tree*, when the Berlin Wall fell, walls all over the world fell, too. What resulted is what Friedman calls "the democratizations of technology, finance, and information—which have changed how we communicate, how we invest, and how we look at the world."[9] In other words, the birth of true globalization.

Ideological Winds versus Sunshine

My father used to read me a fable about the sun and the wind arguing over which one was stronger. They decided only a contest could settle the dispute. Seeing a man wearing a cloak walking along a country lane, the wind said to the sun, "I bet I can remove that cloak." "I bet you can't, but that I can," replied the sun.

The wind went first and began to blow—harder and harder, trying to blow the cloak from the man's shoulders, and very nearly succeeding. But the stronger the wind blew, and the darker the angry sky became, the tighter the man clasped the cloak around his neck and lowered his head into the wind as he bravely trudged on. After a while, the wind gave up, admitting defeat. "Let's see you try," said the wind. And the sun began to shine—brighter and brighter, hotter and hotter—until the man was so warm he removed the cloak himself.

What felled the Berlin Wall was not so much the strong gale of ideological winds as the bright, hot light of information.

Aided in huge measure by the Internet, people behind walls all over the world began to see what had been kept from them for so many years and decided they'd had enough. They wanted their piece of the pie. The Berlin Wall—literally and figuratively—collapsed from internal pressures, brought about by external information, knowledge, and awareness. And other walls around the world quickly followed suit. In political psychology, this is called the Revolution of Rising Expectations. In economic espionage, I call this the Revolution of the Have-Nots, and it shows no signs of weakening.

"The world has become an increasingly interwoven place," says Friedman, "and today, whether you are a company or a country, your threats and opportunities increasingly derive from who you are connected to."[10] I agree with Friedman, but would add this: When we talk about economic espionage, the threats derive not only from connections, but from who merely knows about you, too. With globalization, one company just knowing about your company—even if you have never heard of them—makes you two connected, especially if the other company has you targeted for economic espionage.

Friedman goes on to define globalization in a way that is most relevant for our discussion as "the inexorable integration of markets, nation-states, and technologies to a degree never witnessed before—in a way that is enabling the world to reach farther, faster, deeper, cheaper than ever before. This process of globalization is also producing a powerful backlash from those brutalized or left behind by this new system."[11] One such backlash is an increase in economic espionage by those who fear being left too far behind.

In a national business story on economic espionage, *USA Today* reporter Del Jones wrote, "Even governments of U.S. allies look the other way, or even sponsor the espionage . . . . Seeing the USA thriving in an economically troubled world, [these countries] fear falling behind in technology and efficiency. Theft is seen as necessary to level the playing field."[12]

"As a consequence," according to Freeh, "foreign governments, through a variety of means, actively target U.S. persons, firms, industries, and the U.S. government itself, to steal or wrongfully obtain critical technologies, data, and information in order to provide their own industrial sectors with a competitive advantage."[13]

Shifting Paradigms

MIT Professor Dr. Robert Solow, in a study on economic growth for which he was awarded the 1987 Nobel Prize in Economics, concluded that during approximately the first half of the last century, some 90 percent of our nation's increase in economic output was the direct result of technological change and advancements. Thus, as our nation's knowledge base has increased so, too, has the country's per capita income. Professor Chandler, an economic espionage authority, observes "that economic growth is demonstrably linked to the production of intellectual property."[14]

But Chandler warns, "[T]here is now a grave threat directed against American industry. That threat is economic espionage, the clandestine theft of business trade secrets. These thefts threaten both the life of industry and the economic health of our nation."[15]

The United States is the undisputed leader in the creation of intellectual property, spending ten times more on R&D than any other country in the world. In fact, we spend more money on research than all of the other G-7 powerhouse nations (Canada, Japan, Britain, France, Germany, and Italy) *combined,*[16] as every conceivable industry group and business enterprise fiercely compete to bring new products and services to the global marketplace at an ever faster rate. The further the United States rockets ahead, the further in the dust we leave someone, and the more desperate they are to catch up.

Those who are left behind—and those who fear being left behind—must seek ways to catch up. But if you've been behind a wall for so many years, how do you catch up quickly? How do you get in the game? How do you become competitive? What avenues are open to you as a company or, in many cases, as a country?

"There is little surprise . . . that other nations and their businesses have targeted the United States, its secret laboratories, and its business secrets as essential sources of new scientific and new technological information," said Chandler, who considers our nation's intellectual property as nothing less than "critical natural resources"[17] that are at serious risk.

Let's face it, the paradigms have shifted dramatically. Once, we catalogued the world by such contrasts as friends versus enemies, democracies versus dictatorships, free market systems versus Communism, the United States versus the former Soviet Union, and North America versus Europe and Asia. Since the fall of the Berlin Wall, the new paradigm makes us all simply *competitors.* Where we are located no longer matters. All that matters is, can we play the game? Can we compete? What do we have to do (or *steal*) to remain competitive?

The New Geography

As a definition and a function of competitive business territories, maps are fairly meaningless in a world of globalization. Geography, in many ways, is a subject taught in school. Where a business is located is a fairly moot point, except in the case of getting goods to market. The only essential question is: Can the business operate globally?

In 1999, I took a telephone call in my Los Angeles office from a prospective manufacturing client in Tennessee. The communication quickly evolved into a flurry of e-mails. This company was expecting a specific crisis to befall it and was inquiring about my firm's crisis management and crisis communications services, and our ability to get the company geared up and media-trained. The client was very parochial in terms of geography: The CEO's 20th-century thinking maintained that a California crisis had to be handed by a local firm. In reality, my clients are located all over the world, and I frequently find myself on airplanes flying to see a client or handle a crisis in remote locales. I took this assignment and was able to manage the issues in Tennessee while traveling on an extended European trip with my laptop computer. As it happened, none of the work for this client was actually performed in Los Angeles.

A Dangerous Backlash of Envy

Unless you're delivering morning milk to a customer's door, or need to be closer to your customers to reduce shipping costs, geographical proximity to your clients, customers, or competitors doesn't mean what it used to. And that increases both your opportunities as well as your risks.

If we can conduct legitimate business globally via the Internet as easily as if we were sitting in the same office, those who engage in economic espionage can do so as well. Time zones mean nothing; maps mean nothing; geography means nothing; walls don't exist anymore.

"In the globalization system," says Friedman, "the United States is now the sole and dominant superpower, and all other nations are subordinate to it to one degree or another."[18] The more we brag about how much money we spend as a nation on research, the more crosshairs in which we find ourselves. The boastful expenditure of the nation's vast resources makes *all* U.S. companies lucrative, high-profile targets of economic espionage from perpetrators the world over. And, you're at risk even if you're not doing any of the bragging. The fact is, these technological innovations and the nation's unsurpassed growth have engendered a backlash of envy, greed, and larceny from all corners of the world. We shouldn't, therefore, be surprised that our companies are desirable targets of economic espionage, but these firms don't have to be easy marks, too. Sadly, though, they are. As a nation, we have been essentially unarmed and at serious risk—easy pickings for the crafty as well as the clumsy. And globalization puts U.S. companies even more at risk.

Risks Are Everywhere

While banks are sturdily built and staffed with alarm bells and armed guards to prevent holdups, people continue to commit armed bank robbery all the same. Mom and Pop convenience stores don't usually carry a lot of cash, but that doesn't keep them from being held up day in and day out. Just because you're a giant in your industry doesn't mean you're impregnable, and just because you're small doesn't mean you're not a target.

Regardless of whether you can be competitive on a global basis, the fact remains that others can be and are, and you need to deal with them and the threats they pose. Remember, too, that your threats of economic espionage are not just from the competitors you know about, but those you've never heard of and can't even see on your radar screen. Remember, in the age of globalization, we are all connected.

Assume for a moment you are a U.S.-based technological leader in your field of high-speed widgets. You've been featured on the cover of *Widget World Weekly* numerous times, bragging about how your latest state-of-the-art widget technology is going to revamp the entire widget industry. You think you know who all of your competitors are and, therefore, from where you may be vulnerable to economic espionage risks. But unless you think globally about economic espionage, you're probably wrong. And being wrong here could be costly, because if you don't see the risk, how can you guard against it? If a small, struggling, criminally minded widget maker in Asia or Europe needs a fast jump start, they may target you for economic espionage, even if you've never heard of them.

Chances are, economic espionage spies would follow Willie Sutton's timeless advice and try to steal new technology from the companies of the dominant superpower—the United States. It's where the money—and the technology—is.

And, even though I said that geography doesn't matter when it comes to stealing, a non-U.S. company has an added motivation to steal from an American firm: difficulty of criminal prosecution as well as civil litigation on foreign soil. Avery Dennison had to face this problem in the Four Pillars case, as we'll see later. So, while the distance doesn't stop a company from committing economic espionage, it can make it harder for you to go after your trade secrets and those who stole them.

If you're thinking, "I'm so big, nothing bad can happen to me from companies I've never heard of," you're very wrong. While we'll examine factors that motivate people, companies, and countries to steal, businesses intent on reducing or managing their risk of economic espionage need to be on guard from attacks from all possible sources—internal spies as well as from outlets they've never heard of.

Companies are under attack, plain and simple. Your company, and your country, is under constant unrelenting attack from forces domestic and foreign and from countries known and unknown, hell bent on stealing your most valuable business trade secrets.

Sometimes the criminals are independent, rogue employees, but other times the wrongdoers are heavily financed, well-equipped, sophisticated agents of competitors (foreign and domestic) and even foreign nations seeking to gain an unfair competitive advantage.

The economic espionage risks to your company are everywhere, across the street and across the globe. And you might want to worry most about the risks you can't readily see, along with those right under your nose. Like the guy on the next bench in the lab—that small, quiet, mild-mannered person you would least suspect of ever betraying your trust.

CHAPTER | 3

STICKY FINGERS
Anatomy of a Spy

When Victor Lee was called into his boss's small conference room on March 6, 1997–less than two months after he had been videotaped removing and photocopying that incriminating document–his boss was already sitting at the round conference table with three other gentlemen, who wore dark suits, white shirts, and ties. When Victor came in and was told to take a seat, his boss simply told him that these gentlemen have some questions for him. Then he left without saying another word.

Victor is short and slender, with gray-speckled black hair combed in wavy clumps across his forehead. He wears oversized, aviator-style, black-rimmed glasses, which seem to slip constantly halfway down his nose. His heavily accented English requires close concentration on the part of a listener. He took the offered seat and found himself sitting face to face with Michael Bartholomew, Special FBI Agent since 1985, and two other Special FBI Agents.[1]

At this point, the FBI actually knew very little. In late 1996, Avery Dennison had received a tip from a curious Taiwanese source that someone inside the company was sending secret formulas and other trade secrets to Four Pillars. The inside spy was never completely identified. Some internal sleuthing turned up Victor Lee as fitting a likely profile, but on March 6,

1997, all Special Agent Bartholomew had was a videotape of Dr. Lee taking a report from his boss's filing cabinet. What did that really prove?

Bartholomew is a beefy, self-effacing man in his 40s, with a likeable, nonthreatening face, neatly trimmed beard, and nearly bald head. He identified himself in his low-key voice, kept the conversation somewhat casual, and politely told Victor, "(W)e were involved in determining whether someone had gained unauthorized access to some information. I referred specifically to the business plan."[2]

Bartholomew intentionally kept the conversation broad, merely asking Victor when was the last time that he had actually seen the plan. He gave Victor no immediate reason to believe that he, himself, was under any suspicion. But guilt weighed heavily upon him.

Victor may have been an accomplished thief, but it didn't take too long for him to crack. He first said that he remembered seeing it just once during the January meeting, but not since. Bartholomew then shifted the focus to whether anyone else had access to it and Victor quickly coughed up some names. But the FBI agent then took Victor on an unexpected U-turn and asked him if there was any reason that his fingerprints might be on the document? This question made him nervous.

Victor insisted that he had never read it and spontaneously declared that he didn't even know what information was in the plan. He maintained that he was a "technical guy" and "did not know how to turn technical information into an economic benefit."[3]

Victor reviewed his situation and asked Bartholomew, the lead agent, if he could speak with him alone. The other agents left the room.

Alone with Bartholomew, Victor nervously asked, "How much trouble a person could be in who had done this sort of thing."[4]

Bartholomew explained the statutes involved, primarily dealing with Section 1832 of the Economic Espionage Act, theft of trade secrets, and that someone convicted of that crime could get up to ten years in prison. However, the agent and Victor had not yet discussed whether Victor had taken anything or not. The discussion at this point was purely hypothetical, but the Taiwanese scientist just didn't have the stomach for any more.

Victor took a deep breath and began to spill the beans.

Over the next three months, the FBI managed to extract Victor's incredible saga. The breadth and depth of his exploits shocked the FBI and officials at Avery Dennison. Most economic espionage spies limit their activities to one or two treasures or limited areas. Victor's courage had grown with each theft.

His full confession took nearly three months, as he eventually detailed the incredibly sensitive secret formulas, trade secrets, and proprietary technical information that he had passed on to Four Pillars over a span of eight long years.

Victor had essentially turned over to Four Pillars the crown jewels of Avery Dennison.

Seeds Are Planted

Why?

Why *did* Victor Lee commit economic espionage?

"Why?" is often a luxury question, meaning the answer may be informative and instructive, but because it doesn't alter the facts, it changes nothing. Taking the time to ferret out "why" to a question sometimes is a luxury you can't afford. In Victor's case, however, it might be helpful to know "why" if knowing helps other companies learn if they have any "Victors" on their own payrolls.

In many ways, Victor was a part of my life for nearly two years. During that time, I read his signed confession, watched hour after hour of videotape of him involved in an egregious act of economic espionage, and listened to every word of his testimony for more than a week in a packed federal courtroom in Youngstown, Ohio. Victor's story, in his own words, is designed to evoke sympathy. Judge for yourself, but remember, at the end of the day, he's still a confessed spy and a thief.

Victor was a poor boy, born in 1950 and raised on the hard scrabble streets of Taipei. His father died when the boy was three years old.[5]

As he worked his way through schools in Taiwan and abroad, money was never very plentiful. He was educated first at National Taiwan University, where he received a B.S. degree in chemical engineering in 1973. He came to the United States on a student visa and attended the University of Oklahoma, where he earned his M.S. degree in chemical engineering in 1978; then on to Texas Tech University for his Ph.D. in Chemical Engineering in 1982; and finally the University of Akron where he earned his M.S. in polymer science in 1986. He joined Avery on May 19, 1986 as a Research Associate in the firm's Concord, Ohio, facility at a starting salary of $33,600.[6]

Then, in 1989, Ta-ShenWang, a former classmate of his from Texas Tech University, invited Victor to deliver a talk on his work in the area of pressure-sensitive labels to the Industrial Technology Research Institute (IRTI) in Hsinchu, Taiwan. IRTI is a government-sponsored organization that has an affiliation with Taiwan's Department of Economics. Flattered, Victor accepted and traveled to Taiwan in early July, 1989. He neither told nor asked permission of his superiors to give the presentation. In the audience was T.W. Chong, an employee of Four Pillars Enterprises, one of Taiwan's leading companies.[7]

The next day, C.K. Kao, a Four Pillars vice president, who had heard of Victor's presentation from Chong, contacted the Avery Dennison scientist while he was still in Taiwan and invited him to deliver the same presentation to his company. Flattered again, he accepted and delivered the presentation the next day to a small group of Four Pillars officers and technical employees, including Hwei Chin "Sally" Yang.[8]

Unfortunately, Pin Yen "P.Y." Yang, the founder and chairman of Four Pillars, who happens to be Sally's father, was unable to attend that session. So, about two days later, Kao again contacted Victor and invited him to a small dinner party in a leading restaurant in Taipei. Victor was told the dinner was in his honor, but in reality the entire affair was arranged so that P.Y. and Victor could meet. Toward the end of the dinner, 71-year-old P.Y. invited Victor out on the balcony and put his arm around the young man's shoulders.

You are in a position to help us, P.Y. informed Victor in so many words. By sending us information we need, you could be a valuable consultant to us, and we would pay you well. P.Y. continued to talk, saying, "No one needs to know about this,"[9] while Victor listened attentively.

Although Victor never verbally agreed to do or send anything to Four Pillars, it is the acknowledged custom in Taiwan that silence indicates tacit acceptance. Victor did not say, "No."

The young scientist was now officially on the payroll of Four Pillars Enterprise Co., Ltd., of Taipei, Taiwan, and two days later he received a check for $25,000—at the time more than half of his annual Avery Dennison salary. The check was given to him by C.K. Kao at Four Pillars' San Chung City research and development facility.[10]

To cover its tracks, Four Pillars made the check payable to Victor's mother-in-law and had Victor deposit it into the bank account of his sister-in-law (without the sister-in-law's knowledge).[11] Four Pillars even remembered to deduct $1,500 for the 6 percent Taiwanese withholding tax[12]—a neat bit of bookkeeping that would come back to bite them when a convincing paper trail was displayed for jurors in Ohio. Oh, yes, Victor was definitely on the payroll.

Why?

Victor, once he began his months of confession and during his grueling six days of testimony in court, never wavered from the fact that he stole valuable, highly sensitive, highly confidential Avery Dennison trade secrets and shipped them to numerous people at Four Pillars. He said he agreed to be a consultant because *consultant* is a title of distinction and high honor in Taiwan. He said he agreed to help Four Pillars because he considered P.Y. the father he never had.

And while he is an acknowledged and confessed thief who must have curled the hair on the heads of Avery Dennison management and employees when they realized the full extent and length of Victor's treachery, he eventually maintained that he never did it for the money—although, according to Bartholomew, in their first meeting in March 1997, Victor painted a picture of abject poverty as a youth in Taipei and "was always concerned with never having to borrow money again."[13]

So, did he do it solely for the money? Probably not.

On the one hand, Four Pillars had cut the deal of a lifetime. In exchange for cutting edge technology and trade secrets worth perhaps hundreds of millions of dollars in saved research costs, which netted them who knows how many millions in undeserved profits according to trial testimony, Four Pillars paid Victor a total of $160,000 over eight years. That's so low—an average of $20,000 per year—that it should be frightening for any company to think that its most important secrets could be had for such a small bag of beans. Looked at this way, of course Victor didn't do it for the money. He could have asked for and received a king's ransom for the swag he sent.

On the other hand, when Victor was first approached by P.Y. in 1989, the young researcher was earning about $40,000. So the $25,000 paid to him initially by Four Pillars was 60 percent of his annual salary in one lump sum. Looked at that way, it is difficult to believe that money played no role.

Except for one thing: There is no evidence that Victor ever asked for *any* money, or for more money, at any time during his eight year crime spree. He took what he was given. Could it be that he didn't know the value of the material he sent? Oh, no—he absolutely knew.

In a July 31,1989 letter to P.Y. Yang, sent almost immediately upon his return to the States after being introduced to P.Y. and Four Pillars at that fancy dinner in Taipei, Victor wrote to his new benefactors that Fasson [an Avery Dennison division and the one where he worked] "has 40 percent to 45 percent share of the label market in the U.S. because it has a unique technical service department, which is absolutely an important key link and worth our learning." He went on to say in the same letter that "most" of the information he would provide would be "taken from Fasson/Avery, so please make sure to treat them [sic] as confidential material." Trying to make a good impression on his new Taiwanese employers, he closed by promising that he would do his "utmost to collect data" in order to "benefit Four Pillars."[14]

True to his word, two days later, Victor provided his initial shipment of material, which he characterized as the "first batch of data." This initial shipment included proprietary "mastercurves"—sort of like fingerprints of some of Avery Dennison's adhesive products— that could allow products to be cloned, provided you knew how to interpret the extremely technical information and could match it with the right formula. Victor also provided "a summary of his work in rheology between May 1986 [when he first started working at Avery Dennison] and April 1988."[15]

Less than a week later, Victor sent Four Pillars two highly technical rheology reports prepared by Dr. E.P. Chang of the Avery

Research Center. Dr. Chang, a senior research scientist in Avery's employ, is an internationally recognized expert in his highly technical field of rheology. The two reports, clearly stamped *CONFIDENTIAL*, were, Victor explained in his letter to Four Pillars, "extremely confidential" and constituted "the fruit of painstaking work of Avery Research Center over a period of years." The reports, as well as the two-year summary of Victor's work, were so technical that Victor did not expect Four Pillars to be able to decipher them completely, and so he promised "to explain in detail how to use these two reports" soon.[16]

How about his claim that being a consultant was a title of honor and that he agreed to help Four Pillars for "the honor"? Would that be a motivating factor? Hardly, because whom could he tell besides the handful of senior Four Pillars executives and research scientists who already knew? It's not as though he could have had business cards printed up that on one side listed him as a senior research scientist for Avery Dennison and on the other a paid consultant to Four Pillars.

Another consideration cannot be discounted: loyalty to his native country. If this likelihood has any merit—if it is possible for companies like Four Pillars or even countries to tap into the patriotic pride of its citizens laboring in technology-rich U.S. companies— then a frightening argument could be made that any company that employs someone born in a foreign country—or, perhaps, in *certain* foreign countries—runs a higher degree of risk of economic espionage. For what it's worth, Victor never copped a jingoistic plea.

I think it was ego and power that made him do it.

He began his espionage after working for Avery Dennison for only three years. At the time, he was a very small fish in a huge, 16,000-fish pond. But at Four Pillars, a much smaller company, one where they spoke his native language of Mandarin Chinese as well as Taiwanese (a specific Chinese dialect), he was the conquering hero, personally anointed by Mr. P.Y. Yang himself. And even though Victor rose over the years in the Avery Dennison research pantheon to the ultimate position of senior researcher engineer at a base salary just under $60,000, he could not have stopped spying even if he had wanted to, which he did not. The more his star shone in Ohio, the brighter his entire firmament in Taiwan.

You will meet other espionage spies in this book who stole for money, for greed, for revenge, for their native countries, or for opportunity.

But Victor is not one of these. Victor was on an eight-year ego trip that could have continued indefinitely, had it not been for the wrath of a scorned Four Pillars chemist named Dr. Jong "John" S. Guo.[17]

Pot Calling the Kettle Black

Avery Dennison and Four Pillars were not strangers to each other. They had tried to conduct business and even considered a joint venture around 1993. In fact, Four Pillars tried to use the anemic joint venture defense during their trial, claiming that what it was accused of stealing, Avery Dennison had actually freely passed across the table during lengthy joint venture discussions in Taiwan.

Avery Dennison had received the résumé of Dr. Guo, a talented young scientist at Four Pillars in Taiwan. There was no direct connection at all between Dr. Guo and Victor, and in fact, the two never met during any of Victor's numerous trips to Taiwan to brief Four Pillars on Avery Dennison secrets, but the name *Dr. Tenhong Lee* or just *Tenhong* was well known in Four Pillars as an almost mythic folk hero.

Dr. Prem Krish, one of Avery Dennison's research team leaders— and, strictly by coincidence, Victor's direct supervisor—was assigned to communicate with Guo and developed a good rapport with him. On May 15, 1996, Dr. Krish wrote to Dr. Guo in Taiwan and tendered a formal offer of employment as a research associate in Concord, Ohio, at a starting salary of $70,000. Guo wrote back and accepted on May 24.[18]

But when Victor learned that a Four Pillars employee from Taiwan had accepted an offer to join Avery Dennison in the research facility in Ohio, he feared exposure. He immediately notified Four Pillars of the impending time bomb, which set off a firestorm of anxiety halfway around the world.

So concerned was Four Pillars about this risky dilemma, that no less a grandee than P.Y. himself immediately got involved as soon as he was informed. On June 6—just two weeks after Dr. Guo accepted Avery Dennison's offer—Yang fired off a protest letter to Alan Camp- bell, vice president Pacific Basin, Avery Dennison Materials Group, with a copy to Kim Caldwell, who at the time was in charge of the Material Group Worldwide. In the letter, which began cordially enough, P.Y. soon got down to the business at hand. P.Y. complained about the offer of employment to Guo (whom he referred to as Dr. Chung-Hsin Kuo), because Guo had signed a one-year noncompete clause. P.Y. complained that Avery Dennison lawyers had apparently told Guo that no laws would be broken and that he could accept the offer. This did not sit well with P.Y., who maintained that the employment offer violated Avery Dennison's obligation to adhere to "business ethic and industry harmony," and was putting Four Pillars' proprietary information at risk.[19]

On the surface, Yang's intervention was puzzling. Why would the chairman of Four Pillars be involving himself in the middle of a relatively innocuous, midlevel employment decision? Avery Dennison had hired any number of employees from rival companies over the years, and the company routinely tells new employees not to impart—either willingly or unwillingly—any trade secrets belonging to their former employers.

The company patiently explained all of this to P.Y. in its June 20th reply and assured him that hiring Guo would not pose any sort of competitive risk to Four Pillars, because Guo's work-related activities would be restricted to products that did not compete with Four Pillars.[20]

But if Avery Dennison expected the letter to mollify P.Y.'s concerns, it was wrong. The letter only served to raise P.Y.'s rhetoric and his implacable position that Avery Dennison must not hire the young man. In his reply of June 25, P.Y. strongly reasserted that hiring Guo would pose a significant competitive threat because he had access to "valuable proprietary information" and would breach Guo's "noncompetitive agreement" with Four Pillars. Moreover, P.Y. stated that hiring Guo would jeopardize the friendly relationship that currently existed between the two adhesives manufacturers.[21]

Not content with that tack alone, P.Y. then threatened both Guo and Avery Dennison with civil and criminal proceedings unless Avery Dennison backed down and cut Guo loose.

In what can only be termed a classic example of Taiwanese *chutz-pah*, P.Y. lectured Avery Dennison on how diligent his company was in protecting its trade secrets and that the company's continued financial health and prosperity depended on that protection.

"I don't believe your company has any bad intentions toward us," P.Y. summed up, but it would be "impossible to prevent the unintentional use of our trade secrets . . . unless you refuse to hire him."[22]

Good for the Goose, Good for the Gander

In a little known bit of irony, but one that did garner some media attention at the time in Ohio, not long after this employment issue with Guo arose, Avery Dennison sued one of its own managers for taking a job with a competitor under similar circumstances. Christopher G. Lower, an Avery Dennison plant manager in its Painesville operation, resigned October 31, 1997, to accept a job as vice president of manufacturing at Arlon, a small company based in California. Both Arlon and Avery Dennison make marking films, which are reflective, pressure sensitive materials used to manufacture such things as reflective highway signs and logos for trucks. And both companies operate internationally in the same general markets.

When Lower joined Avery Dennison in April 1988, he signed a contract prohibiting him from working for a competitor for up to two years without his employer's written permission. This was pointed out to him in a letter written by his supervisor, Teddy P. Chung, Avery Dennison's vice president and general manager at its Painesville facility, which concluded, "We assume that, in light of the above information, you will be returning to your current role with Avery Dennison."

When he didn't, the company filed for an injunction to prevent him from accepting the job at the competitor, contending in court documents that such a move was a breach of contract and "will result in irreparable harm, injury, and loss to Avery Dennison." The company maintained that Lower's access to confidential manufacturing information, including equipment design and cost strategies, would be economically beneficial to Arlon.

And, around the same time, 3M slapped a complaint on Avery for taking one of *its* employees. But, unlike Four Pillars, the heads of these other companies did not get involved in the disputes.

The Phone That Never Rang

Meanwhile, Campbell was traveling when the letter from P.Y. was received, so Avery Dennison did not fashion an immediate response. Moreover, the company wasn't ready to abandon Guo. Then, Krish had a brainstorm: he suddenly remembered that one of his subordinates was planning an upcoming vacation to Taiwan in July. Krish asked his employee to look up Guo when he was in Taiwan and to meet with him to find out more about what was really going on. Krish explained to his subordinate that Guo was a talented research scientist at a company called Four Pillars and Avery Dennison had just offered him a job in Ohio, but there seemed to be a snag with his current employer. Guo would be working in Krish's group. Krish then contacted Guo and told him to expect a call from . . . *Victor Lee!*

Victor, of course, agreed to contact Guo, who waited in vain for a call that Victor was too petrified to make. When he returned in mid-July, Victor told Krish that Guo never answered his phone (although it was disclosed later that Victor simply never made the call).

Campbell, now back in Ohio, decided to fire off one last message to the crafty P.Y. On July 18, Campbell put forth the strongest argument he could muster outlining what possibly competitive areas Guo would specifically *not* be assigned to, and concluded by conveying his sincere belief that hiring Guo "poses no competitive threat to Four Pillars."[23] Of course, only P.Y. knew just how much of a threat it *would* pose. P.Y. had to stop the deal at all costs.

So, working both ends against the middle, in addition to the litigation threat hanging over Guo's head if he accepted Avery Dennison's job offer, Four Pillars simultaneously informed the star-crossed scientist that the company was withholding his pension and a $12,000 severance package from his wife and family, who would be staying behind in Taiwan as he traveled to the United States. If Four Pillars couldn't persuade Avery Dennison not to hire Guo in the interest of "business ethic and industry harmony," it would do all it could to force Guo not to accept the job offer. It was a heavy hammer falling on Guo's unprotected and unsuspecting head.

If you were Avery Dennison and were looking at this exercise strictly from a human resources perspective, you would be confused. After all, how valuable could one young scientist be that the founder and chairman of a sizeable company halfway around the globe would take the time to get involved in a relatively small dispute such as this? The events only make sense if you examine it as an economic espionage problem, and Avery Dennison simply was not looking for a spy.

Looked at through the prism of time, Four Pillars and P.Y. Yang had no alternative but to throw down the gauntlet to prevent Avery Dennison from hiring Guo and, simultaneously, do all it could to prevent Guo from taking the job. Presumably, the risk was that Guo would somehow uncover that there was an inside spy and blow the whistle. What Four Pillars had no way of knowing, though, was that Guo already knew there was a spy.

Avery Dennison bit the bullet and made the embarrassing decision to withdraw its offer of employment, no doubt concluding that it wasn't worth going to war with Four Pillars over one prospective employee.

Dr. Guo, who already anticipated that he would not be able to accept the Avery Dennison job offer anyway, was not amused. As a parting shot after the job offer fell through, he informed his Avery Dennison contact, Prem Krish, that there was a spy in Avery Dennison's ranks, working in Ohio, and dropped a dime on "Tenhong Lee."

Guo did not know the name *Victor Lee*, which was how Krish referred to the spy when he told Guo "to expect a call from Victor Lee." It was probably a good thing, too, because had Guo blown the whistle right then and there, Lee and his family might not have returned to the United States after their next trip to Taiwan. There, they could have been safe from the long arm of the FBI and Avery Dennison.

Guo went on to tell Krish what little he knew (which wasn't that much in the overall scheme of things, even if it did begin to unravel the conspiracy). Lee had been a so-called consultant for more than seven years (at the time), he had initially provided material to C.K. Kao; then Sally Yang became Victor's handler after Kao was promoted to a senior sales and marketing position and later had a falling out with P.Y. Guo also said that he had seen Avery Dennison confidential documents, with the company's distinctive paper clip-like triangle logo, in the possession of officials of Four Pillars.[24]

But who in the world was Tenhong? Avery Dennison had more than one Lee on its vast, 16,000-employee payroll. It took time to narrow it down to Victor. But then, that didn't seem to make sense either.

Victor, at the time of the exposure, had been by all accounts a faithful, trusted, and respected employee who had risen steadily in the ranks to a position as senior research engineer. He had been employed by Avery Dennison for more than a decade, earning considerable recognition along with several awards for his work. His annual performance reviews were stellar. His work was cutting edge, and he was one the world's leading experts in the highly technical, arcane field of rheology. Avery Dennison needed to excel at this field to maintain its market dominance. And Victor was the company's rheologist guru.

But the information from Dr. Guo couldn't just be ignored.

An investigative firm was brought in for some very preliminary sleuthing, which ultimately led to the decision to contact the FBI. The result was that on an otherwise ordinary winter's day, Victor was called to a meeting in the office of Thomas E. "Tom" Allen, technical director of Avery Dennison's Fasson Roll Division—the division where Victor was employed. Also attending the meeting was Victor's direct supervisor, Dr. Krish, and another research scientist. The meeting was held on January 14, 1997.[25]

There, Tom Allen told the small group of Avery Dennison's top secret plans to expand its operations into Asia, starting with India and rapidly moving eastward into China, Korea, and Taiwan. The

plan was clearly marked *CONFIDENTIAL* and *For Internal Eyes Only.*
Victor was told that he was to be part of the team tapped to explore
the company's expansion into Asia, but he was told that for now, no
one except Dr. Krish, his supervisor, would have access to the written plan. Tom Allen emphasized to the participants that the binder
contained extremely sensitive, detailed information that had to
remain strictly confidential. Moreover, they were told the information was so sensitive that even conversations concerning the plan
must not be repeated outside of Allen's office.[26]

The binder, they were informed by Allen, contained specific
plans and details for each country named, and only Dr. Krish would
have copies of the layouts and diagrams of plant facilities, buildings, machinery, and other equipment.

Any and all written communications about the plan were to be
marked and treated as confidential and highly sensitive. No copies
could be made of the plan or any portion of the documents. Allen
told the group that even though only Krish would keep a copy of the
plan, the other members of the team would receive limited information and access to the plan on a strictly need-to-know basis, and they
would be advised when they needed the information to perform
their duties.

It was abundantly clear that this Asian expansion was enormously
important to the company and that it represented one of the largest
strategic and monetary investments the company had ever made in
its 65-year history. The trap had been baited for Victor Lee.

When the meeting concluded, Victor accompanied Krish back to
his office, located in a different building from Allen's office. They
spoke briefly as Victor saw his boss holding the one copy of the plan
in existence and saw him purposely put the file into his filing cabinet. The meeting then adjourned.

It was a meeting unlike any Victor had ever attended in all his
many years with Avery Dennison, and his mind reeled with the
knowledge of how important this document would be to Four Pillars. There was no conceivable way that Avery Dennison's Asian
expansion plan—including the specific inclusion of Taiwan—would
not directly affect Four Pillars. He just had to get that plan to Four
Pillars.

Later that night, after everyone had gone home, Victor silently entered his boss's office. Slowly, he made his way over to the file cabinet, where he very quietly opened one of the drawers and furtively peered inside. The document he sought was still there, but he did not disturb it.

The next day, Victor made two surreptitious visits to Krish's office and gained access to the file drawer each time. Approximately 15 minutes after the close of business, he entered, turned off the lights and locked the office door. Cautiously, he looked around to make sure he was alone, looked out the window, and closed the blinds. He removed the plan from the file drawer and held it up to the light streaming in from the sides of the window as he quickly scanned several pages. But then, unexpectedly, he replaced the plan, quickly closed the drawer and fled the room.

Did he hear something that made him withdraw so suddenly? Did he have a change of heart concerning what he was about to do? Whatever it was that caused him to retreat so abruptly, it did not deter him from his ultimate mission.

Victor returned after a short while, slipped on heavy, black, winter gloves, and removed the plan from Krish's file drawer. He left with the document carefully tucked under his arm and soon returned. Then, he replaced the original document in the file cabinet and casually went home to his wife and family on a wintry Ohio evening on January 15, 1997.[27]

Another job well done, he thought.

CHAPTER 4

National Security versus Foreign Policy

"They have re-aimed their guns."

—FBI Supervisory Special Agent Loren Brand, supervisor
of foreign counterintelligence, explaining the economic
espionage activities of both friendly and hostile nations

In the opening of Stephen Ambrose's book, *Ike's Spies,* the author relates an interesting account of the early days of World War II, when British Prime Minister Winston Churchill invited General Dwight D. Eisenhower to visit him at Chequers, the PM's country home. In June 1942, Churchill decided the time had come to trust the Allied Commander with Britain's greatest wartime secret.

Churchill had called Ike to him because the time had come to introduce the future Supreme Commander to the wizard war, that silent backstage ballet between the British intelligentsia and the German intelligentsia that was as critical as it was unknown. [Eisenhower, even though a professional soldier] knew almost nothing about codes or code breaking, about new weapons, or about spies, counterspies, covert actions, or any other aspect of the dark arts.[1]

Churchill first told Ike about the elaborate British spy network, including the French underground, that had been supplying the Brits with reliable intelligence information since long before the war began. Eisenhower was astonished, and impressed. The United States had nothing like it, nothing at all. We didn't spy in those days. Former Secretary of War Henry L. Stimson had abolished the Army's small code-breaking network back in 1929, declaring "gentlemen don't read each other's mail." Churchill, however, told Eisenhower that everyone spied.

He then made Eisenhower swear that he would never allow himself to be captured alive during the war, because what he was about to tell him was so secret that the Germans must never learn of it. Ike swore. Then Churchill told Eisenhower about ULTRA, the British code name describing their successful spying activities with the German Enigma machine. Enigma was the elaborate machine the Germans used to send coded messages, and the Nazis considered it absolutely unbreakable because even if the machine fell into enemy hands, it was useless, they thought, without the codes. What the Germans didn't know was that the British had captured an Enigma machine, and the resident geniuses at Bletchley Park had successfully broken the codes. Thereafter, the Allies were able to intercept, read, and decipher all German communiqués. As long as the Germans didn't know this, the Allies could continue to use Enigma and continue to have the upper hand in the war.

Historians later pointed to the ULTRA project—which is to say spying—as one of the key factors in defeating Hitler.

The remainder of Ambrose's book recounts how Eisenhower began using spies and spy apparatus as he led the Allies to victory in World War II, and how he implemented the concept and the reality of government spying and built up the CIA and other intelligence gathering agencies when he occupied the White House.

Churchill had it right: *Everyone spies.*

Just Competitors

What do you think happened to so many elaborate spy networks around the world in the post Cold War era? Do you think they just folded their tents and stole off quietly into the night after the fall of the Berlin Wall? Or do you think they were actively put to other uses by their own design or that of their governments? No one put it more succinctly than Loren Brand, cited at the beginning of the chapter, who spent a lifetime career tracking the espionage activities of foreign nations: "They have re-aimed their guns," he said.[2]

"When the Cold War ended," agreed U.S. Senator Herbert H. Kohl, "our former enemies, and even our long-time allies, began retooling their spy operations. They didn't fire their spies; they simply changed their targets from military to economic secrets."[3]

Foreign governments that had invested heavily since World War II in espionage services and infrastructure were not about to cast aside such valuable assets. Today, nations who have long been considered American allies, as well as those who were not, are lined up using economic intelligence activities against U.S. companies.

According to Edwin "Ted" Fraumann, former special agent with the FBI, the end of the Cold War simply served as a catalyst for morphing military espionage into economic espionage. Fraumann says, "Increasing international economic competition has redefined the context for espionage as nations link their national security to their economic security. Spying conducted by intelligence services is expanding from its primary focus on military secrets to collecting economic secrets; i.e., conducting economic espionage."[4]

But it would be naïve to think that no such foreign government-sponsored economic espionage had occurred previously. Various governments pass along much of the information they collect to the key industries of those nations to help the companies—and the countries—stay competitive. Remember, no one wants to be left behind, which only increases *your* risk.

For the purposes of describing our nation's vulnerability, the FBI defined *economic espionage* as "foreign-power-sponsored or coordinated intelligence activity directed at the U.S. government or U.S. corporations, establishments, or persons for the purpose of unlawfully obtaining proprietary economic information."[5]

The FBI believes that foreign-engineered economic espionage is far more damaging to national and corporate interests than business-to-business espionage, which in no way is meant to diminish the latter, especially if you're the victim. But if a foreign power is conducting the espionage and passing its ill-gotten gains along to its own national industries, who compete with you in the global marketplace, what is the real difference as to who is actually doing the spying when you get right down to it? Your trade secrets are still winding up in someone else's hands.

When you're being mugged, the identity of the person holding the gun on you matters not at all; what matters is that the guy now has your wallet.

In 1998, the FBI confirmed that it was conducting more than 700 separate investigations involving economic espionage by foreign countries.[6]

"There are no friends or allies in this international spy game," says Fraumann.[7] Remember, the new paradigm in the age of globalization is simply: competitor.

Is the FBI Unpatriotic?

The FBI has bandied about phrases likening economic espionage to war. Former FBI Director Freeh called economic espionage the biggest threat to our national security since the Cold War. And, if that is so, you would think that the government would actively help us combat the enemy, wouldn't you? Shouldn't we expect the government to point out the mine fields so we don't get blown up as we cross into new, unexplored territory? If a town has snipers in it, and our intelligence outfits know it, shouldn't they pass the info back to HQ and from there to the soldiers in the trenches?

Isn't that how you fight a war?

Then why isn't the FBI giving U.S. businesses the sort of intelligence they need to stay alive? Why is the FBI intentionally withholding critical intelligence information?

In conventional wars, and even the Cold War, we knew without a doubt who the enemies were. The government recognized the security threat and fortified the nation with armaments, ammunition, and information. Hell, we were ready. So what's the problem today?

When the head of the FBI offers sworn congressional testimony that 23 countries are actively engaged in acts of economic espionage against the United States, doesn't that beg the question, who are those countries? Give us the names of those 23 countries, and let's examine them closely. Are we at war with those greatest-threats-to-our-national-security-since-the-Cold-War, or not?

What are we doing to deal specifically with the economic espionage threat in each of those 23 countries? If American businesses are indeed at risk, don't the FBI and the rest of the government that is supported by tax dollars have an obligation to wise us up?

And, when Freeh said 23 foreign countries were actively engaged in acts of economic espionage against U.S. businesses, did he mean those U.S. businesses actually located here in the country, or did he also include U.S.-owned operations in foreign countries?

Are nearly two dozen countries attacking companies in which I hold stock? Or, is it more like former Representative Dave McCurdy said: not just 23 countries, but 100 of 173 are actively spying against us. Is this accusation on the level? Or were Freeh and the FBI just blowing smoke to escape the sharp blade of the budget ax that was threatening to fly in all directions as part of the peace dividend following the fall of the Berlin Wall and the collapse of Communism? Was sounding the economic espionage alarm just a grandiose way for Freeh to snare an even larger bureaucratic budget for his fiefdom?

While there is no lack of evidence of governmental bureaucracies looking for ways to feather their own entrenched nests with schemes to snag larger and larger pieces of a shrinking pie, foreign policy appears to take precedence over national security.

Three Major Obstacles

People with whom I spoke who are past and present FBI agents and officials, as well as past and present members of the Department of Justice, told me that a constant debate has gone on within the Bureau as to whether or not to provide critical economic espionage intelligence to targeted American businesses or to the American public generally. At least three major problems complicate the disclosure of specific countries engaged in economic espionage activities.

First, the FBI states that its foreign counterintelligence mission is set out in a strategy known as the National Security Threat List, which combines two elements: a Threat List of eight categories (of which economic espionage is but one) that are of a national security concern; and a Country Threat List, which is a classified list of foreign powers that pose a strategic intelligence threat to U.S. security interests. The operative word is *classified.* Because the National ecurity Threat List covers threats beyond just economic espionage, no one department within the FBI is designated to deal exclusively with this specific issue. And the FBI's National Security Division that does investigate the range of threatening activities of foreign countries—including such things as terrorism—will issue its own internal, highly *classified* report as part of its counterintelligence activities. This argument holds that larger foreign policy concerns trump those of American businesses with respect to economic espionage.

Second, assuming it has information that could be shared with U.S. businesses, the FBI questions how it could impart information without appearing to favor one American company over another.

Third, the FBI points to the problem of identifying American ownership in an era of globalization. If a company is physically located on U.S. soil, for example, it could still be owned by foreign interests. That being said, in isolated instances, the FBI has tipped off a U.S. company where there has been a perceived national threat.

So for now, anyway, the powers that be have concluded that gathering intelligence information is more important than prosecuting cases or issuing blanket warnings to beware of one foreign power or another. And the Feds put it just that bluntly.

But I don't think that's acceptable.

Espionage Advisories?

The U.S. State Department regularly and routinely posts travel advisories to the news media and on its Web site advising U.S. citizens where it is dangerous to travel because of government unrest, militant uprisings, or other reasons. Why can't the FBI or even the

Commerce Department do something similar with known cases of economic espionage that are sponsored by foreign governments?

Let me emphasize that I am not advocating the public release of any information that would in any way compromise American national security interests at home or abroad. But I suggest the FBI take a smidge of its multibillion dollar budget increase and create a separate office for proactively helping U.S. businesses avoid known economic espionage risks.

Either economic espionage is the single greatest threat to our national security since the Cold War, or it isn't. The amount of loss, and the fact that what's being targeted is American ingenuity and technology under different names, suggests that it is, in fact, a massive threat to the nation's economic well-being and security.

Businesses whose executives and managers trot around the globe would undoubtedly benefit from being able to dial up a special Web site that alerts them to confirmed reports of spying activities, or airplanes that bug first class passenger cabins, or hotels where laptop computers seem to wander off from their owners with suspicious frequency.

Strategic long-range planners who are looking at countries as investment partners would want to know which countries are routinely committing economic espionage and how. Human resource professionals might be interested to know which countries have sent spies to U.S. businesses posing as students. Top corporate lawyers might want to know from which countries they'd have the best chance of mounting a civil action to reclaim stolen trade secrets, if it should come to that. Average U.S. citizens might decide on their own to boycott travel to such countries.

The point is merely this: if the State Department can announce where it is unsafe to travel without creating some sort of global Armageddon, then the FBI should be able and willing to help U.S. businesses deal with this specific national threat to security. This is not to say that the FBI is not otherwise active in this arena, as you'll see, but much more can and should be done to help businesses reduce their already high global risks of economic espionage.

Will Things Change?

When Congress passed the EEA, it wanted to make sure that the Department of Justice and the cowboy mentality of the FBI didn't ride roughshod out in the wilderness. So Congress included a specific and unusual pre-indictment approval provision that mandated that only the United States Attorney General (or Deputy AG or Assistant AG of the Criminal Division) would be able to sanction the filing of EEA charges for a period of five years after the passage of the Act—from October 1996 until October 2001. But now, U.S. Attorneys in their respective jurisdictions have the power to file EEA charges based solely upon their own local investigations and the facts and evidence they have in hand. No sign-off is required.

The EEA has two key crime Sections: 1831, which is economic espionage perpetrated by a foreign power against U.S. businesses (which could include a business that is owned and controlled by a foreign power); and Section 1832, which is economic espionage perpetrated by anybody or any business, no matter where they are located, here or abroad, against a U.S. business. Getting the Attorney General's okay involved both 1831 and 1832 charges, with 1831 coordination handled by the Department of Justice Internal Security Section and 1832 being run under the Computer Crime and Intellectual Property Section.

The FBI badly wanted Section 1831 included in the bill, and Louis Freeh lobbied hard and successfully for it. The FBI wanted the power to bring charges against foreign powers. But it took four and a half years before a single 1831 indictment was filed. How could that be?

How could 23 countries be actively engaged in acts of economic espionage against U.S. businesses without a corresponding host of EEA indictments against foreign governments? Given the relatively aggressive FBI in that five-year stretch, the facts don't seem to add up.

It remains for the Bureau and the Justice Department to explain why they lobbied so hard for the passage of a bill that would allow the United States to prosecute a foreign company that is owned or majority controlled by a foreign government, if they're not going to use it and use it effectively.

"If the U.S. ever prosecuted a foreign power for economic espionage, our government would have to explain what it knows and how it knows it,"[8] said Neal Wolin, now the general counsel of a major insurance company, who points to that conundrum as one of the compelling reasons why we are reluctant to prosecute. Nevertheless, he has no doubt that economic espionage by foreign countries occurs regularly. Wolin should know, because a large part of his résumé was devoted to government service, including stints as special assistant to two CIA directors (William Webster and Robert Gates), deputy legal advisor to the National Security Council while at the White House, as well as executive assistant to the National Security Advisor.

According to Wolin, when the U.S. government uncovers such acts, certain fundamental questions and broader issues must be considered, such as:

- What are our general diplomatic relations with the country?
- What are all of the other issues, such as foreign policy, on the table?
- How will the economic espionage activity impact these other issues?
- What is the relative importance of the particular issue of economic espionage in the context of the United States's broader foreign policy and national security concerns?

Looked at in this light, it is easier to see why an indictment against a foreign nation would be a relatively rare event. Even though an indictment could be brought against a business that was owned or controlled by a foreign power, the foreign policy sensitivity still cannot be overlooked.

But that doesn't mean American tax dollars are not hard at work combating economic espionage in other ways. Wolin explained that among the actions the government takes to thwart economic espionage are:

- Blocking and tackling, which is taking necessary steps to block the spying activity before it achieves its missions.

- Delivering a message from one of our intelligence services to that of the foreign nation, that basically says, "We know what you're doing, and you had better knock it off before we have to do something about it." Not wanting its espionage to become a public issue, the foreign government will often back down.
- Kicking people out of the country and threatening to publicize the incident.
- The diplomatic approach, where a foreign ambassador is called on the carpet at the State Department and given an ultimatum, similar to the spy-to-spy conversation, but at a higher level.

"Everyone spies on everyone," Wolin candidly explained. "But there is a certain threshold of tolerance." And within that threshold of tolerance is the simple equation of your company versus good diplomatic relations with one of our strategic military and economic trading partners. Is it worth risking the latter in order to protect your business? The government's answer is "No."

But another murky factor blurs the lines, too. How can you tell if foreign-sponsored espionage is benefiting a specific competitor to a U.S. business (making it economic espionage) or a foreign power (making it military espionage), whether directly or indirectly? For example, consider what industries are at stake in the spying operation. "If a country spies to learn about our telecommunications or computer industries," asks Wolin, "how much difference is there between economic and military applications?"

This is one reason why the government has been reluctant to dive into a pool of 1831 indictments, even though it knows how widespread foreign-sponsored economic espionage is.

There's also the problem of motivating the foot soldiers. As one agent explained the rationale of the FBI, agents will say "I'll risk my life for my country, but not for General Motors."

Because countries already know that we are far more likely to handle the situation with a private scolding rather than a public flogging, they don't see spying as much of a risk. "We don't want to embarrass other countries," said J. Michael Waller, vice president of the American Foreign Policy Council in Washington, D.C.[9]

So, when it comes to economic espionage from foreign countries and/or businesses, Americans are on their own in many respects. But whether or not wholesale prosecutions ever occur, the absence of indictments is not the same as the absence of economic espionage. Far from it. In fact, it means that the global risk of economic espionage is not getting any smaller.

To be sure, the government does have some programs in place to issue warnings if it runs across instances of economic espionage being perpetrated against American businesses. The State Department's Overseas Security Advisory Council (OSAC) is run under the umbrella of the Diplomatic Security operations. It was created in the mid-1980s as a joint public-private partnership to work on security issues of mutual concern overseas, including ever-increasing instances of economic espionage. Currently, OSAC—working through its security officers at home and abroad—provides information and warnings to approximately 1,800 member businesses.

The National Counterintelligence Center, which was founded two years before the passage of the EEA, was designed to coordinate the government's economic espionage response. In May 2001, the Office of the National Counterintelligence Executive (NCIX), assumed the functions previously exercised by the National Counterintelligence Center, which ceased operations by that name. It is headed by David W. Szady, a career FBI man. NCIX is housed at the CIA's offices in Langley, Virginia, and draws on the resources of the entire intelligence community. The FBI had started the Development of Espionage, Counterintelligence, and Counterterrorism Awareness (DECA) years ago and changed its name to Awareness of National Security Issues and Response (ANSIR) around the time of the passage of the EEA. (There will be more on ANSIR later.) The program will proactively notify U.S. corporations when it runs across certain types of nefarious activity.

But programs like these usually tell you things reactively, *after* the economic espionage has been uncovered. While knowing the information is obviously better than not knowing it, after-the-fact intelligence may not be enough to help manage the global risk of economic espionage.

Wouldn't it be better, for example, for you to know *in advance* that a given area is known to actively target American business for economic espionage before opening your next plant overseas? If you knew in advance where your business was at risk, wouldn't that information shape or change the way you do business?

Who Spies?

Disneyland has a pleasant little kids' ride called *It's a Small World.* In it, you are seated in a pilotless boat that takes you on a relaxing, mindless cruise through a dark, cool tunnel, as that title song, "It's a Small World, After All" gets drilled relentlessly into your brain. During the cruise, you pass foreign country after foreign country. You see little children dressed in their native costumes, playing native games, displaying native customs, along with friendly native animals. And that by-now annoying tune is being played with various ethnic instruments. It's a nice enough diversion on a hot day at a crowded amusement park.

But let me take you now on the Economic Espionage-land version of It's A Small World. Climb into my boat and hum the tune as we cruise some treacherous waters. One word of caution: these natives only *look* friendly. Keep your hands—and your trade secrets—inside the boat at all times. Because as it turns out, the first Section 1831 indictment against a foreign power has recently been handed down. As you read through the following list of countries actively spying on U.S. businesses, see if you can guess which country's citizens have earned that dubious distinction for their native land.

France

France tops many lists as one of the world's most aggressive countries to engage in economic espionage. Not too long ago, there were reports that the first class cabins of Air France jets were bugged by the French government to eavesdrop on business conversations between Americans (and presumably other nationalities, too) flying to and from France on business trips. Hotel rooms have also reportedly been bugged. Counterintelligence reports reveal that when

French agents target U.S. businesses, the information they pick up goes straight to French corporations, many of which are nationalized. According to Waller, "The French believe they must steal U.S. defense, aviation, and space technology if their own industries are to survive, but they don't show the same interest in consumer manufacturing. They go to astonishing lengths to steal inside information on deals, contracts, and trade policy to help export their products."[10] Peter Schweitzer, writing in *Foreign Affairs*, says France's "well-developed intelligence service [is] one of the most aggressive collectors of economic intelligence in the world."[11] He said that the French had planted moles in companies such as IBM, Texas Instruments, and Corning. The late French spy chief Count de Marenches is quoted by Schweitzer as writing in his memoirs that economic espionage is "very profitable. . . . In any intelligence service worthy of the name, you would easily come across cases where the whole year's budget has been paid for in full by a single operation."[12]

Pierre Marion, former French Intelligence Director, unapologetically told an American journalist, "In economics, we [France and the United States] are competitors, not allies. America has the most technical information of relevance. It is easily accessible. So naturally your country will receive the most attention from the intelligence services."[13]

U.S. counterintelligence sources report that France has recently created an economic intelligence office called the Economic and Strategic Information Bureau. This network of some 30 personnel will track, collect, and strategically disseminate throughout the nation the information it gathers.

France hopes to improve on the collection and circulation of economic information. Armed with this enhanced approach to collecting open source economic intelligence, the French are openly trying to counter U.S. initiatives.

China

China has "made economic espionage a top priority of their foreign intelligence services," according to a report published in *U.S. News and World Report*.[14] China's name appears so often in all types of spy cases that the politically incorrect but nevertheless prevailing belief dictates that if someone who is a Chinese national is suspected of stealing, the Chinese government is somehow behind the crime. When Dr. Wen Ho Lee was accused of stealing nuclear secrets from the Los Alamos Labs, the assumption was that the Chinese government was the beneficiary.

Taiwan

Taiwan is another country often linked to economic espionage. In fact, in a telling article in a local newspaper, the Taiwanese government acknowledged its cultural orientation was such that businesses needed more and better education to learn it was wrong to steal another company's trade secrets.

Yin Ch'I-ming, [Taiwan's] Economic Vice Minister, said . . . that as Taiwan's industries are constantly upgrading themselves, more and more intellectual property issues will emerge. The industries should enrich their knowledge of intellectual property in order to meet challenges from other countries and to protect themselves.

In view of the Taxol case, where a Taiwanese company was accused of stealing the trade secret formula for Taxol from Bristol-Myers Squibb, Yin said that, "[B]ecause Taiwanese companies lack knowledge relating to intellectual property issues," the government needs to offer Taiwanese companies intellectual property training programs "based on the development needs of high-tech industries."[15]

In other words, teach them right from wrong when it comes to stealing someone else's trade secrets. This is particularly interesting in light of the Avery Dennison case and raises questions as to whether Four Pillars believed it was committing a wrong when it received Avery Dennison's trade secrets from Victor Lee.

A careful reading of the article just cited, though, presents a puzzling question. In the first paragraph, the Taiwanese official is exhorting his nation's companies to "enrich their knowledge of intellectual property," and in the second paragraph, he seems to say that Taiwanese companies need to learn right from wrong in doing so. However, taken together, the two paragraphs might advise that companies merely learn the right, or preferable, from the wrong *methodology* to use when seeking a competitor's trade secrets in order to "enrich their knowledge of intellectual property."

Japan

Japan, according to many reports, often masks its economic espionage behind seemingly innocent cameras. Amgen, an American biotech company, was warned by the FBI some years ago that a Japanese television crew, which was visiting dozens of U.S. biotech companies under the guise of filming a documentary on biotechnology, was suspected of being a cover for intelligence gathering. Amgen's then security chief, William Boni, permitted the filming anyway, because the film's director convinced Amgen executives that when the film aired in Japan, it would help Amgen break into the Japanese biotech market. Once inside the company, though, the film makers revealed their true intent by taking pictures of every scrap of paper they could, even company production numbers. "They ran their vacuum cleaner over the U.S. biotech industry," said Boni.[16]

When I spoke with Boni, he confirmed how much the "Japanese want to get into biotech almost any way they can." He recalls the Amgen incident well and said he tried to get his company's public relations people and even the CEO to back off this so-called interview, but they felt it would be advantageous to the company's longer-range plans to break into the Japanese market. Despite the TV crew's solid credentials from Nippon Television—"NTV is the BBC of Japan," said Boni—when the filming took place, the line of questioning was inappropriate right from the start. They asked the sort of technical and competitive intelligence questions that a TV crew would never ask, pursuing information that was proprietary to boot. "And there were about six of them," Boni recalled, "which is more than the average crew. They started wandering around when they should have stayed put, or I saw them filming papers on an executive's desk. I quickly turned the papers over. And one woman pulled out a sketch pad and started drawing parts of the lab, with arrows and notations saying things like 'stainless steel here.'"[17]

When the show finally aired, Amgen was not even mentioned.

Organizations such as the Chemical Manufacturing Association have openly expressed concerns that certain weapons treaties with other nations would open up more than 50,000 U.S. industrial sites to international inspections, thereby giving carte blanche access to sensitive and proprietary information about the U.S. chemical industry. *The Wall Street Journal* called the Chemical Weapons Convention treaty "a bonanza for countries that are in the business of spying on American businesses."

Japan also has a unique public-private partnership between its Ministry for International Trade and Industry and the Japan External Trade Organization (JETRO), according to Peter Schweitzer, who wrote *Friendly Spies*. Schweitzer points to this partnership as supplementing Japan's already well-developed spy-gathering networks created by Japanese industries and corporations over the years. The corporations and the government feed information to each other.

Israel

Israel has long been known as one of our strongest allies but also a country that has routinely engaged in economic espionage.

Wolin's list of countries that spy points to Israel, too, but also, sweepingly, to a big chunk of Western Europe, especially a very aggressive France, plus Japan, Korea, and China.

The American Foreign Policy Council's Waller cites a decoded GAO report that identified Israel as spying "on American business to advance its own industry and to sell stolen American technologies to other countries for profit or political gain."[18]

Waller used various sources to compile a list of countries that spy on U.S. businesses, which also includes China, Germany, Japan, Russia, Canada, France, South Korea, India, and Pakistan.

The Six Most Active?

A CNN news report on economic espionage in 1999 said that the six most active countries for economic espionage against U.S. business concerns were China, Japan, England, France, Canada, and Mexico.

Ira Winkler, author of *Corporate Espionage*, lists in his book Russia (still one of the most active in terms of economic espionage), China, Iran, Cuba, Japan, France, Israel, and Germany.

Around the same time, the American Society for Industrial Security cited the biggest economic espionage risks coming from China, Japan, France, and the United Kingdom, and the highest increase in economic espionage coming from Mexico and Russia.

In a lengthy period covering all of the 1990s, the FBI cited cases of economic espionage being carried out by France, Germany, Japan, Israel, and South Korea.

The "Stans"

Even the "stans" are active, according to Don Ulsch, formerly a director of PricewaterhouseCoopers Global Risk Management Solutions program. Ulsch says countries like Afghanistan, Pakistan, Kazakhstan, Uzbekistan, and others have an underground high-tech movement that is actively probing the global Internet structure to steal information. Ulsch also includes on his list Taiwan, Japan, and China (specifically Shanghai), Singapore, Thailand, and Australia.

Ted Fraumann, a 27-year veteran of the FBI who for a time led the theft of trade secret cases and now is a private security consultant, cites the French, Japanese, and the Germans among our biggest espionage spies.

Given what you now know, what is your best guess as to which country's activities helped spawn our nation's first 1831 indictment involving foreign economic espionage? That dubious distinction, profiled in Chapter 16, goes to our good friend and ally, Japan.

What Do They Want?

"Many foreign governments and/or foreign corporations find it in their interest to collect economic information on corporate negotiating positions, costs, economic feasibility studies, and marketing plans," according to Wayne R. Gilbert, former assistant director in charge of the FBI's intelligence division. "Theft of these confidential corporate trade secrets or reports can in some situations more directly affect the competitive position of U.S. firms than the theft of the firm's actual technology."[19]

But obviously, the countries that target U.S. business interests for economic espionage want everything they can get their hands on to help them stay competitive in the global marketplace. And because, as we discussed, you are in many ways on your own, you need to develop your own information resources. For whether or not everyone spies, you should operate under that assumption and govern yourself and your security operations accordingly.

But just before you prepare to climb out of our *It's a Small World* boat tour of countries who commit economic espionage, I think I see one more country up ahead just before the end of the tunnel. It's a little hard to see; wait, we're getting closer, the fog is lifting and it's . . . it's . . . why, it's the good old U.S. of A.

Echelon

If our former enemies, as well as our allies, retrained their guns after the Cold War, what do you think we did?

It is the stated policy of the United States that our intelligence community will seek to gather economic information from other countries, but for government use only, not for private businesses, according to Wolin. He points to our information-gathering activities all over Europe but is "quite certain it is not being used for commercial applications."

Try telling that to Europe.

Wolin says—and others concur—that the our government won't risk American lives (read: spies) to help American companies gain any sort of economic advantage. "We won't help Ford get a leg up on Mitsubishi, or Boeing gain an advantage on Airbus," said Wolin.

But many in the European Parliament have accused the United States of doing just that—helping Boeing and McDonald Douglas beat out France's Airbus in a $6 billion deal to sell planes to Saudi Arabian Airlines. But we did it without risking any American lives. If you believe the European Parliament, we simply used the most sophisticated listening device on the planet.

The system is called Echelon.

It's run by the National Security Agency in conjunction with four of our allies: Canada, Great Britain, Australia, and New Zealand. The huge spheres, resembling gigantic dimpled golf balls, contain satellite dishes, and are located in strategic places around the globe.

Echelon intercepts and downloads countless millions and millions of voice and data transmissions from satellites, then sends the data to NSA headquarters in Fort Mead, Maryland. Every single intercepted transmission is analyzed in a search for key words or phrases. It's kind of like an Internet search engine.

The sort of words Echelon seeks out are words like *bomb, terrorist,* and the like. Once located, appropriate action is taken.

In early 2000, the European Parliament of the European Union issued a report entitled "Development of Surveillance Technology and Risk of Abuse of Economic Information" in which they charged that " . . . NSA listed all the faxes and phone calls . . . " between France's Airbus and Saudi Arabian Airlines. In so doing, the U.S. government passed the information along to Boeing, who was able to come in and underbid the French airliner to secure the $6 billion sale for itself.

Everyone on the American side of the pond denies it categorically. But Europe is far from convinced.

And the European community pointed to the French company, Thomson-CSF, which suddenly lost a $1.3 billion contract to the U.S. Raytheon Corporation.

Again, the United States denied being in any way involved in corporate spying. Former U.S. State Department spokesman James Rubin categorically rejected the claims, saying, "U.S. intelligence agencies are not tasked to engage in industrial espionage, or obtain trade secrets for the benefit of any U.S. company or companies."[20]

European Parliament President Nicole Fontaine condemned the spy practices and called them an "outrageous move against the privacy of individual citizens" and on the legitimate activities of private companies. "There has been a violation of the fundamental rights of its citizens, and clearly there has also been economic espionage which has probably had disastrous consequences on employment," she charged.[21]

This sentiment was echoed by France's Justice Minister Elisabeth Guigou, who said, "It seems indeed that this network has been diverted towards economic espionage and surveillance of competitors. This means we must be particularly vigilant."[22]

The European Parliament voted to launch its own investigation into whether the United States is using Echelon to commit economic espionage on European businesses.

"I don't know what they think they're investigating or where they intend to proceed," a State Department spokesman said of the European probe. "The notion that we collect intelligence in order to promote American business is simply wrong."[23]

But what the United States *will* admit is that when it comes across wrongdoing, it will pass that information along to the appropriate government and let that government take whatever steps it feels is appropriate.

Former CIA Director R. James Woolsey addressed the Echelon spy charges when he appeared at a Council of Foreign Relations seminar, saying it would be "madness" for the United States to get entangled in economic espionage activities, and in trying to decide which of our nation's companies should benefit from such activity. But if some wrongdoing is brought to light—such as bribery of a government official to benefit a foreign government or business— Woolsey said we will take necessary steps.

In fact, U.S. government sources uncovered evidence that the French were bribing a Saudi airline official to win the lucrative contract. The United States went to the Saudi government and passed along its evidence of the bribery and asked that the contract not be awarded on that basis. But the U.S. government maintains it never turned that information over to Boeing.

In a similar action, via Echelon, the United States uncovered evidence of bribery and corruption involving Thomson-CSF. The United States notified Brazil, which pulled the weapons contract and awarded it to Raytheon Company. But the U.S. government denies it ever passed any information along to Raytheon.

The question may be one of semantics. Even if we didn't pass information along to Boeing or Raytheon, when we pass along the sort of bribery information that we did in the Airbus case, who else could benefit but Boeing?

There is little if any oversight to Echelon, which is one reason why the ACLU sponsors an "Echelon Watch" Web site to stimulate debate over this powerful tool.

So who's right? As Churchill said, everyone spies.

The world of global economic competition *is* a small world, and it's getting smaller. It's almost like being in a crowded elevator at a pickpockets' convention.

CHAPTER 5

STICKY FINGERS
A Perfect Victim, A Classic Villain

In so many ways, Avery Dennison was a perfect victim—almost a sitting duck—virtually unaware of what an attractive target it was. It was a company that was very successful in creating the entirely new self-adhesive, or pressure-sensitive, industry back in 1935. Not many companies in business today can claim that they created an entirely new industry, but Avery Dennison is one of them.

But it's not a critical industry. The company doesn't do anything to save or prolong lives, and if the company as well as the industry disappeared from the face of the earth tomorrow, we could all get along without it and without suffering any hardship.

The products it produces make life, well, more convenient. And it is the convenience we'd miss—especially for those of you who mail out hundreds of Christmas cards each year. Today, Avery Dennison is a true global leader in the innovative development and manufacturing of self-adhesive consumer and office products— such as the popular Peel-and-Stick postage stamps—but it had humble beginnings.

In 1935, R. Stanton Avery invented the first label that could be applied to a surface through simple pressure. Working humbly in his Southern California garage, with his brainchild pressure label and startup capital of $100 (loaned to him by his then-fiancée, Dorothy Durfee), he began his venture during the Depression with nothing more than a cigar box full of glue, strips of paper, a slicer he assembled from a discarded washing machine, and an idea: Kum-Kleen Adhesive Products Co.—so named because the labels could come clean off without leaving a mark.

Before Kum-Kleen, the only commercial method of affixing labels at the time was to use glue or pregummed labels that required moisture, such as with a sponge or your tongue. (Do remember how awful those things tasted?) But Stan Avery pioneered a self-adhesive process that did not require heat or moisture. His first commercial use of the new self-adhesive product was to create labels to mark prices in Los Angeles–area gift shops. The company later grew rapidly through military contracts during WWII, when adhesives were scarce and the government used Avery's labels on "Mae West" life preservers. A new industry was born, and in just a few years those ubiquitous "Hello, My Name Is" labels would spring up at every cocktail party in America.

Today, the company employs nearly 18,000 people in 39 countries around the world. With year 2000 sales at nearly $4 billion, the company increased its 1999 ranking on the national *Fortune* 500 list to number 429 and is the 23rd largest California company by revenue ranking. Approximately 75 percent of its annual revenues come from the sale of its proprietary adhesive components, self-adhesive base materials, specialized labels, and other self-adhesive products.[1]

Ubiquitousness Personified

It is a testament of sorts to the company's success and steady growth that many people don't even know the company exists, even though you can't help but come in contact with their products—or the products they enhance—virtually every day. "Whenever you use something that's self-adhesive, there's a good chance Avery Dennison made it,"[2] the company boasts about itself.

The ubiquitous Avery Dennison manufactures finished pressure-sensitive adhesive products, or supplies raw pressure-sensitive adhesive materials and technology, for manufacturers in every major industry, but primarily:

- Office products
- Health care
- Retail
- Food
- Transportation/automotive
- Data processing
- Apparel/textile
- Industrial/durable goods

The company's innovative technology actually becomes a part of someone else's product. Here are just a few samples of how the company's labels and adhesive products are used across a wide industry group spectrum:

- Self-adhesive postage stamps for the U.S. Postal Service
- Duracell® PowerCheck™ battery labels
- Kimberly-Clark adhesive tabs for Huggies® disposable diapers
- Adhesive tape for Johnson & Johnson's Band-Aid® brand Sport Strip™ bandages
- Kodak film canister labeling
- Coca-Cola's "invisible" labels for glass bottles
- Labels that are used for food products, such as Kraft Foods' Grey Poupon® and French's® mustard
- Labels that are used for health and beauty aid products such as Unilever's Suave® shampoo, Procter & Gamble's Noxzema® skin cream, and Johnson & Johnson's No More Tears™ baby shampoo and Johnson's® baby powder
- Automated retail bar code tags
- Sizing labels for clothes, such as those long, adhesive strips found on Gap jeans
- Reflective highway signs

- Pinstriping on your car
- Computer software (including that which Microsoft embeds right into Word, its word processing software) that makes it easier to print neat envelopes and labels
- And, naturally, all of the well-known Avery® labels—such as those used for decades by office workers putting little labels on file folders or for mass mailings

Get the idea? It's convenient not to have to lick postage stamps, but the world survived without that technology for hundreds of years and easily could again. It's a great bit of marketing to have labels so transparent that you can see the product through the label on the glass container (the company calls it ClearAdvantage™), but you could certainly live without it the way we used to. And how many people do you know who really check how much power is left in their batteries before using them? It's neat to be able to advertise that your product packaging allows it, but you could always live without the technology and simply keep extra batteries on hand—just the way our parents did.

So it's remarkable when you stop to think about it that Avery Dennison has grown from Stan Avery's garage to an almost $4 billion global giant making things that no one really needs.

Stan's Garage

When I attended Stan Avery's memorial service in 1997, at Founder's Hall at Pasadena's Huntington Garden and Library, I remember being struck by how many Avery Dennison people in attendance actually knew and had worked with Stan for so many years. Some of them might even have remembered the garage, but certainly many knew and had worked shoulder-to-shoulder with the company's founder at his first plant in Monrovia, California.

Stan was a hands-on manager and CEO, and even after he retired from active duty and became chairman emeritus, he still maintained an office and a secretary at the company's Pasadena world headquarters. He reported for work every day, and he traveled the world to officiate at most of the company's new plant openings.

Avery Dennison prides itself on being a family type of business, meaning that it is close-knit and communal. And it was in that spirit that many on the workforce considered employment at Avery Dennison as working in an annex of Stan's garage. The company cultivated that open culture and sharing feeling; walking around the facilities as well as the offices was like walking over to borrow a tool from Stan's garage.

But as the company's investments in new technology and new techniques helped it grow over the years, not everyone shared that same sense of bigness or *Fortune* 500-ness. Many still thought of the ever-growing global colossus as a family business, or maybe one step removed from Stan's garage. Perhaps this familial attitude caused Victor to think that he could "borrow some tools"—steal—with abandon for eight years.

A Label Sandwich

Making a label is like making a sandwich. Even with all the different types of labels Avery Dennison manufactures, either as end products or in the form of raw materials, the basic sandwich equation remains pretty much the same. Picture in your mind those "Hello, My Name Is" labels, because they're well known and they are typical of the sandwich. Labels often consist of many razor-thin parts or coatings, sometimes more than a dozen, but typically these four are included:

1. *Face material.* This is the uppermost portion where you read, "Hello, My Name Is." This face material can be pretty much any kind of paper stock under the sun.
2. *Adhesive.* In the case of the "Hello" labels, the adhesive must be strong enough to stick to your clothes, but not so strong that the label can't be removed or will leave a mark or damage your clothes when it is removed.

3. *Release coating.* It's virtually invisible to the naked eye, but this coating allows you to easily peel—release—the face material from the backing or liner. Without this coating, the face material would likely tear when you tried to separate it from the backing.

4. *Liner.* This is the removable/disposable backing. This is what you discard after you peel off your name tag label.

Why are these terms important to our discussion? They are important only insofar as they help you better understand the immense amount of research and development that goes into a seemingly simple, pressure-sensitive adhesive label—a label that you probably never even think about—and why Victor's thefts were so devastating to Avery Dennison.

For example, Avery Dennison has formulas or patents on more then 225 adhesives, and more than 200 different, proprietary release coatings that it uses for a variety of extremely demanding applications. Avery Dennison products have to perform to rigorous use specifications.

Even though you may not give a second thought to a label, upwards of $50 million per year is spent by Avery Dennison to develop new and better labels or adhesive compounds. Why? Well, ask yourself this: Considering that you don't think much about labels now, how much would you think about labels if they *didn't* perform as effortlessly as most of them do? Would you buy Avery labels if their labels tore when you tried to peel them from their backing, or if they kept falling off the surface they were supposed to stick to, or if the labels left a permanent mark when they were removed? Or, looked at another way, would companies like Johnson & Johnson have Avery Dennison make labels for their shampoo bottles if the water and humidity from the shower caused the labels to fall off? Hardly. Would wine growers use Avery Dennison labels for their chardonnays if chilling the wine or moisture on the bottle caused the label to curl or fall off? Of course not.

Adhesives perform differently under different field conditions, as do the other three primary components of the label sandwich. One of the keys to Avery Dennison's success over the years has been their knowledge and ability to reach into their many cigar boxes filled with glue and pick out the right adhesive for each job, or come up with a brand new one.

In a way, Victor's job was to keep you from thinking about labels—to make sure they continued to perform as advertised. Victor's specialty was rheology, the science dealing with deformation and flow of matter. A rheologist is a scientist who studies the flow properties of a given material. Said another way, a rheologist is the expert on the chemistry involved in how different types of materials flow on surfaces (i.e., Does the material flow like water? Like molasses? Does it spread evenly? Does it leave gaps or bubbles or an uneven surface? How can the flow be improved? Can it be speeded up? Slowed down?) In the case of Avery Dennison labels, Victor's job had to do with studying and improving how any of hundreds (if not thousands) of materials flowed and performed in terms of adhesion and high-speed removal—peeling the face stock from the backing. And Victor was one of the best rheologists at Avery Dennison, which given the company's dominance, is the same as saying one of the best in the world.

But rheology plays an even more critical role in terms of profits to be made during mass production and a near final process called high-speed release.

When labels are manufactured, huge rolls of paper (face material) and backing (liner) are used. Think of a gigantic printing press.

During the process, as the face material and liner are zooming though the machinery at hundreds-of-feet-per-second, the adhesive is sprayed onto the back of the face material and the release coating is sprayed onto the liner. The machinery bonds the face material to the backing at incredible speeds. Near the end of the process, you have one gigantic label that is worthy of inclusion in the *Guinness Book of World Records*. But eventually it must be cut down to size and the waste removed in a process called *high-speed release,* and here is where rheology really pays off and profits are to be made.

At the end of the run, the scrap is lifted and peeled away in one continuous effort, at the same blinding, hundreds-of-feet-per-second speed as before. *Without breaking or tearing.*

Think how costly it would be if the scrap didn't separate as it was supposed to in the high-speed release stage of the manufacturing process. Think of all the time and money that would be lost in down time if the manufacturer had to continually shut down the run to unclog the machinery.

This is Manufacturing 101. Whatever you're making, the more you can produce, and the faster, the higher your profits.

This is where the millions and millions of R&D dollars really pay off for a company like Avery Dennison. This is rheology. This is where Victor excelled.

And this is where Four Pillars was out of its league and badly needed help.

The View from Taiwan

There is an old saying that everyone has 20/20 eyesight through the retrospectoscope, so in hindsight one can easily look back and say that Four Pillars had all of the characteristics of a classic villain. They were struggling financially, lagging in technology, and fearful of the Asian invasion by U.S. and European companies. The company and its founder had previously been convicted of trade secret infringement.

At one time, P.Y. Yang had likened Four Pillars' growth to that of his native country, saying, "As Taiwan rapidly rose to become a world economic giant, Four Pillars during the same period quickly grew to become a major global consumer and industrial products manufacturer."[3]

However, in a fit of irony, the company also attributed its growth to following the Confucius credo of "courtesy, righteousness, honesty, and decency in mind. . . ." And, in an example of grandiose hyperbole, the company's mission statement reads in part: "We dedicate ourselves to continuously upgrading the quality and welfare of human life."[4]

In 1954, P.Y. and three of his former classmates[5] founded the Wei Mei Chemical Factory in Taiwan. The company produced cellophane tape. Soon, however, P.Y. and three others[6] founded Four

Pillars Processing Factory, which manufactured paper-backed aluminum foil and other products. In the early 1960s, Four Pillars was merged with the Wei Mei Chemical Factory.

From 1963 to 1971, Four Pillars began developing adhesive tape and pressure-sensitive and protective tape with different backings and coating materials. The company also introduced into Taiwan what was, for the time and the country, state-of-the-art machinery.

From 1972 to 1989, the company grew and two new manufacturing plants were added, along with an adhesive plant in Singapore. At the end of this growth period, Four Pillars was producing more than 1,000 different products, which it attributed to its "dedicated R&D efforts."[7] It also realized that globalization was bringing competitors to its doorstep. Its lucrative but isolated corner of the world was about to be overrun with interlopers.

Remember, no more walls.

And, in 1989, as Four Pillars was feeling the hot breath of outside competitors breathing down its neck, Victor Lee was recruited to the Four Pillars payroll.

From 1990 to 1997—the year Victor was busted—Four Pillars tried to keep up with the fast pace of globalization. They opened four new factories to manufacture and market specialty tapes and label stock—the same category of products turned out by Avery Dennison. Four Pillars maintained at the time that its focus and foundation for growth would remain in Taiwan, but that it needed to increase its globalization efforts in order to forecast worldwide developments better. Many of its forecasts appeared to be coming from Victor, who was supplying the Taiwanese firm with a steady stream of information.

But Four Pillars seemed to have hit the wall in terms of growth. Its revenue from its primary businesses had stagnated at about $400 million. The company got involved in some noncore businesses that failed or otherwise caused a severe drain on the company's resources.

It was no secret that in the early 1990s, Avery Dennison was eager to expand into the burgeoning Asian market. Four Pillars soon became aware—and perhaps nervous—that this behemoth was nosing around. The two were not yet direct competitors, but only because Avery Dennison's presence in Asia at the time was very minor, and Four Pillars' lone customer in the United States was a Cleveland-based company called Manco, a distributor for some of Four Pillars' tape products.

Avery Dennison representatives met with Four Pillars in 1993 and thought the synergy was good for doing some business together, possibly even a joint venture. The two companies began preliminary talks in earnest around 1993.

In hindsight, one question that might be asked is whether a company with Four Pillars particular background was the right company for such a joint venture. For it turned out that P.Y. Yang had a known prior history in Taiwan of trade secret infringement.

In May 1985, P.Y. as an individual, and the Four Pillars company, were "found guilty, by a final court judgment, guilty of criminal offenses for violation of Patent Law."[8] The case accused Four Pillars of counterfeiting some of a competitor's products. According to published reports, the case finally wound up in the Taiwan Supreme Court and "is well-known in the judicial field for the many records [for longevity, for one] that it has set."[9] While the case was settled in 1985, it took until 1997 for the courts to render final damages. Four Pillars was ordered to pay $180 million in Taiwan currency.

Death of a Deal

As P.Y. sat across the table from the Avery Dennison people—and even flew to Los Angeles on one occasion for a face-to-face meeting with the very top Avery Dennison senior management—he still had Victor in his back pocket. As the company was wooed by Four Pillars, the more the Taiwanese firm learned about Avery Dennison, the more anxious it was to consummate the joint venture.

Also, during these discussions, P.Y. presumably became concerned about Victor being found out and directed the spy to curtail his activities. P.Y. was close to the deal of his lifetime, and he didn't want to anything to blow it.

In the midst of the discussions, however, Four Pillars suffered a devastating fire at one of its plants, which severely crippled the company and hurt its profitability. Coincidentally, it was around the same time that Avery Dennison demanded to see Four Pillars' financials so the larger company could judge the wherewithal of its potential partner. And that's where the real trouble began.

At first Four Pillars was reluctant to turn over any financial information. Subsequently it turned over some, but the information was not encouraging.

Due in part to the fire and to the ancillary businesses in which it was involved, Four Pillars was too weak financially, and Avery Dennison broke off the discussions. P.Y. made a last ditch appeal. But the deal died.

Victor said P.Y. instructed him at that time to resume his spying activities.

Big Happy Glue Factory

Avery Dennison was a company that was, in many ways, fat and happy. Business was up, profits were up, its stock was up, its scientists were coming up with newer and better ways to use adhesives, and world markets were expanding. It was also a company that had never before been victimized by economic espionage.

Many companies in that situation tend to operate on the "It can't happen here" philosophy—a seriously flawed viewpoint that is based entirely on history, but not reality. The thinking is: Because it hasn't happened, we're invulnerable.

More companies than you would imagine—unless you're one of them—operate exactly this way. Espionage always happens to the other guy.

And when it does happen, the company in many ways becomes a victim of its own success: a perfect victim, just like thousands of other perfect victims.

Four Pillars, on the other hand, fit a completely different profile of a company that had to keep up technologically or run the risk of being swept aside in a global marketplace. It had talented scientists on staff but lacked the technological know-how that it felt was necessary to compete and grow (otherwise, why have Victor on its payroll?); it had suffered financial reversals and was quickly losing ground; it knew its competition firsthand and what that competition was capable of.

But if you also have larceny in your heart, you are a classic villain, a corporate predator.

And it was only a matter of time before victim and villain collided.

CHAPTER 6

The FBI and the End of the Cold War

"In the post–Cold War world, our national security

is inseparable from our economic security."

—Warren Christopher, former U.S. secretary of state

In the early days of the Four Pillars case, did the FBI have its own agenda? Other than seeing justice served, was there another factor at work?

Walls weren't the only things that crumbled after the Cold War; U.S. budgets dropped—or threatened to drop—like the bottom falling out of a bull market. Bureaucrats everywhere were scrambling for ways to save their budgets. Even the FBI was looking for ways to protect its own spy budgets and fiefdoms from the budget ax, and they weren't alone.

Neal Wolin remembers that, "A whole set of substantive questions were raised after the Cold War dealing with why do we need such a big military apparatus?"[1] It was a legitimate question. We had won the war, so many wanted to send the soldiers home and ratchet down the big spending.

But then budget-cutting started to get complicated. There were essentially three burning issues of the day: terrorism, weapons proliferation, and drugs. All over Washington, an army of bureaucratic ants was trying to carry away as many crumbs from the overall budget pie as they could. When it came to fighting the Cold War, very few people ever expected to win in a way that meant the War would ever end. Yeah, we wanted to fight Communism, but the balance of power kept food on Washington's table and our military-industrial complex gainfully employed.

Now what?

The FBI, under Louis Freeh, actively and aggressively sought ways to protect its turf and its budget. In the early 1990s, it found its own motherhood and apple pie niche: theft of trade secrets, which had always been a big concern for U.S. businesses. It made perfect sense, too. If foreign countries were redirecting their Cold War spies and technology to perform economic espionage, we needed to protect our own national economic security better. Who could argue with that?

Apparently no one. In the eight years of Freeh's reign before he abruptly left office in June 2001, he openly lobbied and cultivated lawmakers who controlled the FBI's budget. Consequently, the agency's budget mushroomed by 58 percent, to more than $3.4 billion a year, and the Bureau hired more than 5,000 agents and 4,000 technical and analytical employees. Perhaps as an answer to the rising threat of economic espionage from foreign countries, Freeh more than doubled the number of overseas FBI offices from 20 to 44.

One of the lobbying tales the FBI related happened in the early 1990s. Still with a Cold War mind-set, and believing that Russian spies were trying to steal U.S. business secrets, the FBI set up a sting of sorts using a cooperative IBM in Silicon Valley. The spies came out of the woodwork, all right, but instead of our former nemesis from the "evil empire," the FBI was shocked to uncover economic espionage spies from one of Japan's leading companies. The Hitachi corporation was exposed as being in possession of highly sensitive IBM trade secrets known as the Adirondack Workbooks.[2]

Over the years, Congress had passed laws protecting various forms of intellectual property: patents, trademarks, and copyrights. But all other intellectual property fell into a vast maw. In fact, prior to the ultimate passage of the EEA in 1996, the only federal law on the books dealing with theft of trade secrets was a very limited statute that provided for criminal penalties for the unauthorized disclosure of trade secrets by a government worker. Nothing on the law books was specifically designed to protect businesses. To prosecute thefts of trade secrets, prosecutors often charged a suspect with violations of interstate transportation law or receipt of stolen goods—a statute that dated back to the 1930s. However, the law required that the stolen goods be tangible, and trade secrets—such as a formula—are often intangible.

It all came to a head when the FBI and the Justice Department got outmaneuvered in a case of economic espionage allegedly perpetrated by two Chinese nationals and a representative of the Chinese government, accused of economic espionage against Ellery Systems, Inc., of Boulder, Colorado.

The Ellery Story

In 1994, Ellery Systems was a leading edge software developer specializing in high-tech systems for a consortium of private and public agencies, including NASA, AT&T, and IBM. It was helping to develop the information superhighway we now refer to as the Internet.

Andrew Wang, a Chinese national in the United States for five years at the time, worked for Ellery as a computer software engineer. In February 1994, Wang resigned and started his own computer firm called DC Nology. He and his wife, Min Zhu, thought they were living the American Dream. Two weeks later the dream came to a crashing halt.

The FBI arrested Wang and charged that he and an alleged accomplice, Jing Cui, also a Chinese national, stole 122 computer files from Ellery, including source code for critical software, to start the competing business. Wang and Cui denied the allegations. But the government wasn't done. The grand jury indictment alleged that Wang was backed by a Chinese government official and a Chinese firm called Beijing Machinery to get more than a half million dollars in funding. The grand jury indictment charged Wang with copying more than 1,700 pages of trade secret computer files to entice his Chinese backers to help underwrite his own firm.

Allegedly, Wang sent a note to Beijing Machinery saying, in effect, they should use the American technology and business practices to beat the Americans at their own game.

"When we heard that . . . we decided that regardless of what the outcome was going to be, that we were going to pursue this case," said Geoffrey Shaw, Ellery's CEO. "Because at that point, we no longer had a case of espionage, we no longer had a case of theft; at that point we had a direct attack not only on us, but on our entire way of life."[3]

It was a valiant speech, but one that fell short of the mark, because the U.S. government didn't have the right arsenal of laws and statutes to pursue the case successfully. Because no specific laws were on the books against theft of trade secrets, the government had to cobble together a complaint based on statutes such as Fraud by Wire, but they failed to stand up to the test. The two alleged spies were set free and took jobs with one of Ellery's competitors. Soon thereafter, Ellery was forced to close its doors forever—a victim of alleged economic espionage, a loss of confidence among its customers, and the government's inability to prosecute economic espionage cases successfully.

The FBI Lobbies Hard

Ellery Systems was not an isolated case, but it stuck in the craw of the FBI and the Justice Department. Stung by the humiliation of what many thought should have been a slam dunk conviction, the Feds knew that they needed tougher and more specific laws to go after foreign economic spies. And such action would be good for business—*their* business. The last time the FBI had the opportunity to chase huge potential hordes of non–Cold War spies and generate lots of positive press was when they ferreted out Nazi Fifth Columnists looking to sabotage U.S. defense installations and businesses during World War II.

As early as 1994—coinciding roughly with the rise and fall of the Ellery Systems case—Freeh began lobbying Congress to pass an economic espionage act. He wanted something with teeth in it.

While you may think this should have been an easy sell, it wasn't. Freeh lobbied long and hard for the EEA and spent a lot of personal capital in the process. But more than two years went by before the EEA was finally passed and signed into law by President Clinton.

Freeh was interested primarily in getting a law passed that would enable the FBI to pursue cases against foreign countries and foreign agents, although he readily admitted that domestic economic espionage was also rampant. Both, he said, directly imperiled the health of our national economy, but he really pushed hard on the need for a law to protect against economic espionage perpetrated by foreign powers.

To demonstrate his resolve, the same year he began lobbying for an economic espionage act, the FBI initiated an economic counterintelligence program, whose specific mission is to detect and counteract threats and activities directed against the nation's economic interests by foreign powers, especially acts of economic espionage. Within two years, Freeh reported a staggering 100 percent increase in the number of economic espionage-related cases.

"Foreign intelligence operations directed against U.S. economic interests are neither unusual nor unprecedented," said Freeh, as he lobbied Congress to pass an economic espionage act. He went on to tell Congress that "foreign companies and commercially oriented government ministries are the main beneficiaries of U.S. economic information" stolen by foreign spies to gain a competitive advantage over major economic rivals.[4]

Freeh then enumerated the key economic espionage targets, starting with high-technology and defense-related industries. He then ticked off biotechnology, aerospace, telecommunications, computer software and hardware, advanced transportation and engine technology, advanced materials and coatings, so-called "stealth" technologies, energy research and development, defense and armaments technology, all manufacturing processes, and semiconductors. He also cited as targets all forms of proprietary business information such as bids, contracts, customer information, strategic business plans, and information—*regardless of industry*.

The FBI director lobbied and buttonholed senators and representatives for two years, promising all who would listen that the country was lousy with economic espionage spies paid for by foreign powers. Just give us the law we need and we'll start to corral the bad guys, he promised.

As the U.S. Senate was poised to decide the fate of the nation's trade secrets, Senator Arlen Specter said, "For years now, there has been mounting evidence that many foreign nations and their corporations have been seeking to gain competitive advantage by stealing the trade secrets, the intangible intellectual property of inventors in this country. The Intelligence Committee has been aware that since the end of the Cold War, foreign nations have increasingly put their espionage resources to work trying to steal American economic secrets. Estimates of the loss to U.S. business from the theft of intangible intellectual property exceed $100 billion. The loss in U.S. jobs is incalculable."[5]

His persuasive argument was aided by Senator Herbert Kohl, who took the floor and said, "Since the end of the Cold War, our old enemies and our traditional allies have been shifting the focus of their spy apparatus. Alarmingly, the new target of foreign espionage is our industrial base. But for too many years, we were complacent and did not heed these warnings. And we left ourselves vulnerable to the ruthless plundering of our country's vital information. We did not address this new form of espionage—a version of spying as dangerous to our national well-being as any form of classic espionage. Today, that complacency ends."[6]

Finally, the Economic Espionage Act was passed, and President Clinton signed it into law on October 11, 1996.

Remember, the bill that was passed was divided into two key sections: 1831 dealt with the sexy part that most interested the FBI, economic espionage by foreign governments; while 1832 dealt with the theft of trade secrets by a foreign or domestic company against U.S. business interests.

Freeh and the rest of the FBI were seeking the sort of cases that would show Congress how rampant economic espionage was in this country, and how aggressive the FBI could be in investigating and ferreting out foreign bad guys and bringing them to justice. But the cases didn't come in over the transom as Freeh had predicted they would, primarily because many businesses were not sure the FBI could be trusted to protect their trade secrets.

There were—and still are—many who openly raise the question of whether the FBI can be trusted. When a spy has stolen a company's trade secret and the company ponders whether or not to call in the FBI, the question often asked is whether it is better to have one individual or one company have the trade secret, or call in the Feds and run the risk that carelessness or lack of trade secret protection or improper handling might expose the trade secret to the whole world, including *all* competitors instead of just the one.

Denial of Service, Denial of Trust

This specific issue erupted anew during a widely publicized instance of computer hacking—just one form of economic espionage—at the start of the new millennium. When computer giants Yahoo!, Amazon, eBay, and other popular Web sites were hacked and their service interrupted, thereby preventing millions of people from gaining access, the FBI tried to launch an immediate and broad investigation into the crimes. But it found little support from the high-tech industry itself. The reason, asserts Charles Piller writing in the *Los Angeles Times* on the computer hacking incident, is that "[M]any in the industry frankly question the FBI's competence and fear the publicity that may ensue from a high-profile agency investigation."[7]

One man who should know about the FBI's skill level in this area, Jim Settle, a Springfield, Virginia, security consultant and former chief of the FBI's national computer crime program, said, "FBI management still doesn't get it. They keep turning over their management and putting people in that have little or no background. . . . Do I have a lot of confidence that they will find the people who did this? No." And Phil Karn, a top security expert at Qualcomm Corp., a telecommunications company in San Diego said, "I'm a little bit paranoid about the FBI."[8]

Partly due to paranoia and partly due to the snail's pace at which investigations occur, less than one-third of large companies and government agencies that were victims of serious hacking incidents reported those crimes to the FBI or other law enforcement officials, according to a 2001 survey by Computer Security Research Institute, a San Francisco–based nonprofit association of some 5,000 information security professionals.

This widespread lack of cooperation and trust was viewed as so serious that the government sent then U.S. Attorney General Janet Reno to a high-tech summit in June 2000 to urge companies to cooperate with law enforcement officials in battling cybercrime. Many companies have been reluctant to involve the Justice Department or the FBI for fear of public embarrassment, governmental red tape, or widespread public disclosure of the company's trade secrets or other sensitive proprietary information.

Fear of government intervention in what the industry sees as largely private sector concerns spilled over into the Oval Office. In a meeting with President Clinton following the most celebrated of the hacking incidents, executives from some of the nation's leading Internet companies told the President that they didn't see a need for increased government regulation, which they feared. "In dealing with the challenge of security on the Internet, private industry must take the leadership role," said Harris N. Miller, president of the Information Technology Association of America, a trade group that represents many of the leading information technology companies.[9]

This wide distrust is excruciatingly frustrating to the FBI. Its National Infrastructure Protection Center (NIPC), designed to protect the nation's multibillion-dollar investment in computer networks, had a budget of less than $20 million in 2000 and a case load that had skyrocketed from 200 in 1996 to 800 just three years later. With this sort of growth rate, and NIPC's awareness that only one-third of all cases are being reported, the exponential growth of economic espionage by computer is staggering.

The feeling of public distrust of the FBI was a sting the Bureau had felt for a while. The FBI desperately needed a high-profile case of corporate economic espionage to show American businesses that it *could* be trusted to protect trade secrets.

Where were the nefarious companies and foreign governments that the FBI had promised Congress were out there just waiting to be collared in a high-profile, top-of-the-evening-news sting? Where were the big name bad guys that the Feds could exploit by busting up economic espionage spy rings and, in the process, help justify the FBI's bloated budget requests? Mistrust of the FBI was taking its toll on a lot of people.

The FBI desperately needed a trophy case to show Congress the spies were where they said they were. And at last, they thought they had turned one up in a small town in northern Ohio.

CHAPTER 7

STICKY FINGERS
The Mighty Kong

After the March 6, 1997, meeting between Victor and the FBI, when the scientist decided to spill the beans, no one—*absolutely no one*—at Avery Dennison or at the FBI had any inkling of the depth or breadth of his treachery.

Prior to the Avery Dennison spy case, the FBI had been involved in only a few other cases of economic espionage under the auspices of the EEA, all of which dealt with single or simple acts of espionage that ended in guilty pleas or plea bargains. These were the kind of cases the FBI was accustomed to handling, even though the EEA was designed with far bigger and broader cases in mind.

To best understand the magnitude of Victor's theft over an eight-year stretch, let's briefly look at the other EEA cases that were active at the same time.

The PPG Case: *United States v. Worthing*

The first EEA prosecution occurred on January 2, 1997, one day after the Act took effect. Two brothers, Patrick and Daniel Worthing, were indicted by a federal grand jury for stealing confidential trade secrets, including production formulas for fiberglass manufacturing, from Pittsburgh Plate Glass. The brothers tried to sell the secrets to a PPG competitor, Owens-Corning. They apparently believed that everyone has a larcenous mind-set when they boldly offered the information to the Owens-Corning CEO without a second thought of being caught.

Patrick had worked for the fiberglass division of Pittsburgh-based PPG Industries where he had stolen some $20 million worth of trade secret fiberglass research material and blueprints on computer disks. Using an assumed name, he and his brother had written a letter to the Owens-Corning chief executive that began, "Would it be of any profit to Owens-Corning to have the inside track on PPG?"[1] Owens-Corning promptly turned the letter over to the FBI.

As things go, and with the cooperation of the two companies involved, this case was fairly easy to work. The Worthing brothers were arrested on December 7, 1996, just as they were about to turn over the PPG secrets to an undercover FBI agent posing as an Owens-Corning employee. The initial down payment they sought: $1,000, of which Daniel was to receive 10 percent, $100.

Soon after the indictment and less than a month after the arrest, Patrick pleaded guilty to the actual theft of trade secrets and received a 15-month prison sentence and three years probation. Brother Daniel, who joined the conspiracy the night before his arrest, pleaded guilty to conspiring to possess and deliver trade secrets, and was sentenced to five years of probation and six months of home confinement.

At no time was any trade secret compromised.

The Taxol Case: *United States v. Hsu*

On June 14, 1997, the FBI arrested Kai-Lo "James" Hsu and Chester S. Ho, two Taiwanese nationals, for attempting to steal and sell the trade secret production formula for Bristol-Myers Squibb's widely successful anticancer drug, Taxol. This was the first EEA case brought against foreign nationals. (Victor Lee, at the time of his arrest three months earlier, was a naturalized U.S. citizen).

In 1996, Taxol generated more than $800 million in sales for pharmaceutical giant Bristol-Meyers Squibb. The company had initially spent more than $15 million in research and development costs to develop what appeared to be a promising drug to combat cancer. Unfortunately for the company, however, the Pacific yew tree—where the taxol herb naturally grows—was put on the endangered species list. The company then spent several hundred million dollars in what turned out to be a successful attempt to genetically engineer a form of taxol that could be substituted for natural taxol. Hsu and Ho tried to buy this formula.

Yen (or Yuen) Foong Paper Company, in Taiwan, had been trying to diversify into biotechnology and pharmaceuticals for some time. At the time of his arrest, Hsu was the company's technical director. His accomplice, Ho, had served in Taipei as a professor at the National Chaio Tung University as well as the Institute of Biological Science and Technology.

Presumably, had their plan succeeded, the Taxol drug would have been manufactured and sold under a different name in Taiwan and perhaps elsewhere in Asia. The buyer's cost would have been a fraction of what the real Taxol would sell for, because no portion of the R&D dollars would have to be recovered for the Yen Foong Paper Company to turn a profit.

Working through an alleged accomplice, Yen Foong Paper's business development manager, Jessica Chou, the company initially tried to obtain the formula from a technology broker. What Chou and Hso didn't know was that the FBI had already launched an undercover operation, and it was actually an FBI undercover agent, posing as the technology broker, that met on several occasions with the two. After the "broker" informed Chou and Hso that the pharmaceutical company would not enter into a licensing agreement, Hsu reportedly said that they'd "get it another way" and directed the undercover agent to approach certain people at Bristol-Meyers to try to pay someone to steal it for them.[2]

The pair openly discussed their plans with the FBI undercover agent and at one point offered to pay $200,000 (later upped to $400,000) plus a percentage of the actual sales generated by Yen Foong Paper Company's sale of the purloined Taxol.

A legitimate Bristol-Meyers executive was recruited to play the part of a corrupt executive willing to sell the trade secrets to Yen Foong Paper Company. An FBI sting resulted in the arrest of Hsu and Ho on June 14, 1997, in a Philadelphia hotel room, where they had gone to make a preliminary payment.

Hsu was charged with attempted theft of trade secrets and other crimes. Ho was charged only with aiding and abetting. On March 31, 1999, on the eve of their trial, Hsu pled guilty to a sole count of conspiring to commit trade secret theft and was sentenced to two years probation and a $10,000 fine. The government dropped all other charges. All charges against Chester Ho were dropped. Taiwan refused to extradite Jessica Chou.

At no time was any trade secret compromised.

The Gillette Case: *United States v. Davis*

On September 24, 1997, a Federal Grand Jury in Nashville, Tennessee, indicted Stephen L. Davis, a former design engineer at a company called Wright Industries, Inc. Wright is a company that designs and builds custom machinery and was working on a new shaving system for its client, Gillette. At one time, Davis was the lead design engineer on the project, which ultimately resulted in Gillette's new and popular Mach 3 shaving system.

For reasons that were never explained, Gillette exercised its client prerogative and asked Wright to remove Davis from the team, which Wright did. But Davis first downloaded more than 600 megabytes of trade secret data, designs, and system drawings onto his laptop computer.

Angry and vengeful, both at Wright and Gillette, Davis sent the secret data, primarily by fax and e-mail, to Gillette's top competitors: Bic Corporation, American Safety Razor, and the former Warner-Lambert (now part of Pfizer), owner of Schick-Wilkinson Sword. Schick cut Davis to pieces by reporting the action back to Gillette.

What's interesting here—and should be especially instructive and frightening to all employers—is that Davis never even asked for money. He was not interested in selling the information; he was angry at his supervisor and at Gillette and fearful of losing his job, and he was looking to inflict damage and to seek revenge. It also came out later that Davis had committed résumé fraud by overstating his education when he applied for his job at Wright Industries. Apparently, Wright never conducted a standard background or credentials verification check on Davis, which would have easily uncovered the deception.

Davis pled guilty and was sentenced to 27 months in prison, three years supervised release, and $1.2 million in restitution.

While trade secrets were indeed compromised, *ultimately no trade secrets were lost.*

The Avery Dennison Spy Case: *United States v. Yang and Four Pillars*

Eventually, with Victor's confession and cooperation, the government was able to build a case against P.Y. Yang and his daughter, Sally, and Four Pillars. But that was still a long way off, because Victor took three months even to complete and sign his confession, so vast was his haul.

Among the trade secrets he stole, of course, was Avery Dennison's Asian expansion plan from Prem Krish's file cabinet—the document the FBI videotaped Victor removing. Later, a modified form of this document was used in a sting to help snare the Yangs, but it became an object of some bemused confusion in the courtroom of Magistrate Judge David S. Perelman, who was trying to understand what document Victor took and what document he gave to Four Pillars. There was Avery Dennison's original legitimate business plan; there was an altered version of that plan which Victor stole from Prem Krish's filing cabinet in the first FBI sting; and there was an additional modified version of that same plan that the Yangs were given in a later, second FBI sting. This last document was altered so that, when recovered, there could be no doubt of its origins. But at a preliminary hearing early on to determine if enough evidence was there to proceed and hold the defendants over for trial, Judge Per-

elman was having a hard time following FBI Special Agent Bartholomew's narrative, so the exasperated judge decided to take a stab
at clearing everything up:

The Court (Judge David Perelman): . . . let's get this straight because
I want to be sure that we have it straight.

The Witness (FBI Special Agent Michael Bartholomew): Good.

The Court: We start with, there was at one point a bona fide business plan being developed. That we know. We know that Avery
Dennison had their suspicions about Lee.

We also know that they took the bona fide business plan and
tailored it a bit to inject elements that would A, not accurately
reveal what their true plans for the Far East market were, and, B,
that if anybody came up with that doctored plan, it had to be
because they saw the one that was being circulated within Avery
Dennison, and the thought was, if that shows up, now we got
them cold.

Later on after Lee has been found to be doing what he
shouldn't [referring to Victor's pilfering the plan from Prem
Krish's office], the doctored plan is supplemented by another
communication or [sic] to an ancillary being issued, and those
are the documents that ultimately find their way to the Yangs,
and if I have misstated your testimony in that attempt to capsulize
it, please correct me.

The Witness: There was the business plan, which is part of what I
understand every business—this is from my own experience as
well as from what Avery Dennison has told me—[sic] performance on an ongoing basis. Information from that plan was taken
and put together into a document.

As I said, I don't know whether that was—those pages were
taken directly from their business plan or the information was
then retyped with the cover letter. There were things in there that
made it unique, so that if a copy of that plan were discovered anywhere else, we would know that it had to have come from that—

The Court: Let's back up. Did Lee—to the best of your knowledge, was Lee privy to—did he see the non-spurious version?

The Witness: Not to my knowledge.

The Court: So, the only version that Lee was made aware of or saw to your knowledge was the version 2, that doctored, altered, version.

The Witness: The extract from the true plan, yes.

The Court: Son of, son of plan.

The Witness: I don't know what you mean by that.

The Court: We have got Godzilla, and we have son of Godzilla. He saw son of Godzilla, right?

The Witness: I don't know what you mean by that, judge. I am sorry.

(Laughter.)

The Court: Let's go back to Kong and son of Kong. The plan is here that the executives developed.

The Witness: Right.

The Court: As far as you know, he never sees Kong.

The Witness: That's correct.

The Court: They then create son of Kong drawing some DNA from that but altering it, and he sees son of Kong. That's the one that he is caught fingering. Is that the scenario?

The Witness: I don't think it accurately describes what occurred, judge.[3]

What Victor Stole[4]

Whether or not you want to join Judge Perelman in his stroll down B movie memory lane, the vast accumulated list of what

Victor stole—ultimately revealed to be a staggering 12,000 research and development documents and 71 adhesive formulas, including trade secret information on 37 specialty adhesive tapes plus 20 label primers—was more than just Son of Kong. It was also Godzilla and the mighty King Kong combined—and then some. Victor's larceny knew no bounds.

According to Victor, Four Pillars not only received stolen formulas, but it used the Avery Dennison trade secrets to "substantially improve its label technology" and, in fact, gave the Taiwanese firm the ability to "improve its technology across its entire product line, including in the production of pressure-sensitive tape products which it sells in the United States."[5]

Larry Mitchell, Vice President and General Manager of Avery Dennison's Release Coated Materials division, and the man who 11 years earlier was instrumental in Victor's hiring and later was his boss, explained that the disclosed materials gave Four Pillars "a significant competitive advantage" with respect to pressure-sensitive tapes and the stolen information "effected essentially a full-scale technology transfer that allowed Four Pillars to become a much more effective participant in the pressure-sensitive label business."[6]

As a result of the thefts, Four Pillars was able to transform itself "from a technologically primitive company to a company with modern—and, in some cases—state-of-the-art technology. It . . . improved the quality and range of its products and reduced its manufacturing costs. While it gained substantial unjust enrichment on a theft-by-theft, product-by-product basis, the cumulative effect was even greater. Its illegal conduct allowed Four Pillars to transform itself from a marginal player in the adhesive industry to one that is now positioned—through extensive thefts of Avery Dennison's trade secrets—to become a significant participant in the global market for pressure-sensitive adhesives."[7]

Also, Victor didn't just put a formula into the mail and consider his job done; he believed he had a responsibility to make certain that Four Pillars' researchers and scientists fully understood how to make the best and most profitable use of Avery Dennison's stolen trade secrets. To further this effort, Four Pillars paid for Victor and his wife and young daughter to travel to Taiwan in the summers, where he held seminars for that company's scientists in 1990, 1991, 1992, 1994, and 1996. Some of the seminars lasted more than a week, during which Victor often gave out copies of Avery Dennison's new, experimental, still-in-development products and processes. In return, Four Pillars often gave something to Victor at these clambakes: a wish list—or shopping list, if you will—of Avery Dennison trade secrets that it wanted Victor to steal in the coming year, according to testimony.

As you peruse the following list of stolen trade secrets[8] and question how Avery Dennison could have possibly been so unaware for so long, remember this problematic axiom that faces every company, including your own: A trade secret is the *only* thing that can be stolen and you may never know it's missing.

Highlights of Material Provided in 1989

In July 1989, soon after Victor returned to the United States after initially agreeing to be a spy for Four Pillars, he sent P.Y. an outline of what he would be providing during the coming year under two broad headings: Product Development and Adhesive Formulation. In his first mailing, he included an internal and confidential Avery Dennison training guide for pressure-sensitive adhesive technology. It was, in some respects, a master blueprint for what was to come in years to follow.

In August, he shipped technical detail on *mastercurves* for two specific Avery Dennison products. A mastercurve and its accompanying formula give the owner the potential to manufacture clones of a product.

By sending Avery Dennison mastercurves to Four Pillars, Victor was providing the end result of what Avery Dennison had spent millions of dollars to create. So, without spending a dime on R&D (excluding paltry payments to Victor), Four Pillars was getting the ability to exactly reproduce some of Avery Dennison's most successful products. To judge the *potential* for this sort of activity to take place, you might want to bear in mind that P.Y. and Four Pillars had been found guilty of counterfeiting a competitor's product previously.

It is apparent from Victor's testimony that Four Pillars wanted to improve its technology and its knowledge of Avery Dennison's products and its technology. Did Four Pillars clone Avery Dennison products? Did they have to? As P.Y. said once to Victor, all they had to do was modify a formula to make the technology work for them.

In short, having a mastercurve and the corresponding formula is like having the keys to the kingdom. And Victor made certain that Four Pillars had plenty of keys on its key ring.

In August of that year, Victor sent Four Pillars the two highly technical rheology reports (referred to earlier) prepared by international rheology expert Dr. E.P. Chang of the Avery Research Center. These reports constituted "the fruit of painstaking work of Avery Research Center over a period of years," as Victor had explained in a letter to P.Y. Yang. The reports, as well as a two-year summary of Victor's own successful work in rheology, were highly technical. Consequently, Victor and Four Pillars began making plans for Victor to spend his next summer vacation in Taipei so that Victor could hold the first of many summer seminars for Four Pillars' scientists to teach them how to use the information in the two reports as well as other highly technical information that he would send over the next eight years.

In September, Victor mailed the secret formulation for one of Avery Dennison's emulsion adhesives and the exact trade secret formulation of how to make one of Avery Dennison's most successful commercial products. In a cover letter, Victor described the product for which he had provided the formulation as "a new weapon marketed as recently as September of this year."

Just before Halloween, Victor mailed P.Y. Yang the secret test results of two new products not yet in the market, along with ten sheets of special paper specifications. He also sent Four Pillars a technical internal Avery Dennison software program that he had written.

Early the next month, a Four Pillars scientist wrote to Victor asking him to run tests in the Avery Dennison research center to determine if a particular mastercurve that Victor had sent could be used for electronic data processing labels. So, to add insult to injury, not only was Victor sending trade secrets to Four Pillars, but he was also using Avery Dennison labs to conduct tests on behalf of Four Pillars. It would not be the last time.

In December, Victor sent Four Pillars highly confidential 1989 sales data for Avery Dennison's Fasson Roll division and a discussion of Fasson's trade secret hotmelt adhesive technology. At the time, hotmelt technology was a core competency of Avery Dennison's. As a bonus, he told Four Pillars that he had in his possession "four or five [of] Fasson's hotmelt PSA [pressure-sensitive adhesive] formulas that are highly profitable, and I can provide them at any time."

For his services in 1989, Victor received the $25,000 (less taxes) cited earlier—the check made out to his mother-in-law after he initially agreed to spy for Four Pillars. The mother-in-law, remember, was depositing the money into her daughter's account, but without telling the daughter.

So far, Four Pillars' investment was paying off. But this was just the tip of the adhesive iceberg.

Highlights of Material Provided in 1990

Victor said that Four Pillars wanted to know how some of its products stacked up against some of Avery Dennison's, so the Taiwanese company asked him to run competitive tests. In February, Victor complied and sent P.Y. a side-by-side comparison between a Four Pillars adhesive and an Avery Dennison adhesive—compliments of Avery Dennison's state-of-the-art research facilities in Concord, Ohio.

Later that month, Victor took a little road trip to a Newark Airport Holiday Inn, where he met with Sally, Paul Huang, a Four Pillars research engineer, and K.M. Chang, a Four Pillars executive—not to be confused with Dr. E.P. Chang, Avery Dennison's internationally renowned rheology expert. The purpose of the meeting was for Victor to hand over more trade secrets that he had stolen, including a complete set of current Fasson paper specifications and application sheets, along with the instructional detail of how to use them. These specifications gave Four Pillars the ability to reproduce exact copies of Avery Dennison paper face stock. Victor said that one of the purposes of the two-day meeting "was to educate Four Pillars on the potential uses and values of hotmelt technology."

For good measure, Victor also provided the Four Pillars team with three new testing methods for silicone.

In mid-March, Victor sent P.Y. test samples demonstrating the coverage effect of silicone on 16 different Avery Dennison products, to better enable Four Pillars to refine its own expertise in silicone coverage.

In the label sandwich, silicone is a critical layer in pressure-sensitive adhesives. It is the silicone release coating layer that is peeled back to expose the adhesive. Obviously, this is a vital trade secret that is as essential to the commercial success of an adhesive product as the actual adhesive itself. The 16 test samples Victor supplied comprised virtually the entire library of Avery Dennison's silicone chemistry samples and gave the holder immediate access and interpretation of essential silicone tests that had taken Avery Dennison years and years and millions and millions of R&D dollars to develop on its own.

Victor was quiet for the next several months, but in July he and his wife and daughter traveled to Taiwan at Four Pillars' expense to deliver the first of five technical seminars to the company. On American Independence Day, Victor continued his treachery by giving a presentation on polymer rheology and pressure-sensitive adhesive mastercurves to a group of senior Four Pillars executives and scientists: Sally Yang, C.K. Kao, and C.M. Chang. Periodically, chairman P.Y. Yang would make an appearance. Victor's intent was to bring Four Pillars a better understanding of Avery Dennison technology in these critical areas.

The next day Victor lectured on adhesion and peel mechanics.

On July 6, he taught the same group all about silicone release coating, and specifically high-speed release. (Recall the critical importance of high-speed release during the production process.)

Over the next few days, Victor continued revealing Avery Dennison trade secrets, and on July 10, he visited a Four Pillars plant to gain a better understanding of the company's technological strengths, weaknesses, and limitations.

At the end of his productive week in Taipei, he gave one final presentation on pressure-sensitive formulations, including acrylic, hotmelt, and styrene butadiene rubber. He admitted that he was showing off because he wanted to impress his Taiwanese colleagues with the breath and depth of his technical knowledge and sophistication. He ended the day by disgorging a number of specific trade secret formulations for commercially successful Avery Dennison products, including various emulsion-based, solvent-based, and hot-melt-based adhesive formulations.

Before Victor boarded the plane for his return trip to the United States, he said that Four Pillars told him they were interested in developing their ability to work with direct thermal label products and needed Victor's assistance to improve their position in the marketplace. Accordingly, in early September, the spy sent his Taiwanese masters samples of Avery Dennison's new thermal paper product.

Ever the tutor, Victor gave Sally a refresher course in the materials that he had provided when she visited him in Ohio the previous October.

As long as Victor was receptive to receiving out-of-town visitors, C.K. Kao flew to Ohio to meet with the spy two months later. Kao had previously told Victor to obtain the composition for a specific Avery Dennison product, and during their December meeting, they had a long discussion about it and its performance. Victor obtained and mailed the formula to Kao in mid-December, and said in his confession that Four Pillars hoped to prepare products based on this secret formulation. The two also had an extensive conversation about Avery Dennison's ZPE-1000 high-speed release tester, this still being a topic of immense importance to Four Pillars. Remember, one of the keys to profits in labels is a trouble-free high-speed release at the end of the production line.

Victor also sent Four Pillars third quarter sales, business, and research and development reports from Avery Dennison's Fasson Roll division and similar reports from July and August for the Specialty Tape division. He also shipped them two reports he had written himself on release curves of pressure-sensitive labels.

And a special bonus: highly technical reports on remoisturization, modeling, curl control, and moisture measurement, prepared by one of Avery Dennison's top scientists, Dr. Kyung Min. Suffice it to say that because the production of labels requires fluids, the process of optimizing drying and remoisturizing paper are critical to the development of a commercially successful adhesive product.

Dr. Min is a research fellow at the Avery Research Center, the highest level scientist at the company, and an internationally recognized expert in his field. Avery Dennison maintained that the information in those reports—the results of years of labor and millions in R&D dollars—existed nowhere else in the world. Whoever held this nugget in their hands would immediately be able to reduce the costs and expenses of its entire line of products.

In 1990, Victor received a total of $18,000—$3,000 in July, which he deposited in the United States, and $15,000 in September, which he sent to his mother-in-law for her to deposit for him in Taipei.

Highlights of Material Provided in 1991

The first half of the year began quietly, but in July Victor traveled to Taipei to give an eight-day seminar to senior executives from Four Pillars. In an effort to conceal Victor from other employees at Four Pillars, the company arranged for him to speak at private meeting room at the Department of Chemical Engineering at the National Taiwan University. In attendance were Sally, her husband Ed Yin, several high-level Four Pillars scientists, and from time to time P.Y. himself.

As part of its open culture, every year Avery Dennison's top researchers from around the globe meet at an Annual Technical Symposium. The best and the brightest of the company's scientific minds share the fruits of their labors internally with their colleagues at these high-level conclaves. Most of the scientists prepare papers highlighting achievements and breakthroughs, as well as hopes for technology still in the lab. The company's most promising research is revealed and attendance is severely restricted. Awards are presented for the best papers and, in his career, Victor had received such an award one year.

As the first order of business at the 1991 seminar, Victor turned over to Four Pillars a four-inch binder containing confidential reports and papers that had been presented at the Annual Technical Symposium that year in Concord, Ohio. One of the papers was Victor's own on high-speed release technology.

During his seminar week in Taiwan, Victor became a self-styled marketing authority and consulted with company executives on the best ways for Four Pillars to develop its label business. He had no background and no expertise in marketing, but that didn't stop him from holding forth on the subject for two days, offering his untrained opinion on which avenues would be most profitable for the company.

Returning to a subject closer to his field, Victor next disclosed trade secret formulas for two Avery Dennison removable adhesive products. What is interesting here is that these products were out of Victor's area of expertise completely. According to the Avery Dennison complaint, he had pilfered them from a colleague. In an effort to continue to demonstrate his worth and his value to Four Pillars, Victor had decided to branch out beyond his own ken.

This last bit of information, said Victor, was greatly coveted by Four Pillars, but the company needed information on the primer that would be used to formulate these products. Victor said he would provide the information when he returned home.

Another of Avery Dennison's divisions is Specialty Tape, such as the diaper tape used on disposable diapers. Victor had nothing to do with Specialty Tape, but that didn't stop him from branching out on this subject, too. At the seminar he provided the hotmelt adhesive formulations used in diaper tape.

Before Victor left Taiwan, he again met with Four Pillars executives who told him what they were most interested in obtaining. In late August, Victor sent P.Y. his outline plan of what he would try to send from Summer 1991 to Summer 1992. It was an ambitious undertaking and included:

- The formulas for five separate removable adhesive products
- The primer for one specific product
- Information on coating methods, equipment and machinery
- Viscoelastic mastercurves of 20 separate Avery Dennison adhesives

- Compositions for emulsion acrylic adhesives
- Compounding, storage, and test methods for hotmelt adhesives
- Additional information on Avery Dennison high-speed release
- Samples of a new top secret Avery Dennison product still being developed
- Handouts on Avery Dennison's rheology work in emulsion and colloid
- Avery Research Center's monthly individual and group status reports

Victor was largely successful in meeting his plan. In this shipment, Victor was thoughtful enough to include the trade secret formulizations for the primer coating that Four Pillars had specifically requested before he left Taiwan. He added a note that with the formula Four Pillars should be able to develop "a very profitable product." For good measure, he threw in information on two other Avery Dennison adhesives along with instructions for optimum manufacturing conditions.

In October, Victor sent Four Pillars specifications of three types of Avery Dennison products for internal transfer papers. These key specifications are so secret that Avery Dennison does not even provide them to its paper manufacturers.

Sally was Victor's house guest later that month, when Victor said he provided her with the viscoelastic plots for two new Avery Dennison products, along with a high-performance permanent solvent adhesive sample for high-speed release calibration. This sample, unavailable outside of Avery Dennison, would allow Four Pillars to accurately calibrate its new equipment—equipment that had been purchased under Victor's direction and guidance.

So, a new feather in Victor's hat: research scientist, marketing guru, and now purchasing agent. Plus, of course, master spy.

And for his services that year, Victor received $14,100 in travelers checks in July, which was deposited in the United States. Later that year, he received a $3,000 expense check, deposited in the U.S., and $15,000 (before taxes) mailed to his mother-in-law for her to deposit in Taipei.

Highlights of Material Provided in 1992

The year began well for Four Pillars. Not only did Victor send the trade secret formula for adhesive monomer composition and surfactant, but the spy added a belated Christmas present: two internal Avery Dennison Specialty Tape division reports on competitive benchmarking. These reports represented Avery Dennison's test research conducted on competitive products. So now, in addition to everything else, Victor was providing the Taiwanese firm with access to Avery Dennison's research and analysis of *its* competitors' best products.

Just so there's no misunderstanding, what Avery Dennison was doing in its competitive benchmarking is an example of *competitive intelligence* which, you may recall from the Introduction to this book, is completely legal. But taking Avery Dennison's internal competitive intelligence, or competitive benchmarking, studies and reports is economic espionage; it is completely illegal.

In July, Victor and his family again traveled, expense-free, to Taiwan for another of his seminars. The same attendees as last year were present, and the seminar again was held away from Four Pillars' headquarters to protect knowledge of Victor's existence. This time, the seminar was held in a private meeting room at the San-Shin Cooperation Bank in downtown Taipei.

Much of the presentation centered on high-speed release technology, which was now one of Victor's specialties at Avery Dennison. It should be pointed out that high-speed release equipment, which can be purchased on the open market, is not, in and of itself, proprietary or a trade secret. However, the specific methods and applications used by Avery Dennison are very much trade secrets. Victor disclosed this proprietary information at the seminar.

He also gave a silicone chemistry presentation, along with additional detail on Avery Dennison's formulation and analytical methods. Victor felt Four Pillars was weak in this last area and attempted to shore up its knowledge base.

In late 1992, Four Pillars suffered a serious fire at its main production plant in Taipei. The company's rehabilitation demanded the attention of all key executives, so their attention to Victor was diverted for a time.

Nevertheless, he received $9,500 in travelers checks when he was in Taipei in July. The amount was intentionally under $10,000, the limit under which no customs declarations is required. Late in 1992, $18,700 was mailed directly to his mother-in-law.

Highlights of Material Provided in 1993

Much to Victor's surprise, he was informed in early 1993 by Four Pillars vice president C.K. Kao that Avery Dennison and Four Pillars were engaged in possible joint venture discussions. In fear that he might be found out, Victor was told to curtail his espionage activities until further notice.

Nevertheless, he wanted to maintain ongoing channels of communication with his benefactor, so he continued sporadically to send some technical—but, for the most part, publicly available—information.

No seminar and no trip to Taiwan took place that year. However, from Victor's perspective, things started to look up again soon. While touring Avery Dennison's Ohio facilities in August of that year, P.Y. himself paid Victor a visit. P.Y., whom Victor looked up to as a father figure, told him to plan to come to Taiwan in the summer of 1994 to have more discussions with Four Pillars officers and scientists. Victor was elated.

Victor's comparatively idle year was reflected in his payment from Four Pillars of a mere $1,200, reimbursable expenses for books he had purchased and mailed from the United States.

Highlights of Material Provided in 1994

Once again, as P.Y. had promised, Four Pillars paid for Victor and his family to travel to Taiwan in July of 1994. It was time for another seminar. The seminar, attended again by the same cast of characters, was held at Four Pillars' former executive offices in San

Chung City. A side trip was arranged for Victor to visit, observe, and comment on Four Pillars' Tao-Yuan plant.

Of all the material Victor had sent to Four Pillars, the piece that was most highly prized was the deBoer Report—a highly technical, very expensive, extremely confidential, and absolutely proprietary document about five-roll silicone technology.

Rob deBoer was a senior scientist consulting with Avery Dennison. He worked in Europe but came to the United States to teach Avery Dennison all he knew about five-roll silicone technology—which was more than anyone else in the world. Just to understand how to use this technology, which Avery Dennison referred to as a combination of art and science, takes years of experience. This report, which Avery Dennison valued so highly, laid out deBoer's years of experience in minute, confidential detail.

Victor turned it over to Four Pillars without batting an eye, and the company launched an immediate effort to get into five-roll silicone coating production, which in addition to providing a marked quality improvement over other production methods, also lowers manufacturing costs in the long run. Two years later, thanks to Victor, Four Pillars purchased and installed a brand spanking new five-roll silicone coater, but then needed Victor's help on which paper release liner to be used with its new prize.

For work in 1994, Victor received a check for $15,100. However, in a bizarre coincidence, the check that P.Y. gave Victor was actually a U.S. check from Monsanto Corporation made out to Dr. John Guo—the very same Guo who in 1996 would be barred by P.Y. from accepting the tantalizing Avery Dennison job offer and ultimately blow the whistle on Victor. Guo had endorsed the check over to Four Pillars and P.Y. had endorsed it to Victor, presumably so as not to leave a paper trial of payments from Four Pillars to Victor. Ironically, in 1996, when Guo was unable to accept the Avery Dennison position, he took a job with Monsanto.

In October, another $20,000 was deposited by Victor's mother-in-law in Taipei. I believe this large deposit was actually an advance payment for 1995, because no payments were recorded that year.

Highlights of Material Provided in 1995

This was a quiet, low production year for the spy, even though he continued to provide information to Four Pillars throughout the year. He met with P.Y. at the Holiday Inn in Westlake, Ohio—a hotel that would soon figure prominently in Victor's and P.Y.'s lives.

But in December, according to Victor, P.Y. asked him to obtain needed information on some specific printing testing equipment and the two discussed the status of Four Pillars' new silicone coater.

Just before the end of the year, Victor sent P.Y. information on the IGT printing equipment he had requested.

Highlights of Material Provided in 1996

In April, Victor shipped a package of materials, including a Fasson Roll division confidential internal report on thermal silicones, a confidential summary of silicone development, and a confidential design of an experimental plan. Some of the silicone material had actually been prepared by Victor, silicone now being on of his growing list of specialties.

The 1996 summer seminar went off like clockwork with the usual Taiwanese crew in attendance. That year, the seminar was limited to just one day, at Four Pillars' office in Taipei.

Victor had missed—or not been invited to—the Annual Avery Dennison Technical Symposium earlier that year. But, not wanting to show up at the July seminar in Taipei empty-handed, he requested of an Avery Dennison employee—*and received!*—a binder of presentations and technical research papers that had been presented at the 1996 Technical Symposium. This included highly technical papers from nine of the company's most talented scientists from around the world.

In addition, Victor had learned of a top secret product in development at Avery Dennison called the Aquarius Project, a waterproof label project on which the company had spent more than $10 million in R&D costs. Only a tiny handful of people at Avery Dennison even knew of it. Even though Victor was not working on it, he knew people who were. Using a technique known as *social engineering*—the ability to sweet-talk information out of an unsuspecting pawn, a subject we will examine in some detail later—Victor learned all he could from his unsuspecting coworkers who were involved in the top secret project and revealed it at the seminar in Taiwan.

Victor's final payment from Four Pillars was $13,000. His total, including some expenses not listed here, was calculated at about $160,000.

An Explosion of New Products in Taiwan

Victor's economic espionage was indeed Godzilla, Son of Kong, and the Mighty Kong himself! It was the whole damned monkey house. The fruits of Victor's espionage amounted to a wholesale transfer of millions and millions of dollars of technology and trade secrets, almost as though Victor had backed an 18-wheeler right up to the back door of the company in broad daylight and began to fill the semi to capacity. These were the crown jewels of the company.

It was economic espionage writ large.

And it turned out later that he had taken lots more that no one knew about!

Testimony at the civil trial (more so than at the criminal trial) revealed that Four Pillars took much of the Avery Dennison technology and built "new" or modified products straight off the Avery Dennison platforms. The whole Four Pillars/Taiwanese market just exploded with new products thanks to the economic espionage.

Avery Dennison would soon face a potential public relations, business, and financial nightmare unlike any the company had ever experienced. The whole crisis was about to explode and reverberate around the globe, because shortly before Victor's July 1996 seminar in Taiwan, unsuspecting Avery Dennison unwittingly ignited its own fuse by innocently offering a job to that young Four Pillars scientist, Dr. John Guo.

And what motivated Guo to ultimately expose Victor was a psychological provocation that's been around since time immemorial: revenge.

CHAPTER 8

Fear and Loathing in the Workplace, Fear and Loathing in the World

"If you prick us, do we not bleed? If you tickle us,
do we not laugh? If you poison us, do we not die?
And if you wrong us, shall we not revenge?"

—William Shakespeare, *The Merchant of Venice*

Someone I knew some years ago, fresh with a Ph.D. in biochemistry under his arm, surveyed the corporate landscape and decided to accept a job offer from consumer goods giant Procter & Gamble in Cincinnati, Ohio. When I asked him why, he replied that, according to his research, in all the years P&G had been in existence, the company had never laid off a single worker. Being newly married, his primary rationale for taking the position was job security.

In 1999, Procter & Gamble declared it would eliminate 15,000 jobs by the year 2005, and in early 2001 announced it was laying off 9,600 workers, or 9 percent of its workforce.

On April 1, 2001, I sat at my computer and typed in a search for the word *layoffs*. In a matter of seconds, I had retrieved 129 stories that went back just 30 days. When I increased the search to 90 days, the number of stories jumped to 478.

In addition to P&G, here's a small sampling of one month's misery, consisting just of companies whose names are probably familiar to most of you:

- Delphi Automotive Systems. 11,500 jobs (7,600 in the United States, representing 10 percent of its U.S. workforce)

- Solectron Corp. 8,200 jobs
- Motorola. 7,000 jobs (a *second* announced cutback)
- Compaq Computer Corp. 5,000 jobs
- Cisco. 5,000 jobs (11 percent of its workforce)
- Walt Disney Co. 4,000 jobs (3 percent, largest layoff in the company's history)
- Cable and Wireless. 4,000 jobs
- MarchFirst. 3,500 jobs (50 percent!)
- Charles Schwab Corp. 3,400 jobs (approximately 12 percent)
- Gillette. 2,700 jobs
- AOL Time Warner. 2,000 jobs (2 percent)
- H.J. Heinz Co. 1,900 jobs (4 percent)
- *San Jose Mercury News.* 1,700 jobs
- Conexant. 1,500 jobs (20 percent)
- TRW. 1,000 jobs (1 percent)
- Texas Instruments. 600 jobs (a plant closing)
- NBC. 300 to 600 jobs (between 5 and 10 percent)

In the first half of 2001, more than 300,000 tech jobs were eliminated, representing about 40 percent of the U.S. total, according to outplacement firm Challenger, Gray & Christmas.[1]

These numbers are actually more frightening than they appear. In the preglobalization days of Bush I (as opposed to his son, Bush II), these numbers would have presaged a certain recession in the United States. But in the age of globalization, not all of these cutbacks translate into U.S. job losses. The tremendous growth this nation enjoyed for more than a decade enabled American businesses to expand manufacturing plants and offices worldwide. The Manufacturers Alliance, a Washington, D.C., trade group, estimates that more than half of all U.S. manufacturers today are operating on a global basis.[2]

By the way, if we were to just count U.S. job losses in that same month, there were 86,000 layoffs, while the government had been expecting to *add* 58,000 jobs nationwide.[3] This was the second biggest U.S. job reduction since Bush I in November 1991, in the days of the nation's last recession.

But the layoffs and other cost-cutting moves announced by U.S.-based companies are, in many cases, spread worldwide. We are, in effect, spreading our pain by exporting our slowdown, mostly to Europe and Latin America. When Delphi announced it was laying off 11,500, that included thousands of workers and some plant closures in Mexico, France, Italy, the United Kingdom, Germany, and Brazil. Besides closing a plant in Georgia, Solectron's 8,200 job cutback includes closing plants in Mexico and Hungary. And the list goes on. So why is that bad news for the United States?

In the age of globalization, a larger-than-ever boomerang factor that we never had to consider before is at work. When Compaq Computers lays off 5,000 workers, the ripple effect is far reaching. Take the case of Creative Labs in Malvern, Pennsylvania, formerly makers of the popular SoundBlaster sound cards for computers. Its parent company was Creative Technologies in Singapore. But, because of a drop in sound card orders, directly caused by a drop in computer sales by U.S. computer manufacturers, the Singapore-based parent company recently announced a 10 percent cutback in its workforce—its *global* workforce—and that included all of the 150 workers in Malvern. As we export our slowdown, so, too, does the rest of the world. What goes around comes around.

But this is bad news for the United States for another reason, one that more directly concerns our discussion. One of the known key sources of economic espionage is current or former employees—the proverbial inside job. How much loyalty can you expect from a laid off worker? Not much, that's for sure. Revenge or retribution is frequently becoming the order of the day.

With the right motivation, anyone can be inspired to become a spy.

Retribution from Within

The right motivation is a very powerful force. And revenge is among the most potent. Remember, too, that the notion of stealing trade secrets is often considered just a way of doing business in certain parts of the world. In short, if we as a nation are exporting our economic slowdown around the globe, we are also importing an increased global risk of economic espionage.

Employees like Victor Lee, who commit economic espionage over a period of time and without any sense of urgency, are in one group. Employees who are suddenly and without warning thrown out of work may be motivated to seek drastic solutions to put bread on their families' tables immediately. Ethics go out the window; necessity is often the driving force. And economic espionage is too often the fuel that drives the engine of necessity.

Also, agreements not to divulge trade secrets are enforceable only if the former employee, or the employee's new company, is caught. Because, as pointed out before, a trade secret may be stolen without a company knowing that it is "missing," a company's competitor can use it for economic benefit, and the victim may never even know it.

As an example, a glut of technology workers on the market means a feast for those companies who are hiring tech workers. When Lucent Technologies announced in January 2001 that it was laying off 2,000 workers, other technology companies began to scramble to attract some of the best and the brightest that Lucent was turning loose. But dislocated workers, with thousands of others elbowing them at a prospective employers' gate, may seek *any* edge in getting in the door—including divulging trade secrets from their former employer.

And let's not overlook employees at other companies who already have a corrupt mind-set reaching out and trying to entice your key workers. Do you think that is unlikely? Do you think your employees are so loyal that they would never be lured over to "the dark side"? Think again.

Let's say your company recently laid off 10 percent of its global workforce. How confident do you think the other 90 percent are that *their* jobs are secure? If an executive at one of your competitors targets one of your key workers for recruitment—one of the current lucky 90 percent—and paints a doom and gloom scenario for her of her current position and current employer, how loyal do you think she'll remain and for how long? What will she do? Will she report the improper overtures to you, hoping the revelation will ensure her future with your company? Or will she cross over, taking your best trade secrets with her? What motivates her? Loyalty to you, or the cost of putting braces on her daughter's teeth?

And finally, among the list of companies at the beginning of this chapter who have laid off workers, save a special place for Computer Associates. According to published reports,[4] the company was accused of firing workers for "poor performance"—even those with outstanding annual reviews—to save the cost of severance and health insurance that accompanies most layoffs. Dismissed workers accused the company of disguising a mass layoff as individual firings for poor performance. The company denied it, *but if employees believe it, the perception is more important than the reality.* I can only imagine the sense of "loyalty" those Computer Associates employees feel toward their former employer.

In short, there is genuine fear and loathing in the global workplace, and that only raises the risk of global economic espionage. How high a risk? According to the FBI and other sources discussed in detail in later chapters on risk, some 80 percent of economic espionage is done by insiders—employees, vendors, contract employees, partners—people with knowledge, access, and frequently an ax to grind.

Cold, Cruel World

Earlier, I pointed out that U.S. economic growth has engendered envy among the world's nations. Of course, with that envy comes the backlash of economic espionage, as companies seek ways to keep pace with the United States. But some of the mind-numbing, rearward decisions of the current administration, almost bringing back vestiges of the Cold War, are doing more to provoke a concentrated *global* backlash against this nation than anything done previously. You can't be an isolationist in an age of globalization.

"Bush II has reeled backward so fast, economically, environmentally, globally, culturally," said Maureen Dowd of *The New York Times*, "it's redolent of Dorothy clicking her way from the shimmering spires of Oz to a depressed black-and-white Kansas."[5]

In 1997, the United States signed what is commonly referred to as the Kyoto Treaty, or Protocol, which calls for signatory countries to agree to legally binding targets for reducing emissions, mainly carbon dioxide, created by burning fossil fuels like oil that contribute to global warming.

Bush II—many of whose big money backers come from the oil industry—announced at the start of his term that the United States was not going to honor the Kyoto Treaty or the nation's word to abide by the terms of the Treaty. (The Treaty, agreed to in the Clinton administration, had not been ratified by Congress at the start of the new administration.)

The president made it clear that he felt the Kyoto Treaty would be a bitter pill for certain businesses, and he considered the U.S. economy more important than the Earth's environment. Whether or not he's right is not part of our discussion, and I don't want to get mired or even sidetracked in politics. The perceived heavy-handed, America-first way in which he made the announcement raised the ire of the world's leaders, who immediately attacked the United States in venomously strong language.

"The court of world opinion delivered a harsh verdict . . . on President Bush's decision to put the U.S. economy ahead of global climate protection. Politicians, environmentalists, and commentators accused Bush of arrogance, isolationism, and being 'just not big enough for his job,'" wrote the *Los Angeles Times* in a story about the reaction of the world's leaders to Bush II's decision. Declaring that withdrawing from the Treaty would damage the United States as well as its image, leaders of Europe, China, and Japan said it was "a moral lapse by the world's biggest polluter."[6]

German Chancellor Gerhard Schroeder said, "The U.S. [must] accept its responsibility for the world climate [as] the heaviest energy consumer," and Swedish Environment Minister Kjell Larsson criticized Bush by saying, "No individual country has the right to declare a multilateral agreement dead." A member of Britain's Parliament, Alan Simpson, more bluntly described Bush's decision as being "equivalent to launching a nuclear attack whose missiles will land across the globe over the next 30 years." He then called for an international boycott of American products.

According to a global roundup report in the *Los Angeles Times*,[7] Tokyo's *Shimbun* newspaper denounced Bush for "great-power greed." France's daily newspaper *Libération* said that Americans were promoting "hostile opinions and an explosive diplomatic isolation." And the Portuguese newspaper *Publico* said Bush was acting with "the arrogance of someone who thinks he owns the world." Many world leaders openly threatened economic retaliation against the United States unless Bush reconsidered. Even the presumably nonpolitical Council of Churches said the United States was betraying its "responsibility as global citizens." And even China—*China!*—called *us* "irresponsible."

But our oldest and closest friends, the British, leveled the most devastating slings and arrows our way. An editorial in Britain's *Guardian* newspaper called the United States an "unrepentant outlaw" and went on to say, in part:

> George Bush's decision to trash the Kyoto global warming treaty is appalling . . . Mr. Bush, clinging to his "national interest" credo, seems incapable of seeing the big picture. He does not grasp the basic truth that America's national interest is inextricably intertwined with the global interest. . . Instead of leading the community of nations, Bush's America seems increasingly intent on confronting it . . . [saying] we do what we want, for ourselves, regardless of the consequences for you. And if you don't like it, well, tough. . . .[8]

A few days later, Polly Toynbee, in a column in *The Guardian*, naming us "America the Horrible," wrote, "In less than 100 days, [Bush] has turned America into a pariah [and] made enemies of the entire world . . . ." Citing some 45 editorials from around the globe critical of America, and referring to us at one point as "the evil empire," she said, "The rest of the world draws instinctively together in its repudiation of the Bush Junior White House."[9]

This is the reaction of the global community (and some in the president's own party) to a U.S. action other nations consider wrong-headed, self-serving, and most assuredly antiglobal. Not since the community of nations banded together to verbally and militarily attack Iraq during the Persian Gulf War has such a unifying outcry occurred against a single nation.

And global loathing over the administration's America-first attitude does nothing but stoke the fires of increased economic espionage.

This administration's nationalistic mantra that it must soften environmental regulations and allow increased pollution to prevent a recession and spur the country's economic growth, only "revives the insupportable notion that economic progress and environmental protection are incompatible."[10] You don't have to look any further than the nation's unprecedented economic growth during the environmentally friendly Clinton administration to disprove Bush II's position.

A national poll taken by the *Los Angeles Times* on the heels of this global flap showed that 53 percent of the nation favored protecting the environment over protecting jobs, and said that if economic growth required environmental degradation, improving and protecting the environment should take precedent. The newspaper said Bush II had a "tin ear" on the environment.

Even if the White House suddenly reversed course, the world's community of nations views America as believing that it can do whatever it wants and the rest of the world be damned. Any capitulation on the part of the White House now may be viewed as too little too late.

If the nations of the world had it in for us before, the Bush II position on the environment gives them license to steal. It was one thing when we were envied and/or hated because we were successful in our research, development, innovations, and economic growth. But now, Bush II has paved the way for global economic espionage to be perpetrated against U.S. businesses by foreign companies and countries that think that our success is being floated on the back of the world's environment. When Bush II says the Kyoto Protocol is bad for the U.S. economy and, therefore, he won't support it, how does he *expect* the world to react? This administration's policy and attitude was not well received anywhere in the world. And if we are, indeed, globally viewed as an "unrepentant outlaw," why should foreign countries and companies care a damn about the legal boundaries set forth in our Economic Espionage Act? If we're environmental outlaws, other nations and companies may reason that they have the right to be economic espionage outlaws: espionage tit for environmental tat.

Trouble at the United Nations

If you want more evidence that the nations of the world have their long knives out for us, consider this unprecedented humiliation. In May 2001, for the first time, the United States was denied a seat on the prestigious United Nations Human Rights Commission. This mortifying defeat came after the United States had received written assurances from 43 of 53 eligible voting countries that they'd vote for us, but when the secret ballot was counted, we had received only 29 votes. Even many of our allies voted against us.

The New York Times said the U.N. rebuff came about as a direct result of inattention on the part of the Bush administration and "rising resentment abroad" toward America and its policies.[11] Using even blunter language, the *Los Angeles Times* called it "payback time for what a growing number of states deplore as a new go-it-alone approach to global affairs."[12] And The Associated Press cited Chinese state media and progovernment experts who hailed our loss "as a rejection of U.S. attempts to bully other nations."[13]

Secretary of State Colin Powell expressed shock and dismay at the vote and said he blamed it on some unease over certain U.S. initiatives around the world. That is an understatement.

In retaliation, outraged members of Congress threatened to withhold payment of $244 million in back dues to the U.N., unless we regained our seat at the next election, scheduled for spring, 2002. Oh, yes; we have been reviled for years for not paying our U.N. dues—which at one point far exceeded $1 billion. You can imagine how well that extortionist threat went over.

Almost overlooked was another embarrassing downfall. On the same day, the United States also lost its seat on the U.N. International Narcotics Control Board. Not only were we instrumental in the founding of this important board in 1964, but a senior American diplomat had cochaired the group for the past decade. As before, we had obtained written assurances of support, but received few votes. Again, many of our allies abandoned us in the secret ballot.

Taking us to task publicly, Sweden's U.N. ambassador Pierre Schori, whose country was among those that won seats on the human rights panel, said, "Global problems need global solutions. You can't go it alone any longer in this globalizing world."[14]

And former Secretary of State Madeleine Albright, who previously served as our ambassador to the U.N., called it "a sock-back for the unilateralism . . . that this administration is developing."[15]

Bad for Business

Teddy Roosevelt used to say that America should walk softly and carry a big stick. But we're no longer doing that and haven't been for some time; we're stumbling around like a loud, belligerent master of the house who's drunk on power—military and economic.

No matter how you slice it, we now have genuine fear and loathing in the world directed squarely at us. It *is* payback time, and one of the most effective payback weapons is economic espionage.

Even if the United States eventually ratifies the Kyoto Treaty, the damage has been done. The Bush II administration has sent a clear and unmistakable signal around the globe that it is simply not comfortable in an era of globalization. The *Los Angeles Times* wrote:

> [T]he administration of course has the right to act in what it sees as the nation's best interests. But as a world leader and senior partner in the Western alliance, the U.S. also has an obligation to consult with its friends and prepare the way diplomatically when it knows its plans are controversial. It is its manner of acting—not just its actions—that evokes resentment.[16]

What Bush II has tried to do is erect a unilateral wall that has long since lost any hope of foundation. In time, the forces of globalization will make the administration realize that on the environment and other, future issues, this nation needs to recognize—and live up to—its preeminent position in the world in a responsible way. We have long been a target of the world's envy because of our wealth, power, and technology, but the administration's actions have only served to open the floodgates for increased economic espionage activity. Every setback—such as losing seats on U.N. commissions, acts of terrorism against U.S. embassies abroad or ships at sea, and, of course, acts of terrorism carried out on our own soil—cause us to be perceived as vulnerable and easy pickings. All of these things combined, which make the United States seem like just another country as opposed to the soft-walking-big-stick-carrying superpower of another era, put U.S. companies even more at risk for global economic espionage.

And far more than strict environmental regulations, becoming a global target for economic espionage is definitely bad for U.S. business.

CHAPTER 9

STICKY FINGERS
The Crisis Manager

I've been helping companies manage their crises and the communications of their crises since my involvement on the Three Mile Island crisis management team in the administration of then Pennsylvania Governor Dick Thornburgh. And one thing I can tell you is that I've never had a boring day. I get the most intriguing phone calls you can imagine, often leading me into the most out-of-the-ordinary situations—from the greasy kitchens of fast food restaurants suffering from a nationwide E. coli or salmonella outbreak to the once pristine waters of Alaska's Prince William Sound afflicted with a massive oil spill.

The phone call I received from Avery Dennison was like other calls I've received, except Avery Dennison was not a new client. Over the years, I had been called in to help the company manage a number of their crisis situations. But this call was slightly different. Instead of telling me what the new problem was, I was merely told I needed to be on a plane to Cleveland as soon as possible and would be briefed en route.

Issues of client confidentiality preclude a full discussion of events that transpired, but I can tell you that while the Avery Dennison/Four Pillars case was pure economic espionage, it was also a classic crisis management situation very familiar to me from past experience. Any crisis holds both the reality and the perception of that reality, a dynamic we will look at closer later on.

Because of the importance perception plays, one of my immediate concerns when I learned of the economic espionage was how Victor Lee's wanton thefts would be viewed by the news media and, through them, others in the outside world. I was concerned that my client not be viewed as careless with their own trade secrets as well as potentially those of any of their major customers who were soon named in many national news stories.

While you may know Avery Dennison's consumer goods products[1]—such as a wide variety of Avery labels—the company makes some of its largest profits in its business relationships with its corporate manufacturing clients. If you were in Avery Dennison's shoes, try to imagine how corporate giants like Duracell, Johnson & Johnson, Kimberly-Clark, Coca-Cola, or many others might react if they woke up one morning and read in the newspaper or heard on the news that a major trade secret involving their best known products had been stolen. How do you think Wall Street and the overall investment community would react to that news?

And don't forget the United States Postal Service. Avery Dennison developed the technology that allows the USPS to sell pressure-sensitive postage stamps, across the post office counter and in ATMs.

I was concerned about any careless listing of Avery Dennison clients by name and links to specific stolen trade secrets, as well as what uncontrolled exposure of such news might do to the stock prices of some very major, public companies—including, but definitely not limited to, Avery Dennison.

One of Avery Dennison's strengths over the years has been its innovative ability to partner with a new or existing customer in the design phase of a new product's packaging, creating custom adhesive formulas for many customers. That raised a question in my mind: While Victor had stolen Avery Dennison trade secrets, was it possible that some of the adhesive formulas developed exclusively for a particular company might be owned or co-owned by that cus-

nity, employees, and customers? Think about these things if you ever find yourself in a similar situation.

If you are in this sort of situation, suing the spy would accomplish little in terms of damage recovery, when your damages are so high and your spy is a salaried worker bee. Your spy would be unable to provide adequate restitution.

Clearly, for any civil damages to be recovered, you would have to sue your spy's masters. But bringing a successful suit in a foreign country always involves difficulties, especially in Asia. Just getting the case onto a docket in Asia is problematic.

The United States has the kinds of laws on its books that could help you in civil litigation, but you need to serve court papers on your foreign competitor. Hiring a law firm or a local process server in Asia to serve papers would be an exercise in futility. How are you going to force a foreign company you are suing that doesn't have any facilities or personnel in the United States to come here to face a civil trial on your home turf?

If you were fortunate enough to be able to serve papers on the foreign masterminds when they were in the United States, court papers could be served on them here. But so what? They could just board a plane and return home. Of course, they could be tried *in absentia,* but good luck collecting if you prevailed in court.

Soon, you may very well come to the realization that you need to bring in the FBI, even though you lose control.

And, the FBI wanted this trophy case. The government went so far as to tell Avery Dennison that it would be doing a great patriotic service by going forward with the prosecution and by leading the way for other American businesses that had been victimized by economic espionage. It was risky, but it was also time for an American company to take a stand, and Avery Dennison was apparently willing to bet "Stan's garage" on the outcome.

But, initially there were several pressing considerations such as keeping Victor focused on his confession and keeping him under wraps. For appearances's sake, he had to continue "working" at Avery Dennison, lest Four Pillars get wind of anything out of the ordinary. Consequently, Victor stayed on the payroll, but he was quarantined from the general Avery Dennison employee population. He was put "on assignment" to a senior Avery Dennison executive and was housed in a trailer as he met daily with the FBI and worked on his confession. Also, it was important that Victor maintain a status quo relationship with Four Pillars. For the time being, Four Pillars had to believe—as it had for the past eight years—that Victor was still on the job and in its pocket.

Meanwhile, my company began drafting the master crisis management plan, never knowing if we'd need it tomorrow or six months from tomorrow.

But all this planning was predicated on a factor that was totally out of everyone's control: if and when anyone from Four Pillars would arrive on our shores.

CHAPTER 10

Cybercrimes
Electronic Economic Espionage

"The Internet was never designed with security in mind."

—Former U.S. Deputy Defense Secretary John Hamre

The Internet is the fastest growing technique for foreign firms to obtain sensitive business data, according to the former National Counterintelligence Center (now the National Counterintelligence Executive). The anonymity and ease of use of the Internet makes it incredibly simple for industrial spies or terrorists alike to obtain open-source data.

Hacking is sometimes played out like a game of kidnapping and ransom. Not too long ago, one hacker managed to break into Visa's computer network and demanded a $10 million ransom. That hacker was eventually caught.

Not long ago, two Swedish hackers—one age 15, the other 17—broke into a communication company's network systems and downloaded the company's five-year plan for its cellular systems. Then they demanded $2 million to destroy the information. Ultimately they, too, were caught and prosecuted.

Revealing—or threatening to reveal—credit card information is a big risk. In early 2000, an extortionist disclosed some of the 300,000 customer credit cards he stole from online music retailer CD Universe.

A 19-year-old Welsh hacker gained access to e-commerce Internet sites in five countries—the United States, Canada, Britain, Japan, and Thailand—and stole information on more than 26,000 credit card holders. He said he did it to demonstrate that Internet security is inadequate. In July 2001, he was sentenced to three years probation and psychiatric treatment.[1] Before he was arrested, he made at least one Internet purchase with the stolen credit card information. As an in-your-face gesture, he ordered a bottle of Viagra® and had it shipped to Bill Gates.

One person who is very familiar with the risks posed by hackable computer systems to the companies that rely on them is Kevin Mitnick. Probably the most notorious hacker in history, Mitnick claims he never hacked into any computer for profit. His motives, to hear him tell it, were more about the fun, excitement, and challenge he got from hacking. But, at one time, his exploits were so daring and costly to some three dozen of the nation's largest and most well-known companies, that he occupied a place of honor as the FBI's most wanted cyber criminal. The government and his victims estimate that Mitnick's hacking cost the businesses hundreds of millions of dollars in damages.

How could one man do so much damage? According to Mitnick, it was easy. Maybe too easy. Mitnick scaled or broke through any number of computer firewalls. This fact should sound an alert that you cannot assume your company's computer firewalls are sufficiently protective or foolproof.

Of course, Mitnick wasn't foolproof either. His 13-year crime spree came to a screeching halt in 1995, when he finally was arrested and sentenced to five years in prison. The sort of crimes that Mitnick committed would make him an ideal candidate to be charged with violations of the EEA, except for the fact that his hacking spree and his arrest and conviction occurred before the EEA became law. Moreover, nothing suggests that he would have necessarily been deterred by the EEA even if it had been on the books. It might only have stiffened his sentence.

Mitnick was so skilled that the only way the FBI could take him down was to hire a cyber sleuth, Tsutomu Shimomura, who knew all of the tricks that Mitnick used and turned them against him.

"I saw myself as an electronic joyrider having a great time on the information superhighway," Mitnick said after he was released from prison. "It was a big game to me."[2]

Game or not, he knew that what he was doing was wrong. But he claims the challenge compelled him. Anytime a company put up a new firewall or other sophisticated defense barrier that companies use to protect their most precious trade secrets, Mitnick saw it merely as a challenge to be conquered.

Mitnick's trail of fallen victims were electronics firms, and most were computer firms. You would expect these firms, in particular, to have the latest, toughest, and most elaborate security apparatus imaginable. Mitnick claims he broke through software company Novell's firewall in a matter of minutes.

While Mitnick considered his activities a hobby, the U.S. Department of Justice considered him nothing less than a cyber economic terrorist. Among the companies he terrorized with his own brand of economic espionage, besides Novell, were Motorola, NEC, Sun Microsystems, Qualcomm, Finland's Nokia, Digital Equipment Corp., and Japanese computer giant Fujitsu.

"The companies that Mitnick broke into," reported Ed Bradley of *60 Minutes*, "claim that by illegally copying their software and other trade secrets Mitnick was . . . stealing their intellectual property and compromising the security of their entire networks, causing them to redesign their systems. All told, the companies estimate Mitnick cost them $300 million in damages."[3]

Mitnick claims he never sold or profited from the software he copied, nor did he actually deprive any companies of the use of the software. For these reasons, Mitnick actually questions where his hacking caused any harm.

But here's where Mitnick's logic falters. If one hacker can get into just one small area of your network, your entire security procedure is compromised. By and large, hackers operate by locating, uncovering, and exploiting security flaws in your systems that then need to be plugged immediately.

If your trade secrets are at risk, so is your company. In most hacking instances, you are probably going to have to shut down your entire network until the security breach is repaired. While a hacker may try to justify his or her actions as a harmless joyriding prank, the reality is that hacking does major harm and even greater potential harm once it gets going. Can you stop an avalanche after it gets rolling?

How much do you rely on the Internet today? Other than routine e-mail, do you conduct business over the Internet? Do your customers access your sales and product catalogs over your network, check their orders on your network, or make payments to their accounts over your network? How much would it cost to shut down your networks for hours, days, or weeks? Costly shutdowns and system redesigns are only a portion of the damages just one joyriding hacker can cause.

In 2001, worldwide Internet use by companies to reach employees, customers, and suppliers reached $260 billion worth of business, according to Thomas Friedman of *The New York Times.*[4]

Mitnick, by the way, was only 17 when he started hacking, and he didn't even own a computer. He used the ones at Radio Shack.

Denial Is a Problem

David Schindler, the former Assistant U.S. Attorney in Los Angeles who helped put Mitnick behind bars, thinks companies can do a lot to better protect themselves just by doing a little. "One of my golden rules is: A good checkup on the front end can avoid major problems on the backend," he says. One reason Mitnick succeeded was that companies did not have in place the kinds of alarms that would keep a hacker out or tell a system administrator that someone had gotten in.

"When we send in 'tiger teams' to see if a client's networks are properly protected," Schindler told me, "we make sure they're installing the kind of trip wires you expect to have in order to spot intruders. But even today many companies still do not have alarms because they don't think in those terms. They don't expect to be the victim of a crime."

Schindler, who also served as the Department of Justice's computer crime and telecommuting coordinator and now is a private attorney in Los Angeles, feels that companies have a lack of awareness about how much information on their business operations is stored electronically, which makes them so vulnerable. He also noted that many "insurance companies offer a premium reduction to companies that take steps to protect themselves, the same as they do for cars and homes that have alarms and other security measures."[5]

Netspionage

Some hackers are out for revenge or retaliation. In the first week in May 2001, in retaliation for an incident involving a U.S. reconnaissance plane, Chinese hackers attacked and defaced more than 650 Web sites of U.S. businesses and the U.S. government. One attack targeted a popular U.S. medical Web site that advises doctors on cancer studies and drugs vital to treating patients. The hacking attack shut down the Web site for days, leaving physicians and their stricken patients dangerously in the dark.

If these presumably amateur hackers can cause this sort of damage, just imagine what could happen with real pros—say, business competitors with money to spend on the best hacking technology—at the keyboard?

Netspionage involves seasoned pros who make their living working for unethical companies. Their job is to break into a competitor's network and steal trade secrets over the Internet.

Over half of 600 companies responding to a survey conducted in 2001 by the Computer Security Institute[6] said they felt their competitors were a likely source of cyber attack, claiming more than $60 million in losses to cyberespionage. The survey is conducted annually by CSI and the Computer Intrusion Squad of the FBI in San Francisco.

The findings of the survey confirm that the threat from computer crime and other information security breaches—including theft of trade secrets—continues unabated and that the financial toll is mounting. The survey indicated that 85 percent of respondents detected computer security breaches within the last 12 months. Thirty-five percent quantified their financial losses as exceeding

$377 million. As in previous years, the most serious financial losses occurred through theft of proprietary information.

No Point in Wasting Good Intelligence . . .

Cybercrime consultant Bill Hancock tells of a case of netspionage that involved a U.S. cordless telephone company believed to have stolen designs from one of its archrivals. Hancock states that an engineer from one company hacked into the computer network of its rival and swiped its trade secret designs and drawings. The story eventually surfaced when the greedy engineer next tried to pass the work off as his own where he worked, but his supervisor recognized that the engineer's skill level was insufficient to have created the work for which he was claiming credit. Once uncovered, what do you think happened? They liked the designs so much, *they went ahead and manufactured the phones anyway!*

Sometimes, the practitioners of netspionage use amateur hackers to do their dirty work. If the hacker is caught, nothing links the activities back to the ultimate corporate spy. Most often, though, because these arrangements are made via the Internet and other anonymous ways and means for obvious reasons, the hacker doesn't even know the identity of the person paying him. Hancock cited the case of a 17-year-old U.S. hacker who was paid $1,000 down and $10,000 to come for stealing kitchen appliance design documents from certain U.S. firms.

In some of these cases, the real culprit—the so-called netspionage brains of the outfit—is across the world, safely ensconced in a land with different laws, a different culture, different extradition treaties, and different business ethics. Maybe *no* business ethics at all. Maybe they work for your competitors, or maybe for a foreign power.

"More and more hacking for the sake of trade secret theft is going on," said Richard Power, who conducts the annual Computer Security Institute survey. The numbers are on the rise, and the reason should come as no surprise. According to the Information Technology Association of America, the global marketplace for information-related technology is expected to surpass $3 trillion by 2003.

But, while theft is on the rise, victims are still reluctant to talk about their losses. Former U.S. Attorney General Janet Reno—who also pushed hard for the passage of the EEA when she was in office—implored businesses to be more aggressive and forthcoming and to report cybercrimes, indicating there was no way to catch criminals if crimes go unreported. "We must share information about vulnerabilities, so that we can each take steps to protect our systems against attack," Reno said. "We have a common goal: to keep the nation's computer networks secure, safe and reliable for America's citizens and its businesses.[7]"

One reason for her plea, discussed earlier, is the lack of trust that many computer and Internet firms have toward the FBI. But another reason lies in the fact that while computer crime quadrupled in the last three years of the 20th century, funding for prosecutors remained stagnant. This is no way to motivate the good guys.

InfraGard

In January 2001, the FBI announced a program to enlist private businesses to work with its 56 field offices around the country to share information about computer crime and ways to thwart it. Established by the FBI's National Infrastructure Protection Center (NIPC), the four-year pilot program is called InfraGard and had 518 company members at its inception. At the time the program was unveiled, then FBI Director Louis J. Freeh explained the need for the program when he noted, "Computer crime is one of the most dynamic problems the FBI faces today." He said the InfraGard initiative would open communication lines among the public and private sectors and the law enforcement community.[8]

Openly recognizing the distrust that for years existed between private businesses and law enforcement agencies, InfraGard is designed to build better bridges between the two groups, specifically, in tackling the daunting challenge of hacking and netspionage.

Michael Vatis, the group's director, believes the effort is already bearing fruit. He cited a statistic that FBI investigations into com-

puter intrusion—from amateur hacking to full scale netspionage—
had grown from 450 cases to over 1,200 between 1998 and 2001.

Specifically, InfraGard concerns itself with three types of attacks:

1. *Unstructured threats,* encompassing threats or attacks generated
   from insiders, recreational hackers, and institutional hackers
2. *Structured threats,* emanating from organized crime, economic
   espionage from competitors, and terrorists
3. *National security threats,* coming from the intelligence agencies
   of other countries and so-called information warriors

InfraGard members receive three levels of infrastructure warnings—alert, advisory, and assessment—which are developed and distributed consistent with the FBI's National Threat Warning System.

More information may be found on the NIPC Web site, which is
included in a list of many useful Web sites in the Appendix at the
back of this book. I have included a comprehensive and up-to-date
listing of Web sites that deal with the broad subject of economic
espionage and places where you can find help or additional information.

Dealing with Cybercrime Is Critical

Even with greatly improved deterrence and security, hacking is
in many instances a sport of adolescence, or arrested adolescence.
The *hacking* problem may be a reflection of our 21st century technological age, but the *behavioral* problem is as old as the adolescent
game of "I dare you."

The more obstacles the government and security experts put in
the hackers' paths—in effect saying, "I dare you to break in, now!"—
the more determined the hackers and netspionagers are to show
that they're smarter than the business or government agency that
thinks it has built a better firewall.

So when the government said, in effect, "We dare you," the hackers attacked and brought to their knees such stalwart commercial
Internet companies as Amazon, Yahoo!, eBay, and E*Trade and

paralyzed them. Customers who tried to log on were greeted with "denial of service" messages.

Within a month, the FBI director and the attorney general acknowledged that hackers and hacking threats had outstripped the government's efforts to keep up with them.

In 2000, Reno testified before a Senate panel on Internet security and further reiterated the necessity for an even stronger and more coordinated law enforcement strategy. "How we deal with cyber-crime is one of the most critical areas we face," she said. She then proposed a five-year plan to crack down even more by invoking tougher penalties for hackers.

However, security expert Bruce Scnheier gives a blunt assessment: "The hacking community treats countermeasures as road-blocks and goes around them." In terms of stealing trade secrets, if you don't want it copy-able, he advises, don't make it digital.

Private Industry Efforts and Risks

While the government publicly announced its plans, private industry is still not doing enough, according to Don Ulsch. Now an independent consultant, when Ulsch was a director of Pricewater-houseCoopers Global Risk Management Solutions program, he worked with companies on ways to fight Internet attacks, among other things. He cited a PWC-sponsored survey that put the overall cost to global businesses for Internet attacks such as hacking and netspionage at $1.6 trillion in 1999.

"Since the advent of the Internet," Ulsch points out, "it is difficult for companies to discern what might be the actual motive of an attack—economic espionage, such as theft of trade secrets, other types of theft, planting a bug or virus, and so on."[9]

At the top of the list of high-interest trade secrets from companies are customer lists. They are one of the easiest things to identify on a computer network and, if stolen, one of the hardest things ever to prove was stolen.

If one company steals technology from another company, there are any number of ways to prove who the ultimate creator was of the pilfered piece of technology or formula. But consider the difficulty of proving the source of a customer list. Think of all the obstacles you might face in court to prove to a legal standard of certainty—or even just a preponderance of evidence—that the *only* way your competitor got the Acme Widget Company on *its* customer list was by stealing it from you.

So companies that do business with lots of anonymous repeat customers are at extremely high risk for electronic economic espionage. These might include Internet firms and Internet service providers, software firms, banks, cable-TV firms, and so on. A business that usually maintains extensive customer lists in its databases is a prime candidate for electronic economic espionage.

Any business that maintains financial information and other personal data on customers is a prime target. Also, research and development departments are at high risk.

Law and investment banking firms, especially those engaged in mergers and acquisitions (M&A) work, are also at the top of the list. An effective technique, and one not easy to spot, is when a hacker learns of an upcoming merger of two public companies and then trades on that information weeks in advance of the deal. Despite the SEC's sophisticated ability to spot insider trading, if a hacker with no connection to either of two companies involved in a big deal starts trading on knowledge gleaned from hacking, it is difficult if not impossible to find her out. This explains why M&A firms are high payoff targets in the world of electronic economic espionage.

Consider how valuable it might be to hack into the networks of big accounting firms who represent publicly traded companies, or the office of the chief financial officer of a public company, just before quarterly earnings are reported. Again, if the hacker has no ties to the firms, this information could easily translate into a big payday for the hacker.

Electronic Pearl Harbor

But high-tech and financial firms are not the sole target of hacking and netspionage. Far from it.

The average *Fortune* 2,000 company is attacked by hackers two to three times a year, according to Ira Winkler, president of the Internet Security Advisers Group. But he believes most companies are unaware that they've been attacked. When competitors come out with a similar product, service, or production method, victimized companies often chalk it up to fierce competition or dumb luck, but they should examine their security procedures. "Usually companies have policies for that, but rarely do they enforce them."[10]

Ulsch believes it will take "an electronic Pearl Harbor to get the attention of management," which he thinks is essential before any real progress will be made in getting companies to take steps to reduce their risk of electronic economic espionage. He thinks convincing the CEOs, the boards of directors, and the general counsels of companies one at a time is essential before the companies will step up to the plate.

Human Social Engineering

But is electronic or technical security enough? Sadly, no, according to—who else?—Kevin Mitnick.

In an ironic twist of fate, just weeks after Mitnick was released from the federal penitentiary in Lompoc, California, in January 2000, he was asked to testify before the Senate Governmental Affairs Committee. The committee was investigating how to keep business and government computers safe from hackers. A frustrated U.S. Senate turned to one of the world's most notorious hackers to suggest solutions to the problem. Acting as someone who has seen the light, Mitnick was only too glad to comply, but what he said underscored the age-old maxim (highlighted in Chapter 24) that it's hard to get good help today.

"I have gained unauthorized access to computer systems at some of the largest corporations on the planet and have successfully penetrated some of the most resilient computer systems ever developed," Mitnick said. And he did it largely by social engineering.[11]

Social engineering is the art of sweet-talking and manipulating a person into doing or divulging something that he wouldn't otherwise be inclined to do by making that person believe that the social engineer is trustworthy. In the hands—or the mouth—of an accomplished slick talker or con artist, social engineering can be frighteningly easy and effective. In the lore of social engineering, Mitnick was among the best. He told legislators of various times he had duped victims of major corporations into voluntarily relinquishing their own passwords and even sending him trade secret software blueprints.

Mitnick never really used ultrasophisticated technology to do his hacking. He was definitely more skilled at social engineering than computer engineering. This suggests that he has as refined a feel for people as for machines and flies in the face of the hacker-as-computer-nerd stereotype.

One of his most successful acts of social engineering involved Motorola. Knowing that Motorola was about to introduce a new ultralight wireless telephone, Mitnick—who loved telephones—was determined to get his hands on the plans. He called Motorola and asked who was in charge of that project, and the receptionist gave him the project manager's name, adding that the manager was on vacation and would Mitnick instead like to speak to the assistant project manager.

Mitnick said sure and, *armed only with the name of a person on vacation* (let's call her Sue), he told the assistant (let's call her Mary) something like, "Hi, Mary, Sue said I could get a copy of the source code for the new ultralight from you if she was on vacation when I needed it." Mary said, "Okay, where shall I send it?" And Motorola's hottest trade secret was e-mailed to Mitnick within 15 minutes, compliments of a socially engineered assistant project manager.[12]

He regaled the U.S. Senate committee with the time he called an AT&T receptionist and, just through the art of social engineering, persuaded her to fax to him an important password. If you would have asked that young woman an hour earlier if she knew the importance of protecting her password, she almost certainly would have said, "Yes."

"I was so successful in that line of attack that I rarely had to resort to a technical attack," Mitnick said. "Companies can spend millions of dollars toward technological protections, and that's wasted if somebody can basically call someone on the telephone and either convince them to do something on the computer that lowers the computer's defenses or reveals the information they were seeking."[13]

This is certainly one area where a company's greatest assets are and, at the same time, often its greatest source of vulnerability: its people. The human element, simply put, always adds an element of risk.

To keep pros like Mitnick and social engineers like him thwarted, the solution lies in effective education and training of your vulnerable employees.

Another witness called the well-publicized "denial of service" hacking attacks "mere pinpricks on the body of e-commerce," and told the Senators that worse was possible.

He's right. And one reason is that it is now possible to engage in a form of electronic social engineering.

Electronic Social Engineering

It happened to Microsoft toward the end of 2000 in a highly publicized hacking case in which an intruder gained access to its networks, systems, and source codes for anywhere from two to five weeks (it depends who you ask). But the scary part was how easily the hacking was accomplished and that it happened to computer behemoth Microsoft.

Microsoft is at the top of every hacker's dream list of companies to hack, and the company knows it. So you would think they'd go to extravagant measures to protect their systems. But this was not the usual amateur hacking attempt, according to the victim. Microsoft states that this successful penetration was at the hands of someone specifically seeking the company's commercial and trade secrets. "We are very confident in describing this as an act of industrial espionage," said Microsoft spokesman Dan Leach.

Microsoft almost has to say this. How would it look if an amateur hacker scaled Microsoft's security wall? Microsoft president Steve

Ballmer confirmed that part of its source code was accessed by the intruder.

A breach of Internet security at the world's most powerful software company demonstrates more than anything how what used to be amateur hacking by computer nerds and geeks has evolved fully into a tool of electronic economic espionage. "The élan of the hacker, the adventurous culture of the hacker—we've moved on from all of that," said the Computer Security Institute's Richard Power. "There are corporations and governments and freelancers that are going straight into your systems, taking the secrets they want, and using them [for] research and development, or to sell them."[14]

But whether this was amateur hacking or full scale netspionage, some reports indicated that the method used in the intrusion was not highly sophisticated at all. How could an unsophisticated method of intrusion get past Microsoft's safeguards?

Here's how. Most likely, the intruder used a specific program that relies on electronic social engineering. In this case, not unlike what Mitnick described, the program has the ability to fool a computer user into running what may seem like a benign or harmless program, but that actually performs a surreptitious task without being detected. Once this program is installed, it can open an electronic back door on the affected computer that allows it to search for networks to which the machine has access.

Because so many of Microsoft's employees work at home and gain access to the company's network either by remote access or a virtual private network, one theory is that an e-mail sent to a worker's home computer could have launched the backdoor program on their machine. Then, when that infected computer logged onto the Microsoft network, the social engineering aspect of the program takes over via the now open electronic backdoor. Further, this program allows a hacker or netspionager to commandeer those machines remotely and break into the network.

"If this can happen to Microsoft, this could happen to anybody," said Sandra K. England, president of PGP Security. "I think this will cause companies to reevaluate their own security policies and their own security infrastructure."[15]

CHAPTER | **11**

STICKY FINGERS
Crisis Communications

Shortly after the Tylenol crisis, I had lunch with an academic acquaintance of mine who had a truly bizarre theory he wanted to bounce off of me.

As most of us remember, the now classic textbook Tylenol crisis management case involved a terrorist—who has, to this day, never been caught—who laced Tylenol capsules with lethal cyanide poison, resulting in seven deaths and widespread fear. But my acquaintance was looking at the Tylenol crisis from a psychoanalytic viewpoint to see if it was possible to predict sociopathic behaviors from certain key events in a person's life. He thought that the Tylenol terrorist had been weaned from his mother's breast too early as an infant and, as a consequence, was now acting out. Because I had been widely quoted in the media about the management of the Tylenol crisis, and had analyzed the company's laudatory management of the crisis in my book, *Crisis Management: Planning for the Inevitable,* the breast-weaning theorist was eager to share his theory with me and to have me put forth his theory to the folks at Johnson & Johnson.

After I told him that it would be the FBI, not J&J, to whom he might want to talk, I assured him that at no time while the company was wrestling with the crisis did anyone on the crisis management team ever ponder at what age the terrorist got yanked from his mother's breast. The company was too busy managing the crisis. I took a pass on passing along his theory to either J&J or the FBI.

I advise clients in crisis situations to avoid overanalyzing if possible. In a crisis, you must get to the heart of the matter—what I call the *Keystone Crisis*—as quickly as possible and *not* spend time needlessly debating into which of several holes a given crisis may fall. Companies who do not or cannot act swiftly fall into a black hole known as *analysis paralysis,* which in crisis management terms, can be fatal.

Most crises—regardless of type—can be categorized into headings that are much simpler and easier to deal with, such as *long-fused crisis* or *short-fused crisis.*

A short-fused crisis is one where the company has little or no time to prepare and is thrust almost immediately into the acute stage of a fast-breaking crisis. I have been involved in more of these over the years than I can count.

But a long-fused crisis is different. You prepare for it and manage it differently. In a long-fused crisis, you know what's going to happen and sometimes you even know when. I have been called in, for instance, for cases of labor strife in the midst of intense contract negotiations. We know if a contract isn't ratified, a strike or work stoppage will likely take place. We know when the current contract runs out. We know, in other words, when the acute stage of the crisis may be upon us and what the reaction from the other side will be, and we can manage the acute stage of the crisis appropriately. This is a classic long-fused crisis.

And, while the fuse is burning, we have our work cut out for us. We know from experience all the things that must be done to protect the company in a strike, for instance, so that the company can to the best of its ability continue to operate its essential business under strike conditions. You hope for the best but prepare for the worst.

In the Avery Dennison spy case, after Victor had been caught and had confessed, Avery Dennison's crisis dynamic changed drastically and began to revolve around time. How much time would we have, and could we do all that needed to be done within that time frame? In other words, we had to answer the same question we consider with all clients in a crisis: how long is our fuse?

Preparations

It is always wise to operate as though the acute stage of the crisis will break immediately. Initially, my company wasn't at all sure which of a variety of potential scenarios might play out, but good crisis communications prepares for them all in the broadest possible way. As it turned out, the situation that did occur was Victor's lengthy confession, his cooperation in maintaining a status quo relationship with Four Pillars as though nothing out of the ordinary had happened, and his cooperation with the FBI in the ultimate sting, which resulted in the arrest of P.Y. and his daughter Sally.

Using secret code names for the taskforce, my own personal binder became a crisis management and crisis communications bible in the tension-filled months ahead. Every conceivable contingency that could be foreseen was updated continually. Ultimately, of course, the whole situation became public within 24 hours of the FBI sting, arrest and booking of the spies, and the FBI press conference. The objective was to deliver tightly coordinated announcements to *all* Avery Dennison constituencies immediately following the FBI arrest, without suffering a loss of confidence, customers, or share price. It was essential that news of the economic espionage to those identified constituencies come *first from us.*

As with other clients in similar situations, the types of information required followed a certain format of anticipating what could happen and what would be needed to respond.

The team members. In any crisis setup, it is essential to have not just the list of essential team members but the means to contact them. Therefore, everyone has to surrender all of their many telephone numbers—home, office, pager, cell, car phones, vacation homes—and all their e-mail addresses. In other words, the communications works. If someone has to be reached during any phase of the crisis, you need to know *in advance* how to make contact.

Message points and media strategies. One advantage of a long-fused crisis is the ability to prepare communications in advance. You always want to have a media strategy to tell your story quickly and accurately, before incorrect speculation runs rampant. In this manner, we were able to immediately confirm the FBI's announcement at its press conference but strictly limit the release of additional information that was off the main point. The messages that we conveyed in response to reporters' questions were:

- Avery Dennison initially uncovered the espionage and alerted the FBI.
- The company places the highest priority on the protection of its trade secrets (a message designed for Wall Street and its customers).
- The extent of the damages to Avery Dennison would not be determined until the trial (even though the FBI created their own monetary estimates and the media ran with them).
- Avery Dennison still views Asia Pacific as a key growth area (a message intended for the investment community).

It is always preferable to have a company speak with one voice, rather than many conflicting voices, especially in a large company. Steps should be taken to centralize communications and media inquiries. To that end, the company's weak and ineffectual public relations department in Ohio was removed from the media loop at this stage. Initially, we wanted all communications coordinated out of the corporate communications office in the company's Pasadena headquarters or Lexicon Communications in Los Angeles.

News release drafts. If you are planning for different contingencies, you need to have different drafts of news releases targeted to each contingency. In a breaking story, the media are on constant deadline and can't wait for you to figure out what to say. That's why the advantages of a long-fused crisis should be used to the maximum. In this case, no matter what happened, we made sure the company was prepared for it.

Internal and external Q&A. A most effective way to disseminate information quickly and accurately—especially in a large company— is through a Q&A document, usually designed for management. It is effective, too, as a way for managers to answer questions posed by subordinates as well as outsiders, such as customers and vendors. Companies often err by not communicating, and silence often fuels rumors. Plus, when you know certain questions will be asked, you should arm people with the appropriate responses on how they should be answered. Avery Dennison was no exception: we *wanted* questions to be asked, and we were fully prepared to answer them with accurate information.

One of the most anticipated media questions in the Avery Dennison case had to do with Victor's actions. Therefore, we prepared a succinct timeline of all relevant actions, from the time Dr. Tenhong Lee joined Avery Dennison to his involvement with Four Pillars to his arrest and ultimate termination.

Employee notification. Do not overlook one of your most important assets, your employees. They should not read shocking news in the paper; they should hear it first from you. This serves two purposes: it helps avoid undue concern, and it gives you an army of informed soldiers who can help overcome rampant rumor and speculation when they hear it from others. We drafted a two-page letter, signed by then Avery Dennison CEO Chuck Miller, that was sent to all 16,000 employees. The letter was designed to convey the facts directly and candidly to help ensure that if the employees were going to talk about it—and we knew they were, especially with their friends and families—they talked about it accurately. We wanted to avoid rumor and hyperspeculation as much as possible. The letter, in part, read as follows:

Dear Avery Dennison Employee:

I want to convey to you the brief facts surrounding an incident of international industrial espionage against our company. A Taiwan-based competitor—a company called Four Pillars—has been stealing trade secrets and other proprietary information from Avery Dennison for a number of years.

What makes this act all the more deplorable is the fact that Four Pillars could not have accomplished its theft without the aid of an Avery Dennison employee. Dr. Victor Lee, a senior Avery Dennison researcher in our Concord R&D lab for more than 11 years, has confessed to stealing and selling Company trade secrets to Four Pillars over a period of years. Dr. Lee was in a position of great trust and responsibility within the Company—a trust that he willingly chose to violate, purely for personal gain. That violation—against the Company and against each and every employee of Avery Dennison—has cost Dr. Lee his career, his reputation, his friends, and all of the money he collected through his reprehensible actions.[1]

The letter was communicated by company mail, e-mail, voice mail, and video to ensure that as many employees as possible received the message simultaneously.

Financial community. If yours is a publicly traded company, as Avery Dennison is, maintaining the health of your company's stock price is always a paramount concern. As with inquiries from the news media, you need to prepare yourself with the necessary ammunition, Q&As, and directions to deal forthrightly with any inquiries from the investment community, including preparing in advance letters that might have to be sent to shareholders.

In this type of crisis, as with so many others, we advise clients who will be speaking to the financial community or any outside group:

- Do not assume.
- Do not conjecture.
- Do not offer opinions.
- Do not lay blame.

Key customers. What could be worse than having nervous customers? If your company is about to make headlines as the focal point of a crisis, and especially if your customers may be mentioned, too, do you want them to hear it first on the news, or from you? A long-fused crisis allows you time to prepare. As stated earlier, the careless and misleading naming of key customers was one of my major concerns in the Avery Dennison case. My advice was to have the primary customer contact briefed and instructed to call the client at the first mention of their name. One thing you certainly want to avoid is having your customers getting calls from reporters, blindsiding them with awkward and uncomfortable questions.

Vendors/suppliers. Similar to the situation with customers, you never want a vendor to worry about the health of one of its customers, because it might suddenly want to change terms on you, for example. Anything vendors or suppliers are going to learn about your crisis, they should hear from you, first and accurately.

Tennis Anyone?

During this long preparatory process, as information came out in testimony and various court documents, Victor had one or two conversations with P.Y., asking the old man if he was planning a trip to the United States in the future. In May and then June, P.Y. indicated he might be coming soon, but later changed that. Victor told him that he had some important documents that he wanted to hand to him, rather than send by mail.

Subsequently, P.Y. expressed a desire to travel to the United States in early September to see tennis star Michael Chang play in the U.S. Open. Good corporate citizen P.Y. was the head of Taiwan's youth tennis association.

Finally, the phone call came. P.Y. called Victor at the end of August to say he'd be leaving Taipei September 1, bound for Los Angeles and then Cleveland. Then, he'd travel to New York for the U.S. Open.

It seemed like everything had fallen into place. Except the FBI—incredibly—nearly missed the landing party, and all because they'd never read Jules Verne.

The Kodak Moment

*"The camera can be the most deadly weapon since the
assassin's bullet. Or it can be the lotion of the heart."*

—Norman Parkinson

Let me tell you about Harold Worden, a quintessential company
man who spent nearly three decades as an engineer at Eastman
Kodak, until he retired. (Some say he was downsized, but Kodak
officials denied that when I spoke with them.) At any rate, Worden
left the company, but he didn't leave empty-handed.

While the relevant acts in the Worden case happened just before
the EEA was passed, and its conclusions occurred after, it was not
prosecuted as an EEA case because the law does not permit retro-
active charges. Nevertheless, by our definition, it is classic economic espionage. And how Kodak reacted to—and the unusual way
they dealt with—the case is a tale worth telling.

Kodak in recent years has gone through some tough times. Once
the only name in films and film developing, it has been battered by
competitors like Japan's Fuji Film and Germany's Agfa. Additionally, the rapid rise of digital (read: filmless) cameras and scanners
has hurt the company, even though only about 10 million digital
cameras are in use today compared to some 300 million film-eating
monsters. The company has laid off 20 percent of its U.S. workforce
since 1995; just in Kodak's corporate company town of Rochester,

New York, the company went from its peak of some 70,000 employees in the early 1980s down to about 30,000 in 2001.

Many observers point to the Harold Worden spy case as the
beginning of Kodak's decline. Whether or not that's true, what *is*
true is that Kodak was not smiling for the cameras when the
Worden case was exposed.

The 401 Machine

For the last five years that he worked at Kodak's Rochester
campus, Worden spearheaded Kodak's top secret manufacturing
project called the 401 Machine, a piece of multimillion dollar
machinery the size of a city block and four stories tall. It's purpose
was to speed film manufacturing while improving film quality, and
thereby better position Kodak in the marketplace against its fierce
global competitors.

Like many manufacturers, the basic nuts and bolts of Kodak's
manufacturing process—spreading photosensitive emulsions on
sheets of acetate, which afterwards are then cut into strips to make
rolls of film—is not a real secret. But Kodak spends more than $10
million a year on R&D, and again, like many manufacturers, the
R&D enhancements and improvements Kodak makes to its various
film processes are entitled to trade secret protection. This is where
the 401 Machine comes into play.

The 401 was Worden's baby. He oversaw every bit of its design,
the multimillion-dollar prototype, and the onset of its construction
before he retired. Ultimately, the Machine became a wonder, producing a virtually defect-free acetate with a smoother surface. To
ensure the highest level of secrecy, people worked on the 401
Machine in parts, and only a small, select handful of people knew
the whole picture. Not only was Worden one of these people, but
he was entrusted by Kodak's management and legal staff to help
decide which parts of the machinery and technology should be sub-
mitted to Washington for patent protection and what processes
should remain as a company trade secret.

But Worden left Kodak in 1992 before the 401 was completed and soon set up his own consulting business called Worden Enterprises, Inc. He advertised himself as a "one-man operation serving acetate and polyester clients," but he didn't stay one man for long.

Have Knowledge, Will Travel

Worden raided the Kodak roster of recent retirees and recruited them to work for him and his fledgling company whenever he had a client, anywhere in the world, who needed a particular sort of expertise that one of his associates could provide.

Worden had nearly three decades of experience at Kodak and knew thousands of colleagues with the broadest swath of technical experience imaginable. The Kodak human resources department had already screened and vetted these people years ago, and Worden had worked shoulder-to-shoulder with them as they gained experience at Kodak. Now he had the pick of the litter. Whatever the particular needs of a client of Worden Enterprises, Harold Worden could deliver a custom-tailored team of expert consultants to solve the problem. Within a few years, Worden had some 63 associates in his Rolodex, many of whom also had had access to Kodak proprietary information and trade secrets. Flushed with success, Worden moved his family and business to a picturesque home on the Santee River in South Carolina.

But how can you have 63 associates and not have word get around as to your activities and access to trade secrets?

It all began when a senior Kodak researcher overheard some cocktail party talk about a Kodak retiree named Robert Newmiller who was planning to do some consulting work for Agfa, Kodak's big German competitor. In no time, word had reached the ears of Kodak employment attorney Brian O'Connor.[1] He invited Newmiller to lunch for a meeting, to remind him of his confidentiality agreement, and to find out what sort of consulting work he was planning to do. By the end of the lunch, O'Connor had convinced Newmiller that he would be in violation of his agreements if he were to consult for Agfa.

But before he left the table, Newmiller gave O'Connor indigestion; he told him about Worden and his legion of globetrotting Kodak retirees, all consulting for Worden's many clients. Newmiller had, in fact, been one of Worden's many associates, according to O'Connor, and the German consulting assignment had come from Worden.

So, unlike some other cases in this book where a domestic competitor or foreign company targets an American company's trade secrets, in this case the person accused of committing economic espionage is successfully shopping an American company's trade secrets around the world—wherever there is an open market and a ready buyer.

Do-It-Yourself Sting

The year was 1994, and the Economic Espionage Act was still two years from passage. The path for Kodak was murky and risky, no matter which way the company turned, and O'Connor was unsure of the best avenue. Neither he nor Kodak had ever faced anything like this before. Worden had signed a noncompete agreement, but just consulting for a competitor is not in and of itself illegal nor a breach of a noncompete clause; it all depends on what sort of consulting the individual is doing, what areas are being covered. Nevertheless, "You're always concerned when someone is going to consult with one of your direct competitors," said O'Connor.

He discussed the situation with general counsel Gary Van Graafeiland and Kodak CEO George Fisher. They turned to Pat Watson, head of Kodak's worldwide corporate security and a former FBI agent. He was new to Kodak but an old hand at espionage. Just before he left the Bureau, he had been assistant director in the FBI's national security division. It is this division, specializing in counterintelligence and counterterrorism, that ultimately became one of the two FBI divisions to deal with economic espionage under the EEA. Under Watson and O'Connor's leadership, Kodak decided to keep the problem in house for the time being and to conduct its own sting operation. If they got the evidence they suspected they'd find, then—and only then—would they bring in the FBI.

For a large, globally known company like Kodak to run its own sting operation is quite rare. But Kodak's management wanted first to find out for themselves if there was any truth to the story, what kind of consulting Worden was doing (it might be all legal and aboveboard), and what trade secrets, if any, were compromised.

No absolute and automatic government protection existed for any of Kodak's trade secrets. The sting was a gutsy move that could easily backfire, leaving the company the subject of ridicule, lawsuits, a drop in stock price, and further erosion of employee morale, as Kodak employees looked at the film giant and wondered, "Is this what I've got to look forward to when *I* retire?"

O'Connor and Watson recruited two accomplices; Joseph Louie, a former FBI agent, was hired to portray the owner of a company called Asia Pacific Resources. The second beard was actually a Kodak employee who played the role of a Chinese official named Dr. Chen Ping. According to the script, Dr. Ping was interested in building an acetate plant in the Shantou province of the People's Republic of China, and Louie would represent Ping in the negotiations.

The Bait

It was a given that Worden Enterprises would have the knowledge and "staff" to help construct an acetate plant, based on what O'Connor knew of Worden's background. But what Kodak needed to learn was how much help Worden would be willing to provide, and whether that included revealing trade secrets. If all Worden offered to do was provide legitimate consulting services to build a plant, solo or with any of his associates, Kodak couldn't do much, even if the company didn't like it.

Two meetings were scheduled in the summer of 1995, both of which were attended by Worden, Ping, and Louie. One meeting in Atlanta, four-and-a-half hours long, was videotaped,[2] and much of what follows is taken from those transcripts.

Ping and Louie jumped right in and told Worden about the acetate plant they wanted to build from scratch in China. Worden immediately rose to take the bait. It sounded to him like a replica of the massive 401 Machine project that he had labored on for so many years at Kodak.

Ping emphasized that the plant had to be state of the art, using only the leading technology available. The way Ping and Louie described their dream plant, it looked like China was about to enter the film market in a big way.

The two role players grilled Worden on what he could deliver, what sort of technology, what sort of experience. "I'm the first barrier," Ping told Worden. "You have to convince me first."

And so he did.

Worden launched into his years of experience working on the top secret 401 Machine project, making sure he properly emphasized the huge role he had played in its design and development. He told them not to be concerned because all of the things they perceived as obstacles he had already run across and solved in doing the same sort of work for Kodak. Referring to himself and his colleagues, he explained, "Anything that we're going to recommend is . . . proven technology. I mean, we didn't just dream it up. The risk of it not working is relatively small."

When Ping asked Worden specific technical questions and expressed concerns about possible problems in the manufacturing process, Worden confidently told him that those problems are already solved, telling him later in a written proposal that building the plant would be "a piece of cake."

"[B]ut now you have to tell me really how" those problems were solved, Ping challenged Worden. In other words, put up or shut up. This contract represented a large six-figure assignment for Worden, so he responded in detail.

At this point, Worden really started to spill the beans and reveal Kodak trade secrets.

In his defense, Worden told Ping and Louie at that Atlanta meeting that while Eastman Kodak was not happy with his consulting, he believed that what he was doing was open and aboveboard.

"[A]s I have told the people at Kodak . . . I'm not in the business of selling secrets, and I'm not in the business of selling formulas," Worden said. "We're using our basic technologies to help people, and those things that we recommend are not covered by patents, or patents have expired. So I don't personally have a problem with what I'm doing."

But, of course, Kodak did have a problem, especially after Worden followed up the meeting with a written proposal, saying in part, "Worden Enterprises, Inc., has all of the technology types that would be required to take on a project of this type." He then listed 41 of his associates and their areas of expertise and technical background. Most of them were Kodak retirees.

Could it be that Worden was sincere when he said he wasn't dealing in trade secrets? Did he truly believe that to be the case? He'd have to be pretty stupid to publicly name some 41 retired Kodak employees with tomes of Kodak's best kept secrets if he thought he was doing anything wrong. Or did he know that what he was doing was economic espionage but think that huge, multibillion-dollar Kodak up in Rochester would never notice a small flea on the banks of the Santee River?

The fact is that Kodak was convinced that its most valuable trade secrets had been ripped off. It was time to bring in the FBI.

The Haul

Despite all the spade work Kodak had done on its own, nine long, agonizing months would still pass before the FBI acted. And those nine months were excruciating for O'Connor and others involved in the sting operation. The FBI took its own sweet time to act on the information Kodak had provided.

Finally, armed with a search warrant, the FBI paid a visit to Worden at his home on the river in May of 1996. The six-hour search yielded some "17 boxes of documents, a very large number of which were either original Kodak documents or copies," according to O'Connor.

Part of the FBI's haul included "a five-inch thick package of confidential Kodak specifications" for a half-billion-dollar film facility. In an affidavit filed in the case, a Kodak engineer who had worked on the 401 Machine stated that the documents indicated that Worden had sold Kodak trade secrets and other proprietary information. Included in the recovered documents was a book containing between 40 and 50 Kodak secret formulas. The engineer stated that, in some of the documents, Worden used liquid correction fluid in an attempt to cover over Kodak's distinctive logo.

Worden was a good record keeper, allowing the FBI to find documentation of sales of Kodak trade secrets for assorted prices and employment records and invoices for his associates.

I asked O'Connor if he believed that Worden had knowledge of his own guilt. Could it possibly be, I asked him, that Worden did not recognize that he was trafficking in Kodak trade secrets? O'Connor told me that he had no doubt of Worden's guilty state of mind. O'Connor also pointed out that, despite what Worden said to Ping and Louie about not being in the business of selling trade secrets, he still pled guilty to the charges.

Kodak subsequently filed civil suits against Worden and other accomplices.

No Regrets

When I spoke to O'Connor several years after the Kodak sting, he said he would do it the same way again if given the chance. He thinks Kodak made the right decision in proceeding slowly with its own internal investigation. "We wanted to make sure of our facts before notifying the FBI," he said.

Despite Worden's guilty plea, some retired Kodak people—including some of Worden's former associates—still think that what Worden did was neither wrong nor criminal. Some held that Worden pled guilty only to avoid the otherwise huge legal expense he would have incurred otherwise.

My own position is that these retired Kodak employees are, for the most part, naïve. On its part, Kodak may very well share some of the blame or responsibility. Perhaps the people who didn't think that Worden used Kodak's trade secrets illegally had never been educated by their employer (or former employer) about what a trade secret is and why it is not a commodity that can be taken or sold by an employee or by a spy. In short, these people may simply have meant that—in their minds—Worden didn't realize that what he did was wrong.

But those retired employees would be wise to remember a few salient points:

- As part of his guilty plea, Worden accepted a 15-month prison sentence and a $30,000 fine. That would be a big pill for any innocent person to swallow.
- One of Worden's tasks on the 401 Machine was to decide what was a trade secret.
- Ignorance is not now, and never has been, an excuse for breaking the law.
- As part of his plea agreement, Worden is still cooperating with Kodak to determine where in the world Kodak's trade secrets have ended up. As a result, in 1997, Kodak sued 3M and one of 3M's Italian subsidiaries, Imaton, accusing them of theft of trade secrets in the advanced manufacturing of film. 3M had been a client of Worden Enterprises for four years, beginning in 1993. According to O'Connor, Kodak also entered into settlement agreements with many of Worden's most active associates.

Fear and Loathing at Kodak?

All of which begs a larger question. Consider it a given that Worden could justify his own activities. Further, assume that he could have one or two or even three accomplices. But if 41 retired Kodak employees jumped on Worden's bandwagon so easily, what does that say about Kodak?

Is Kodak so reviled among its employees that this was payback time? Or was Worden so talented a salesperson that he successfully persuaded more than 40 colleagues that what he was doing—and what they would be doing—was noncriminal and, indeed, legitimate?

Was Kodak negligent in failing to properly educate and train its employees about trade secrets? Could that explain why so many former Kodak employees lined up to consult with the company's competitors? Did those individuals believe they were not breaking any laws or violating any noncompete agreements? If they did, then the company must have fallen down in its job of properly educating its troops about trade secrets.

Today, as a result of the Worden case, the company offers employees one *optional,* three-and-a-half hour seminar on protection of trade secrets. "It's up to each individual business unit within the company to decide whether or not to offer the course to their employees," O'Connor said. "It's not automatically given to each employee. Each manager must do a cost-benefit analysis and decide to what extent the seminar will help the business unit."

This approach is hardly sufficient. Without question, senior management at Kodak and other companies need to pay more attention to the risks of economic espionage. And they need to start by educating and training all employees.

CHAPTER 13

STICKY FINGERS

Blueberry Bagels

As anyone who has read *Around the World in 80 Days* knows, Jules Verne's peripatetic hero, Phileas Fogg, returned to his home at No. 7 Saville Row, Burlington Gardens, London, weary and dejected. Having wagered his life's fortune that he could circumnavigate the globe in 80 days, he was morose that he had missed his deadline by one day and therefore lost the bet. Or had he?

[Note: Those who have never read the book—or seen the movie— and don't wish to have the ending spoiled should skip the next paragraph.]

It took until the last chapter for Fogg to realize that by traveling the globe in an easterly direction from Asia to the United States, he had crossed the International Date Line in the Pacific Ocean, thereby picking up one full day. If you leave Asia on a Monday, you actually arrive in the United States on the preceding Sunday, thereby gaining 24 hours. Fogg unfogged his brain to walk into the Reform Club and claim his prize in the nick of time.

Perhaps the book should be required reading for the FBI.

Father and Daughter

Finally, P.Y. called Victor and, with the FBI listening in, announced that he was leaving Taipei for California on September 1. Sally, who had been traveling within the United States since August 16, unbeknownst to the FBI, was going to meet up with her father in Cleveland. P.Y. told Victor that he had some business in Ohio with his U.S. client, Manco, and would visit with Victor while he was in Cleveland. He would leave for New York and the U.S. Open tennis tournament after his stay in Cleveland.

The FBI planned to be at the airport when P.Y. arrived to monitor his activities. They badly wanted this "trophy case" case, and P.Y. was not going to be out of their sight for a moment.

So the Feds were at the airport on September 1 to meet P.Y.'s flight.

But P.Y., flying from Taipei on September 1, crossed the International Date Line and arrived in this country on August 31—a full 24 hours *before* the FBI even realized it.

While the Feds were cooling their heels in California, a day late and a dollar short, and perhaps thinking that somehow somebody leaked something and P.Y. wasn't coming after all, the old man and his daughter were already in Cleveland trying to arrange to meet with Victor.

Victor stalled and said he would need at least a day to get the information out of the Avery research lab. Then he hurried P.Y. off the phone and called FBI Special Agent Mike Bartholomew.

When I first heard of this near fiasco, I wondered whose heads might have rolled if P.Y. had been able to meet with Victor, pocket the trade secrets, and blow town before the Feds caught wise. Remember, much of what Victor had stolen from Avery Dennison had occurred prior to the passage of the EEA. To prosecute P.Y. and Four Pillars under the EEA—for the FBI to have a trophy case—they had to catch P.Y. in a sting, receiving trade secrets *today*.

Then there was this riddle: If Avery Dennison gave Victor a trade secret to give to P.Y. and Sally, did it still qualify for trade secret status and protection?

An Essential Provision of the Law

When the EEA was passed, the general question of trade secret protection in a criminal matter was addressed. Section 1835, regarding the issuance of court orders to preserve the confidentiality of trade secrets, allows courts to issue orders and "take such action as may be necessary and appropriate to preserve the confidentiality of trade secrets. . . ." This provision was essential to protect a victim's targeted trade secret if the FBI had any hope of ever getting companies to cooperate. Hence, the inclusion of protective Section 1835, whose meaning and intent to preserve confidentiality of trade secrets you would think was crystal clear, but not so.

In the Bristol-Myers Squibb Taxol case (*United States v. Kai-Lo Hsu*), Hsu's lawyers raised a disturbing question about their client's constitutional right to a fair trial. In a trial, the accused has a right to see and examine the evidence against him to prepare for his defense. But the government had filed a motion for a protective order to prevent the disclosure of the trade secret formula for Taxol. The prosecutors' argument was logical: to turn over the formula would defeat the very purpose of the Act. Moreover, the prosecutors argued that because Hsu was not being charged with actually stealing the secret formula, but rather *conspiracy* to steal it, proving the existence of a trade secret was not even necessary. A conspiracy to commit economic espionage—not the success of the conspiracy—was all that was necessary to bring charges under the EEA.

As you might expect, Hsu's lawyers fought back aggressively and said they needed to see the formula to make sure their client received a fair trial. Whereas the government argued that all trade secrets should be reviewed *in camera* (in the judge's chambers), and then released to the defense after they had been redacted, Hsu's lawyers countered with their own motion. They proposed a much, much broader protective order that would, in essence, turn over all designated confidential material that was necessary to help them mount a defense. Presumably, the people receiving this material would include the attorneys, outside experts, and even Hsu—the guy who had been trying to steal the formula in the first place.

Incredibly, the district court ruled in favor of the defendants. However, the government appealed and was successful. In reversing the trial judge, the Third Circuit Court of Appeals said that because Hsu was charged with a conspiracy to steal trade secrets and that he never had the formula in his hands in the first place, he did not need it now for his defense. The Appeals Court understood and explained in its ruling the purpose of the EEA: to provide the nation with a solution to the problem of economic espionage, not to compound the problems that American businesses have. To turn over the formula to Hsu would set a precedent that would deter reporting of such theft in the future.

However, the Appeals Court did not address the question of what happens when the *actual* theft of a trade secret or secrets—more than just a conspiracy—is alleged in the criminal complaint. So, if the Four Pillars defendants were going to be charged with actual theft of trade secrets received in a sting (as opposed to conspiracy to steal trade secrets, á la the Taxol case), did that mean that at some point Avery Dennison would have to turn over to Four Pillars the very trade secret documents the government and Avery Dennison were accusing P.Y. and Four Pillars of stealing? This ice was thin to be sure.

Ultimately, Avery Dennison turned over two documents that it and the government believed qualified as trade secrets, as was reported at the time and as the case proceeded. One was yet another iteration of the secret Asian Expansion Plan that Victor lifted from the file cabinet (the "Son of Kong" version), and the other was a patent application. A patent application—before the patent is granted and thereby protected by patent law—is considered a trade secret. By the time this case came to trial, the patent would almost certainly be granted, so Avery Dennison and the Feds would be able to disclose it in court without the level of concern that Bristol-Myers had with its Taxol formula. The relevant fact was that the Avery Dennison document would still be considered a trade secret at the time Victor turned it over to P.Y.[1]

All that was required now was the sting.

Forget James Bond

If you have the idea that economic espionage spies operate in exotic ways, the way you sometimes see depicted in edge-of-your-seat spy movies, think again. The FBI surveillance tapes of Victor meeting with P.Y. and Sally in a hotel room are like watching paint dry. The tapes themselves, four hours long, are painfully boring and, in my opinion, only noteworthy in a couple in places. The three principals speak a combination of Mandarin Chinese and Tai-wanese, but the video has English subtitles and the whole affair is essentially mundane.

I was struck by how calm everyone was. Not a care in the world, not a rapid heartbeat in the bunch. They are together in the West-lake, Ohio, Holiday Inn for hours, just the three conspirators: Victor, the 47-year-old spy; P.Y., the slight, 71-year-old, patriarchic founder of a leading Taiwanese company; and Sally, P.Y.'s 39-year-old daughter, whose occasional bouts with a queasy tummy and a bad back force her to recline periodically on the couch but still in view of the camera. There they sat, around one of those cheap veneer circular hotel/motel dining tables, looking almost like a happy family, making idle chit-chat for some time, discussing routine, everyday events.

P.Y. starts by suggesting to Victor that he should review documents he sent previously to see what else may be in "the treasure box."

Victor hands over Avery Dennison trade secret materials to P.Y., telling him that he took a special trip to the office that morning and got these things. They relate to adhesives. This was filed for patent on July 31 [just one month earlier]. "Basically, this is a confidential document." Then Victor explains it has to do with "adhesives in tackifier" and running adhesives at high speed.

P.Y., handing some of the material to Sally: "Why don't you read this?"

Victor, opening a bakery bag: "Have you tried the new blueberry bagels? They're very famous in America. Have you heard of it?"

Then Victor and P.Y. discuss their respective false teeth, P.Y. boastfully saying that he has only one false tooth. But, as all three of them dig into the blueberry bagels, the talk turns serious and they discuss adhesive production and processing.

Victor talks about adding a certain compound to the silicone emulsion so the silicone will flow on the surface of the paper. The holes on the paper will be filled. He explains that the advantage of porous paper is that it will not curl.

P.Y.: "What holes?"

Sally: "Paper has holes in it."

Victor elaborates: "Advantage of porous paper is that it will not curl after the moisture is applied."

Sally is uncomfortable and complains that she ate too much when she was in New York. "I was either eating or sleeping," she says, and adds that she caught a cold and hurt her back from walking. "So I lied down for two more days."

P.Y., the dutiful father, admonishes her that she hurt her back "due to lack of exercise."

The talk then turns to Sally's recent sleeping habits the past few days, and then to the U.S. Open tennis tournament, and whether or not tennis star Michael Chang will be playing that night in New York.

Sally assures them that Chang will play that night.

What follows is a back and forth discussion between Sally and Victor of Michael Chang's tennis ranking, while P.Y. continues to study the Avery Dennison documents carefully and pick blueberry bagel bits out of his teeth.

Victor, the gracious hotel room host, then offers chewing gum, but Sally explains she doesn't often chew gum.

P.Y. turns the talk back to production processes: "Can we use the five-roll?" [Remember the deBoer Report on state-of-the-art five-roll silicone technology mentioned in the list of what Victor provided in 1994?]

Victor says it all depends on the products, then likens the process to preparing meat to make it delicious. "It takes technique."

P.Y. and Victor engage in a discussion about the market for products in Taiwan.

Then, as though he suddenly realized he was eating something, P.Y. says: "Hmm. This tastes good. What is this?"

Victor tells him it is a bagel. It is the same bagel P.Y. has been eating since about the time he first arrived in the room.

P.Y.: "Bagel?"

Victor: "I bought them right out of the oven. Leave it out for too long and it will get too hard."

Then, P.Y. stands at the table and reaches into his pocket. He withdraws a small, ornamental pocket knife with a built-in scissors, like a small Swiss Army knife.

P.Y., referring to the Avery Dennison document: "You have to cut it."

Victor disagrees: "It should be alright," telling him it is not necessary to make any alterations to the document.

P.Y. contradicts him: "No. No."

Then, and for hours to come, P.Y. carefully and methodically begins to cut the papers so as to remove the Avery Dennison logo and confidential stickers and other identifying and incriminating language.

While P.Y. engages in his craft, Sally discusses with Victor her upcoming travel plans to Singapore. Sally explains about how much food they've eaten in the past couple of days and when and where their next meal is coming from.

P.Y. carefully begins to crumble up and set aside the papers he cut out of the original documents.

He then stands and walks over to his briefcase and removes a large roll of clear tape, returns to the table, and begins to tape the remaining pieces of paper back together to create a new whole document.

As this is taking place, Sally tells Victor that she's flying home and plans to watch the rest of the U.S. Open on television, "where I can eat ice cream and lots of snacks."

Sally, a grown woman and married, says that she lives in her parents' house. She complains that she wants to stop doing technical work and start working on "life philosophy." They talk about the fact that she has colored her hair.

P.Y. continues his surgery on the documents and takes a big bite of his bagel.

They talk briefly about the recent death of Princess Diana.

But then P.Y. brings the conversation back to business. Indicating the scraps of paper that he has cut away, and apparently not wanting to leave incriminating evidence behind, he tells Victor, "You have to throw that trash out at your home. Take that back to your house."

P.Y. continues his work while Victor and Sally talk of allergies. Then, Victor announces that his high-school-aged daughter, Judy, recently came home with good news: she has become a National Merit Scholar. The proud parent explains that she is in the 99th percentile, one of only four in her school who made it.

Sally asks about possible colleges that Judy is interested in attending.

Victor explains that his daughter "likes to stay with us–no pressure from home."

"Doesn't she want to go away to school like most kids?" Sally asks.

"She's different from most American kids," explains Victor.

Back to business for a moment, as P.Y. asks for clarification on what he's reading, and Victor complies.

Then Victor returns to talk of his daughter's potential, explaining that she likes to study science and engineering.

Back to business. P.Y. asks what an Avery Dennison finishing center is, a phrase that P.Y. just came across in his reading. Victor explains it is where a product is finished, cut, and slit to specific product sizes.

Turning back to Sally, he picks up the thread of conversation about his daughter and the fact that she doesn't like to memorize equations.

Enough bragging. Victor asks if they went to see Manco, Four Pillars' local customer this morning.

Sally: "Yes."

Victor also went to the office this morning, but he had to take his wife to a doctor's appointment because she had some bacteria on her fingers. The doctor took a culture and told them to return in two weeks. Victor was annoyed and thought this was just a ploy for the doctor to charge more money.

Next, Victor makes polite inquires about Sally's husband's new job.

P.Y. asks some more questions about the Avery Dennison document he's reading, and in response to Victor's questions says business is getting better.

As they're talking, P.Y. begins to assemble the new document.

Victor looks over: "So, there are three sheets."

P.Y.: "Yes, three sheets."

He continues taping the pieces of them together and is admiring his handiwork when he says: "Often times, all of a sudden, sometimes I cannot remember which company it came from."

Handing some of the documents to Sally, he says: "Why don't you take care of these papers?" And he goes back to picking bagel bits out of his teeth.

Then Sally begins to cut some of the documents, too, seemingly as though running them through her own "finishing center."

Victor, concerned about the old man's health, asks how his liver is.

P.Y. proclaims that he's in good health, but he sleeps only about five hours a night and then has to get up to pee.

Sally retreats to the couch and begins to read the Avery Dennison documents.

Victor, perhaps conscious that P.Y. has been picking his teeth since he started eating the bagel, tells him to go brush his teeth, and P.Y. says he will.

Later, Victor declares that he still has one bagel left. "Do you want it?" he asks P.Y.

P.Y.: "No. No. I've just brushed my teeth. I don't want it. My teeth are clean now." He then quizzes Sally about what she's reading. "Does it mention anything about surfactant?"

Sally: "Yes, it does. It does mention that."

P.Y.: "That is great."

Sally: "It might be good technology to be used in decreasing the cost."

Later, Sally initiates a discussion about increased staffing at the Four Pillars research centers.

But, P.Y. notes, there are more females than males.

Sally explains what this means: "More gossiping, chatting, and more time talking." Her team, though, "is very busy—no time to chat."

Sally continues her discussions about Four Pillars operations and machinery and staffing. She announces that Four Pillars has the biggest turnover in rheology.

She then takes Victor on a mental excursion of her recent travel in the United States for the past two weeks, including a discussion on her plane being stacked up over Chicago's airport due to bad weather and a driving trip through Detroit where she made a wrong turn and wound up in Canada.

All the while, P.Y. is still hard at work reading the material Victor brought with him from his trip to his Avery Dennison office this morning.

Suddenly, P.Y. gets to something that is particularly interesting to him: Avery Dennison's expansion plans in the Far East.

[This is the document—modified á la "Son of Kong"—that Victor removed from his supervisor's file cabinet under the watchful eye of the FBI surveillance camera nine months earlier.]

P.Y. talks about what he is reading and Avery Dennison's plans, all spelled out for him. He comments that Avery Dennison is starting with a coating center in Taiwan and then expanding into India, China, Thailand, Malaysia, and the Philippines.

P.Y.: "They are not going to start the finishing center until 1998. They do too much at one time, I felt."

Looking at their competitor's Far East plans, Sally observes that Avery Dennison is stealing employees from other companies, including Four Pillars.

P.Y. complains that he's having trouble reading and goes to his briefcase, saying he needs his magnifying glass and calling himself "old man."

Then, they talk and laugh about a maid who used to work at the home of one of P.Y.'s friends in Beijing, with whom P.Y. once danced. Seemingly smitten with her, he declares that she doesn't look like a maid. She's 50 but looks 20.

Sally—perhaps sensitive to her father's comments about another woman—points out that the maid, or baby sitter, easily fools people because she wears a wig and uses a lot of makeup. She does makeup for movie stars, Sally notes. Then she delves into this elaborate story of how P.Y.'s friend would take the beautiful maid to his son's school functions and people at the school would think she was the man's wife, and when the wife showed up people would think she was the maid. And how, Sally goes on animatedly, this maid used to boss around the whole family, and how she watched aerobics on TV at 7:00 AM every morning, and instead of using barbells she would use jugs filled with water to do her exercises.

P.Y. says he had danced with this maid a couple of times in mainland China and that she had a pretty figure.

Back to business: P.Y. wonders aloud if Avery Dennison knew that Four Pillars bought some machinery recently.

Then, P.Y. calls Avery Dennison "unreasonable" over the way it handled the controversy surrounding Dr. Guo, when Avery Dennison offered him a job.

Then, at last, he finishes the final taping of the papers to make a new, intact document.

P.Y.: "Everything is well organized. I have everything. I have had time to do a good study."

Next, *P.Y. declares: "It's time to leave." But first, he asks, "Should we have some soup?"*

Victor has a better idea and offers *P.Y.* the last of the blueberry bagels. Then surprisingly, without any preamble, *P.Y.* asks if Victor has heard about Kai-Lo Hsu–the Taiwanese scientist whom the FBI had recently arrested in the Bristol-Myers Squibb/Taxol case.

P.Y. says he knows the Yen Foong Paper Company in Taiwan and, as *P.Y.* explains it, the paper company sent some 300 faxes to Bristol-Myers trying to do business with them. Then, he continues, Bristol-Myers set the trap for them.

But Sally quickly protests: *"Not so, not so."* She has a different version of events and explains to her father that lots of advertisements appeared in U.S. newspapers about people selling confidential information. Sally says the FBI put the ads in the paper in order to catch *"international spies."* Sally tells her father that Kai-Lo Hsu contacted the FBI himself, not knowing he was contacting the FBI. The FBI set out a lot of bait and he took the bait, she says.

"America wanted to catch the business spies," she tells dad. *"They* [the FBI] *have a special division to catch business spies."*

Interestingly, during the entire time the three of them are in the room, *P.Y.* almost never makes eye contact with his daughter or with Victor. He has been too engrossed reading and cutting papers. But during the discussion of the FBI and the special division to catch business spies, *P.Y.* suspends all work and stares fixedly at his daughter.

P.Y.: "I am a very careful person. Whatever I get, I get rid of it immediately. I don't like to make phone calls, so she [referring to Sally] called you."

Then, as he's packing up to leave, he tells Victor to bring some more samples or new research trends the next time he visits Taipei.

P.Y.: "As a research institute, we do not need to copy the thing, we can modify it. Whatever tomorrow's product, we have to develop earlier. We need to know the future and to know what's the best machine to use."

Victor then drives them to Cleveland's Hopkins International Airport. They are not aware that they are being followed.

This is definitely not James Bond material. And yet, in its own way, I think it is more frightening than a John LeCarré or Len Deighton spy thriller, where you often have high-speed chases, secret drop locations, code names, disguises, and high-tech gizmos made in a secret lab by people named Q.

But in a plain vanilla room at a suburban Cleveland Holiday Inn, amidst the most mundane talk of false teeth, bad backs, overeating, airplane delays, driving mishaps, tennis tournaments and tennis stars, sleeping habits of middle-aged women, urinary habits of old men, hair dye, the death of a princess, allergies, academically proficient daughters, dental hygiene, the work habits of men versus gossipy women, good looking Chinese maids, and, of course, blueberry bagels—*real espionage occurred.* And because it was so routine, it is, in its own way, so frightening.

If espionage happened only once in a while, that would be one thing, but what took place in that hotel room with Dr. Tenhong "Victor" Lee, Pin Yen Yang, and Hwei-Chin "Sally" Yang happens every day, all over the country, with some of the people you would least suspect of committing economic espionage.

But they do it.

They do it with big companies, small companies, and medium-sized companies. But they do it.

They do it for greed or for revenge. But they do it.

They could be your competitor across the street or across the globe. But they do it.

And because they—so *many* of them—do it, it should be more frightening to you than pulp fiction.

In Section Two, we'll look at some of the ways you can fight back.

But, before we leave our Taiwanese friends, let me point out two things that have troubled me ever since I first saw the FBI surveillance videotapes. Maybe you caught it, too.

First, as a parent, I was greatly troubled by the father-daughter relationship between P.Y. and Sally. At what point does economic espionage become a family business, which according to Victor, it was with Four Pillars?

At what point did P.Y. decide to bring his daughter into the practice of economic espionage? If we just take Victor's confession that he began sending trade secrets to Four Pillars and P.Y. eight years earlier, Sally would have been in her early 30s and out of graduate school for a few years. Is this what she expected when she went to work for her father's company as an educated and skilled scientist? According to Victor's testimony, he reported as a spy first to one Four Pillars executive and then to Sally directly. So, besides using her own technical training, she became what, a spy master? Victor's "control"?

How does this happen exactly? What does a father say to his daughter? How does a father explain that the business may not be able to survive unless they break some rules, and he needs her help?

Over the years, people have commented that certain cultures view economic espionage more as a way of doing business than as the crime it is. If that is so, does that help explain Sally's acquiescence?

As Victor was bragging about his own daughter's academic achievements in high school, was P.Y. thinking about what Sally was doing at that very moment, helping to doctor documents so that incriminating logos and confidential stickers would vanish? Did he think of how his own daughter had been particularly bright as a young school aged girl in pigtails, and about how at one time he may have bragged about her school record? Did that cross his mind at all?

I have wondered about that, and it has bothered me. But I have also wondered about something else. I have wondered about the deeper meaning behind P.Y.'s statement when, referring to a document, he said: *"Often times, all of a sudden, sometimes I cannot remember which company it came from."* What the hell does *that* mean?

Could he mean that Avery Dennison was not the only source of Four Pillars' economic espionage? Could the line *sometimes I cannot remember which company it came from* mean just what it seems? Was P.Y. boasting that he is so proficient at doctoring other companies' documents, that when he is finished with his handiwork and examines his counterfeited document at some future time, his inability to recall the origins of the original trade secret—*sometimes I cannot remember which company it came from*—amazes even him?

I don't know.

But consider this: If Avery Dennison wasn't the only company where Four Pillars had a spy on its payroll, what other companies had—*has*—a mole?

And are they still active? Where? Could there be one at *your* company? Or have they gone underground, only to surface after things cool down?

I don't know. Do you?

Does anyone?

CHAPTER 14

Lucent's Falling (Path) Star

"Anything that can go wrong, will go wrong."

—Murphy's Law

"This was a tough year for Lucent Technologies."

That understatement of understatements was delivered by Henry B. Schacht, Lucent's hapless chairman and CEO, at the beginning of his annual message to shareholders in 2001. To say that Lucent had a tough year is like saying the Titanic had a leak.

In just one year, shares of the number one U.S. maker of phone equipment, which was spun off from AT&T in 1996, plunged 81 percent. That translates into a loss of about $80 billion in market value under the short reign of former chairman and chief executive Richard McGinn, who was fired in October 2000. Lucent's stock price plummeted 53 percent in one year. In the first quarter of 2001, the company lost an additional $3.69 billion, its fourth straight quarterly loss. Sales fell 17 percent from a year earlier. Its high profile, highly paid CFO, Deborah Hopkins, quit or was terminated after about a year on the job, as what one wag described as "the last rat leaving a sinking ship."[1] The Murray Hill, New Jersey, company has been battling rumors that it will file for bankruptcy protection.

In a desperate bid to return to profitability, Lucent first announced it would cut some 16,000 jobs, cancel product lines, and shed two businesses units. Then in July 2001, the beleaguered company slashed another 19,000 jobs, bringing the total number of layoffs that year to 39,000.

One bright light in this otherwise dismal business landscape was the company's highly successful PathStar™ system, which had generated about $100 million in sales for Lucent in the previous year. This innovative and proprietary software allows companies to simultaneously manage voice and data traffic efficiently on Internet-based communications networks.

Imagine the temblor that rocked Lucent when the FBI announced the arrest of two of its top PathStar scientists. The scientists, both Chinese nationals, were charged with stealing the source code—the entire PathStar kit and kaboodle—and providing the keys to the PathStar kingdom to a Chinese state-owned company.

Call Me Hai; Call Me Kai

The nabbed Lucent employees were Hai Lin and Kai Xu. Also arrested and charged as a co-conspirator was a non-Lucent employee, Yong-Qing Cheng, a naturalized Chinese-American citizen and vice president of Village Networks, an optical networking vendor in Eatontown, New Jersey. Cheng had served as an outside Lucent consultant working on the PathStar Access Server project.

Until their arrest, Lin and Xu were designated as *distinguished members* of Lucent's technical staff. Both were experts in the source code, software, and the entire design of Lucent's PathStar system, which they worked on and refined. Lin and Xu allegedly conspired to steal and transfer out of the country the highly advanced and profitable Lucent trade secret technology to create a new company, which they predicted would become "the Cisco of China."

Apparently, the lessons of American free enterprise were not lost on the two. While gainfully employed at Lucent, Lin and Xu, along with co-conspirator Cheng, started their own separate company called ComTriad Technologies, Inc., which was incorporated in New Jersey in January 2000. According to the complaint and subsequent indictment, ComTriad was involved in an active joint venture with Datang Telecom Technology Co. of Beijing.

The details of this complicated conspiracy follow, but what is noteworthy here is that Datang is majority-owned by the Chinese government. However, assistant U.S. Attorney Scott S. Christie, who is prosecuting the case, told me that the U.S. government does not know whether Datang knew it was receiving stolen Lucent trade secrets, which—if it did—would have opened the way for a Section 1831 indictment for economic espionage by a foreign government. Consequently, on May 31, 2001, the three defendants were indicted on the more routine Section 1832 counts of economic espionage.

The government's allegations, as detailed in the indictment, illustrate what many companies have experienced over the years: seemingly loyal employees suddenly and inexplicably quit work only to surface a couple of months later as business competitors against their former employers. In the United States or abroad, the new competition offers products whose speed in coming to market can only be explained by the help of economic espionage. That's precisely how Lucent was victimized.

First, the defendants "came to Lucent as scholars, but in reality, they were no more than sleuths," according to statements made by Robert Cleary, U.S. Attorney for northern New Jersey, at the time of the arrests. Elaborating on this kind of educational espionage duplicity, Cleary went on to say, "In the information age, it is difficult to imagine anything more dangerous to a company's business interests" than this type of economic espionage.[2]

Foreign governments frequently pay to send students to college in the United States to study science and technology and to work for U.S. companies whose business units manufacture products or technology that could benefit the sponsoring country. This sponsorship does not necessarily imply or involve economic espionage. However, it does allow for U.S. technological information to be put in practice in the individual's home country, if the individual returns home. On occasions, though, economic espionage by a foreign power *is* the main purpose of the employment.

In other circumstances, the entrepreneurial spirit of the individual spy is the key motivating factor—to learn, and steal, as much as possible with the explicit goal of starting a competing business in the United States or back at home in the foreign country.

It is now almost routine, when allegations of economic espionage are made against foreigners, for representatives of the named ethnic group to rise up in protest, often charging discrimination or unfair treatment. In an attempt to deflect such accusations against the company, Lucent spokesman Bill Price made a point of telling me that Lucent was not treating this as a case of international spying. "This is about two employees who allegedly stole equipment for their own commercial gain," said Price. "It is not about ethnicity or national origin. The fact that they are Chinese is beside the point."[3]

If you are the victim of economic espionage, your first and major concern is the damage to your business. Who commits the crime doesn't really matter. And why the crime was committed—entrepreneurial greed or foreign-backed economic espionage—is also of secondary importance. If you are robbed, you are robbed.

If products based on your intellectual property are being manufactured illegally, you will be hurt economically; the identity of the person (or country) perpetrating the espionage will matter far less than the fact of the economic hit your company will take on its bottom line.

On Second Thought: Call Me Howard; Call Me Roy

In the Lucent case, Hai Lin, also known as Howard, and Kai Xu—Roy—reportedly came to the United States as college students and started working for Lucent around 1996, first as long-term, temporary workers and then as full-time, full-salaried employees. Rising through the ranks to become distinguished members of the technical staff on PathStar, both became experts in the PathStar software and in the entire design and implementation of the system, and each had access to all the system's components. At Lucent, the two had been members of a team that had sought to enhance PathStar's overall commercial effectiveness.

There was, in fact, little or nothing they did not know about Path-Star—a product of such high technical excellence that it was recognized as a 1999 Product of the Year by *Computer Telephony Magazine* and received the 2000 Technology Leadership Market Engineering

Award from an international strategic market consulting, training, and research company. PathStar commands a 93 percent share of the market.

When they started ComTriad, the three conspirators listed themselves as its officers. Every *i* was dotted and every *t* was crossed. Everything appeared to be perfectly legal, except that the actual intent of their conspiratorial venture was allegedly to steal Lucent trade secrets and pass them on to a telecommunications company controlled by the Chinese government. U.S. prosecutors said the three conspirators had started a password-protected Web site to facilitate the secret transfer of information and ultimately PathStar source code.

Datang's principal business in China involves the development, manufacture, and sale of telecommunication products including mobile telephones, indoor wireless telephones, and computer hardware and software to facilitate voice transmissions over the Internet. In short, the company is a perfect customer for PathStar.

Ironically, when the spy story broke, Datang had several ongoing business relationships with Lucent, including the marketing of some of Lucent's products in China. But Lucent did not sell Path-Star to Datang. ComTriad, on the other hand, recognized a huge marketing opportunity. Here's how:

The U.S. government alleges that beginning in July 2000, Cheng (the third conspirator) initiated a series of meetings between Com-Triad and Datang to launch a joint venture in which the Chinese firm would pay $1.2 million in venture capital financing to Com-Triad. The financing was intended to secure the ComTriad technology that was, in fact, the PathStar technology. For its investment, Datang received a 51 percent controlling interest in the joint venture. Once the money had changed hands and the deal was struck, the joint venture was named DTNET.

The U.S. government does not know at this point whether or not Datang or the Chinese government was aware of the conspiracy. But, according to an ambitious business plan created by ComTriad, that company's primary contribution to the joint venture was to be intellectual property, specifically the delivery of CLX-1000, Com-Triad's name for PathStar. However, when the CLX-1000 and its source code were reviewed by Lucent's president and general manager, he confirmed that the product is identical to PathStar.

According to the U.S. government, the stated goal in the new DTNET joint venture business plan was for the new entity to become the leading data networking company in China—"the Cisco of China," is how the business plan put it.

It is revealing that in the section of the DTNET business plan's executive summary detailing the proposed budget for the venture's first fiscal year, no money was allocated for research and development, according to the Feds.

According to the U.S. government, Cheng told Lin and Xu in an e-mail message that the attached PowerPoint presentation was "based on PathStar." Another e-mail message from Cheng to Lin and Xu included a PowerPoint marketing strategy slide show. When Lucent reviewed it, the company said that portions of it were almost identical to part of a PowerPoint presentation developed by Lucent to market the PathStar Access Server. Indeed, the notes accompanying the PowerPoint slides in the document still make references to the PathStar Access Server instead of to the CLX-1000, which would have been expected and far more appropriate in context.

According to revised marketing timetables, the launch date was to be September 2001, and around February 2001, Lin and Xu began transferring source code onto the password-protected Com-Triad Web site.

To get ready, the government says that Lin and Xu decided they needed to distance themselves from ComTriad until they obtained their green cards (they had been working in the United States under business visas, and the green cards would grant them legal residency) and they resigned from Lucent, which they were planning to do sometime between May and August 2001. They also changed the ComTriad articles of incorporation and installed their wives in their places as company directors and officers.

Around March of that year, Lin started using the Americanized name Howard, and Xu became Roy.

The FBI raided the offices of the company hosting the Com-Triad Web site on March 7, 2001, and searched its contents. A review of the files indicated that it contained computer source code prefaced by explicit language reflecting that the information was the proprietary, unpublished intellectual property of Lucent.

Moreover, Lucent confirmed that the source code itself is unique to the PathStar Access Server. A substantial amount of the source had already been transferred to Datang in China, according to Assistant U.S. Attorney Scott Christie. In fact, ComTriad, named in the original complaint but not indicted, surprisingly issued its own news release at the time of the arrest that seemed to confirm the government's accusations.

On May 3, 2001, the FBI arrested Hai "Howard" Lin, Kai "Roy" Xu, and Yong-Qing Cheng. But, strictly as a matter of legal strategy, the conspirators were not charged immediately with theft of trade secrets. According to Assistant U.S. Attorney Scott S. Christie, "It is faster and easier to get arrest warrants for something like conspiracy to commit wire fraud, and charge them later under the Economic Espionage Act." This was in large part because of the extra burden prosecutors had to face until October 2001 to get the approval of higher-ups in the Justice Department before seeking any indictments under the EEA.

According to Lucent's Bill Price, the criminal activity was uncovered by Lucent after its internal security people became suspicious in February 2001. The company reported its suspicions to the FBI, and Lucent cooperated in the ensuing investigation.

A liability of the technological age is the ease with which trade secrets and other proprietary information can be transferred. (See Chapter 10 on cybercrimes.) For example, the government maintains that Lin and Xu transferred the PathStar source code to the password-protected ComTriad Web site, and from there to Datang in China, all via the Internet. But technology works both ways. The government's case is based on evidence investigators compiled by monitoring Lin's and Xu's incoming and outgoing e-mail traffic.

Comment Vous Dites Distraction en Français?

Absolutely, 2000 was a tough year for Lucent Technologies. And it got even worse.

Crises do not usually occur in a vacuum; typically they are not isolated events. More often, crises come in thundering herds. In conducting crisis post mortems with my clients—trying to understand what went wrong and why after a crisis has passed from the acute stage into the chronic stage—we often discover that because of one ongoing corporate crisis, someone had not been paying attention to other things that needed to be watched. Economic espionage, from a purely crisis management perspective, is no different. Crises often occur when management is distracted by other matters. Lucent was certainly distracted by one business setback after another for at least two years prior to the economic espionage case.

One well-publicized distraction at the time of the PathStar crisis was a near purchase of Lucent by the French telecommunications firm Alcatel for a fraction of Lucent's former value.

But if Lucent is looking for partners, it can always consider a merger with Datang, considering the Chinese company already has a good deal of Lucent's trade secrets.

CHAPTER 15

STICKY FINGERS

21 Counts and
a Funeral

Victor dropped off P.Y. and Sally at the curb at the airport and sped away. The Yangs nonchalantly walked through the crowded terminal and approached the airline counter. They had no idea they were being followed.

But, as they stood at the counter, minutes away from boarding a flight, P.Y. and Sally were approached from behind by three people who softly and professionally identified themselves as FBI agents. They told the Yangs they needed to come with them, and father and daughter meekly complied. There was no debate, there was no struggle.

The Yangs had the incriminating documents with them.

And they also had the last of the blueberry bagels.

Ten minutes after the arrest, I took a telephone call from the FBI telling me that the Yangs were in custody.

It was time for the crisis communications plan to kick into gear.

In a situation like this, one of the biggest mistakes a company can make is to allow its key constituencies to read the news in the papers or see or hear it on television or radio before they hear from the company itself. Maintaining control of the message—to the maximum amount possible—is essential to effective crisis management and crisis communications. One of the critical purposes of the crisis communications plan then, was to make sure that all of Avery Dennison's key constituencies—employees, customers, Wall Street, vendors, suppliers—heard the news from us first.

Whatever they heard later and from whatever source—no matter the intent or how it came across—the information would be landing on the soft featherbed of our version of the story.

While Avery Dennison would be embarrassed by having been victimized by economic espionage perpetrated by a highly placed employee for eight years, I wanted to ensure that message also included the fact that the company was not embarrassed by—in fact took pride in—its role in uncovering the crime, reporting it to the proper authorities, and cooperating with the FBI in the arrest of the Yangs.

The FBI was going to hold a press conference at 10 AM, September 5, and it was important to coordinate our internal and external announcements with that event. But we had to start in Asia because of the time difference and because in Taiwan this would be a big story.

Late on the night of September 4 California time, early on the morning of September 5 Taiwan time, Avery Dennison personnel in Asia were notified.

I recommended that Avery Dennison employees in Asia—but especially in Taiwan—keep a very low profile in the event any official Taiwanese government response or reprisal took place. P.Y. was a distinguished and respected citizen in Taiwan, and the last thing I wanted was to have an Avery Dennison employee play the pawn in a revenge plot by being arrested on some trumped-up charge. I could just see myself exchanging prisoners on a dark, fog-enshrouded night on the middle of a bridge at some "checkpoint Charlie."

I had also recommended that all nonessential travel by Avery Dennison employees to Asia be eliminated until further notice.

They were asked not to talk to the news media and to pass all media calls to us in California. But other than the media restriction, there was no prohibition against talking to their friends, family, neighbors, and colleagues in other companies. We knew that people would talk, so we wanted them to have the correct information.

By doing so, we were able to prevent unfounded rumors, gossip, hearsay, and innuendo from taking root. Everyone we could possibly reach was armed with the facts and the story, as *we* presented it.

Van A. Harp, special agent in charge of the Cleveland FBI Bureau, held his press conference on the morning of September 5 to announce the arrest of P.Y. and Sally and the charges. He announced that the Yangs and the Four Pillars corporation were charged with 21 criminal counts, including conspiracy, mail fraud, fraud by wire, money laundering, sale/receipt of stolen goods, and theft of trade secrets. There were several counts of each violation, totaling 21 in all.

When the federal court house opened in Cleveland, Avery Dennison lawyers were there to file the civil suit against Four Pillars. Later that morning, as P.Y. was being arraigned on the criminal charges, he was served in court with the civil complaint.

As we were monitoring the press conference in California via a telephone hookup, we pulled the trigger on the crisis communications plan, and Avery Dennison managers began to make announcements and calls to outside constituencies, as appropriate, regarding the news. CEO Chuck Miller and other managers sent mass voice mails, and Miller's written message was e-mailed to all employees worldwide.

Additionally, a confirming news release was issued the moment the FBI concluded its press conference. The release began:

> Avery Dennison today announced the filing of a civil lawsuit against Four Pillars Enterprise Ltd., a Taiwan-based competitor, for violations of the Racketeer Influence and Corrupt Organizations Act (RICO), as well as Conspiracy, Theft of Trade Secrets, Unfair Competition, Fraud, Unjust Enrichment, and other charges related to allegations of economic espionage.[1]

Best Laid Plans . . .

I considered two issues particularly sensitive. The first—as discussed earlier—was any mention of Avery Dennison's customers in a context that suggested that a customer's trade secret had possibly been compromised. The second was how much money this theft had cost Avery Dennison.

Whether this concern was ever conveyed to the FBI or not, I can't say. But at the press conference announcing the crime and the arrest, Harp freely and somewhat cavalierly mentioned many of Avery Dennison's largest and most well-known customers, such as Duracell, Kodak, and the United States Postal Service. Also, he put the cost of the economic espionage at $200 million.

This snafu might have caused corporate apoplexy had people not been prepared to speak to Avery Dennison's key customers whenever and wherever necessary, assuring them that they need not worry about the company's commitment to protecting its customers' trade secrets.

But the money was also a concern. It's one thing to talk about the theft of a trade secret in the abstract, but to quantify the loss made it seem as though the company had just been robbed of $200 million. This news, obviously, had the potential to shake the confidence of the investment community. What helped keep the erosion of investors' confidence in check was our anticipation, preparedness, and swiftness to react.

In Avery Dennison's then most recent annual report, a line indicated that the company had spent about $200 million on R&D in the past four years or so. While it first appeared that Harp had pulled the $200 million figure out of the air without first checking with the company, the source of his loss estimate was actually the annual report. The line I had crafted and that was used religiously throughout the criminal trial was that the amount of damages would be determined at the civil trial.

As soon as Harp finished his press conference and our confirming release was issued via BusinessWire, the phones in the office began ringing off the hook with calls from reporters and wire services all over the world. We had reached the end of the long fuse at last, and now it was time to put the planning to work.

Candle in the Wind

The expected potential land mines were deftly sidestepped. Based on the FBI's recitation of Avery Dennison's A-list customers, we were expecting and we received many pointed questions from news reporters about what trade secrets actually walked out the door and in what way Avery Dennison was damaged.

First, I explained that a full list of what was stolen would be provided at the trial. I then asserted that the extent of Avery Dennison's damages would be proven at the time of trial. In both instances, I maintained that it was just too soon to know.

Plus, I elaborated, if Four Pillars was proven to have been unlawfully enriched by Victor's thefts, that would contribute to the Avery Dennison damages claim, as well. In other words, if Four Pillars had profited by the thefts, then Avery Dennison was consequently damaged.

The progress of the crisis communications plan was closely monitored around the globe, and by the first day's end, we concluded that the handling of the media had gone very well. Calm prevailed in the Avery Dennison world, and the company's stock price had even gone up.

We also caught a break in the news.

There was no question that the Avery Dennison/Four Pillars spy case was big news, particularly throughout the United States and Asia. But another breaking story dwarfed us the morning after the FBI's press conference. While the world certainly learned of the Four Pillars sting, it was distracted, even spellbound, by the funeral procession of Princess Diana. And understandably so.

Following her tragic death, the world seemed to live and breathe on every Diana story out of Europe—from the car crash in a Paris tunnel, to the tearful, flower-strewn vigil outside her Kensington Palace residence, to her stately funeral procession to Westminster Abbey. As a Westminster church bell solemnly tolled a *D* note for Diana once every minute the caisson rolled on, the world's attention and emotions were transfixed.

Against this background came the media coverage of the FBI's press conference, the timing of which helped keep the sensationalism out of our story. Certainly, enough sensationalism was present elsewhere in the world to satisfy even insatiable media appetites.

In Taiwan, though, the Avery Dennison/Four Pillars story caused quite a sensation and dominated the front page of Chinese-language newspapers for more than a week. But, at least in the States, we clearly caught a break in how the media handled our news.

The quiet lasted for 16 months—and then all hell broke loose.

CHAPTER 16

And the Winner Is . . .

"The Japanese are experts in the matter. . . ."

—Count de Marenches, former director of French
intelligence, discussing international economic espionage

Japan.

Land of the Rising Sun and Lowered Ethics—or so it may seem.

Land of the first Section 1831 indictment our nation has ever filed against "an instrumentality of a foreign government."

How the theft took place is classic economic espionage. But what was stolen is right out of science fiction. The details that follow are based on my interview with Robert E. Wallace, senior trial attorney from the Internal Security Section, Criminal Division, U.S. Justice Department, and from a federal grand jury indictment.[1] (A reminder: An indictment is only a charge, not proof or evidence of guilt, and a defendant is entitled to a fair trial where the government has the burden to prove guilt beyond a reasonable doubt.)

Having said that, let's take a look at the case and see how portable science can be—even without the Internet.

First, Some Basic Background

The Cleveland Clinic Foundation (CCF) is one of the nation's leading nonprofit medical and research institutions, and its Lerner

Research Institute (LRI) is actively engaged in research into causes and treatments for such diseases as Alzheimer's, a disease that affects nearly 4 million people in the United States.

In their cutting edge research, LRI's leading scientists have identified that certain proteins found in the human brain may play a causal role in the development of plaque found in the brains of people who have died from Alzheimer's. The simplified central scientific question then becomes: How does the body produce these proteins? The question focused on an analysis of DNA—the basic molecular building block of life and the material that contains all genetic code, genes, and chromosomes in all life forms.

Alzheimer's researchers at LRI and other laboratories now believe that an identified mutant gene, located at a specific chromosome, might be the cause of one particular type of early onset Alzheimer's disease. Further research has identified two other genes which may pass early onset Alzheimer's from parent to child.

The current science now holds that all individuals who receive a mutated form of one of these three genes from just one parent will develop early onset Alzheimer's disease.

The potential of this remarkable genetic research is enormous. If scientists can identify and isolate mutant genes, they can work toward developing drugs and other methods to modify or correct the genes. Think of the benefit to humankind this innovative research can produce!

Two Gentlemen from Japan

According to the indictment, Takashi Okamoto, a Japanese national and legal permanent resident of the United States, worked at LRI from approximately January 1997 to July 1999. His work involved research into the cause and potential treatment for Alzheimer's disease.

Okamoto's colleague, Hiroaki Serizawa, is also a Japanese national with legal, permanent resident status in the United States. Serizawa worked at the Kansas University Medical Center in Kansas City, Missouri, beginning in 1996. Okamoto and Serizawa had been friends since the mid-1990s.

The Institute of Physical and Chemical Research (known as Riken) is a quasipublic corporation in Saitama-ken, Japan. According to the indictment, Riken receives over 94 percent of its total operating budget from the Ministry of Sciences and Technology of the government of Japan. Its purpose is to "promote creative and advanced research in the physical, chemical, engineering, and biological sciences."

Additionally, Riken's Brain Science Institute was "formed in 1997 as a specific initiative of the Ministry of Science and Technology to conduct research in the area of neuroscience, including research into the genetic cause of and potential treatment for Alzheimer's disease."[2]

Okamoto and his fellow scientists developed designer genes, which are known as *reagents*. These researchers used recombinant DNA techniques to transfer reagent cells into lab dishes, a process commonly known as genetic engineering. The purpose of the transfer is to study how the mutated genes are processed in normal brains as compared with those afflicted with Alzheimer's. For research purposes, the reagents are kept in small vials and have to be stored in liquid nitrogen freezers of minus 20 to minus 80 degrees Fahrenheit.

According to the indictment, Okamoto accepted a job with Riken as a neuroscience researcher in April 1999, with a start date in the fall of 1999.

The same month that Okamoto agreed to Riken's job offer, he provided a handwritten list of reagents to a researcher in his LRI lab in Cleveland. He directed the researcher to provide detailed written instructions concerning how each of these reagents were developed, according to the indictment. Okamoto then allegedly sent e-mail messages to all researchers in the LRI lab, instructing them to transfer *all* of the cell line reagents and constructs upon which they were working to a centrally located liquid nitrogen freezer in LRI's neuroscience department.

Not long afterwards, in the early morning hours of a July day in 1999, Okamoto went into the lab and stole the DNA and cell line reagents and constructs, according to the charges. But that wasn't enough. The indictment further charged that he destroyed and otherwise sabotaged those DNA and cell line reagents and constructs that he did not remove from the lab. Apparently, it wasn't enough merely to steal the trade secrets; but Okamoto also wanted to sabotage CCF/LRI's ability to conduct genetic research, thereby effectively destroying any foothold LRI night have in the race to cure early onset Alzheimer's disease, the government alleged.

Okamoto next shipped the goods to Serizawa in Kansas City. A few days later, after being notified that the DNA had arrived safely in Kansas City, Okamoto tendered his resignation to the Cleveland Clinic Foundation, according to the indictments. A few days later, Okamoto was in Japan working for Riken.

He returned to the United States a week later and traveled to Serizawa's laboratory at the Kansas University Medical Center. There, according to the indictments, he and Serizawa filled small laboratory vials with plain, ordinary tap water and made meaningless markings on the labels affixed to the vials. Okamoto then instructed Serizawa to provide these completely worthless vials to CCF officials if they ever came looking for the missing DNA. Serizawa later claimed that Okamoto had told him it was all a joke. Some joke.

When Okamoto left the country the next day for Japan and his job at Riken, he carried with him the stolen DNA and cell line reagents and constructs, according to the indictments and my interview with Bob Wallace.[3]

On May 8, 2001, the grand jury handed down a four count indictment, including violations of the EEA, theft of trade secrets. Because the intended beneficiary of the economic espionage was Riken, and because it is "an instrumentality of the government of Japan," the U.S. government was able for the first time to seek and receive an indictment—actually two of them—on Section 1831, international economic espionage, along with Section 1832 indictments.

Wallace would not comment specifically on how the acts of economic espionage were uncovered, except that, "The Cleveland Clinic Foundation reported it to us and was very cooperative in our subsequent investigation." Wallace said that the investigation was very long and involved and spanned FBI Bureaus in Cleveland, Kansas City, Boston, and New York.

I asked Wallace why there was no indictment against Riken, especially in light of the fact that the indictments against Okamoto and

Serizawa point squarely to Riken as the beneficiary of the theft of CCF's trade secrets. However, Wallace explained that there is a provision in the EEA which allows for the U.S. government to proceed on foreign soil in cases such as this. He indicated that such an action is (at the time of this writing) under consideration.

Okamoto is in Japan but is not beyond the long reach of the United States. The very broad territorial reach of the EEA, covered in Section 1837, states that the Act may also be applied to foreign schemes, provided that the offender "is a citizen or permanent resident alien of the United States, or an organization organized under the laws of the United States" and that any act "in furtherance of the offense was committed in the United States."

Wallace informed me that the Department of Justice (DOJ) is working with authorities in Japan to file an extradition request, forcing the Japanese government to send Okamoto back to the United States.

New Sheriff in Town?

Despite former FBI Director Louis Freeh's testimony before Congress in 1996 that numerous acts of foreign-sponsored economic espionage were ongoing, no Section 1831 indictments at all occurred under the Clinton-Reno reign. But, less than five months into office, the Bush-Ashcroft regime dipped its toe into those treacherous waters.

Given that the strong EEA oversight was still in existence at the time of this case—meaning any EEA indictment required the approval of the attorney general or a top deputy, as well as approval and coordination by the DOJ's Internal Security Division, in particular before a Section 1831 indictment could be sought—it is a matter of speculation if the current administration will be more aggressive than its predecessor in pursuing indictments against foreign economic espionage.

Loose Lips Sink Ships!

FIGHTING ECONOMIC ESPIONAGE
ON THE HOME FRONT

*"The reason economic espionage is
such a big problem to all Americans
is that we lose billions of dollars,
thousands of jobs, and the incentive
for research and development."*

–Thomas J. Pickard, Deputy Director, FBI

CHAPTER 17

STICKY FINGERS
Perception versus Reality

"It is as hard for the good to suspect evil,

as it is for the bad to suspect good."

—Cicero

In the pitched battle between perception and reality, perception always wins. Avery Dennison came to understand and benefit from this all-important crisis management axiom.

The company also understood—as you should—that economic espionage *is* a crisis. It is a particular type of crisis, but a crisis nonetheless by any reasonable definition of the term. However, the full crisis proportion of economic espionage is not always appreciated by parties involved, be they perpetrators or victims, prosecutors or defense attorneys, corporate departments or outside consultants.

Generally speaking, the FBI and the DOJ treat economic espionage as the crime that it surely is. The civil lawyers view it as the basis for a potential lawsuit, which it can be. The security types treat it as a security issue, which it often is. Public relations people treat economic espionage as a public relations problem, which it may become. If the theft was an inside job, the human resources department will treat it as a human resources issue, which it also is. If someone hacked into your system, your IT people will treat it as a valid technical issue, which it certainly is. And, if you or your company have been seemingly victimized by a particular ethnic group, the espionage can become an international cause célèbre, and even a national security and foreign policy problem, which is also possible.

Economic espionage is a crisis of all of these things and more. It is a crisis that can affect every aspect of your company and should be coordinated as such, rather than allow it to be pigeonholed into any one area or department by any one group or division.

One of the most serious mistakes I have observed companies make in economic espionage cases (as well as in other cases where the Feds are involved) is to give up trying to communicate to their various constituencies. Understand that the Department of Justice and the FBI are interested in one thing: prosecuting a case to a successful outcome. They may not give a hoot what happens to the price of your company's stock. They are unlikely ever to recognize that your customers are nervous and concerned. Or that after an FBI press conference in which your company's name and the phrase economic espionage are used together, those customers—who are your lifeline—may not even know if you're still in business, or will be tomorrow.

The FBI, after all, is doing its job, which does not necessarily concern the same issues that concern you. They want to see justice done. But that doesn't mean that the FBI and DOJ should have no sensitivity to your interests. They should recognize and care, for example, that what they say and do in front of the media might boomerang back and hurt you, maybe even more than the original crime of which you were the victim. The FBI can and should exhibit a degree of care in what they say and how they say it.

Meanwhile, your choice is either to allow the Feds to handle everything in terms of media relations, or to exert your own proactive influence for the sake of what's best for your company. You have ways to communicate what needs to be said to your key constituencies—including Wall Street—that will not compromise the government's case. You or your lawyers should insist on a meeting of the minds with the Feds. Forewarned is forearmed.

Hope for the Best, Plan for the Worst

As the Victor Lee saga unfolded, all the ways in which we could conceivably lose control of our message and wind up in even deeper waters began to crystallize. Some close bullets had been dodged thus far, but there was certain to be more shooting down the road.

One of my biggest concerns had to do with the possible perception that Avery Dennison would appear inept. When you stop and think of all the proprietary information and trade secret documents that Victor took—over eight incredibly long years—you might be inclined to ask how so smart a company could appear so unaware.

When we look at companies that have been victimized by economic espionage, by and large we see single incident crimes. Usually, the bad guys steal some trade secrets and then leave the company, perhaps to start their own business or just to escape with the goods. At any rate, the crime is over and done with, even though the thieves may benefit from the theft for some time to come.

But to date, there has never been an economic espionage spy saga on a scale as grand and protracted as that of Victor Lee. But its scope speaks to the effectiveness of the spy, not the carelessness of the victim. While you can certainly do things to reduce your risk, and this section will discuss many of them, it is important to bear in mind that someone determined to commit a crime will in all likelihood succeed. Whether she gets away with it is, of course, another matter. One reason for Victor's ability to do what he did, for as long as he did, was his high position of trust within Avery Dennison. He had access to almost everything.

So one of my concerns, then, was to disabuse people, including the media, of the perception that Avery Dennison had been asleep at the switch, allowing this economic espionage to go on apparently unfettered and unaware. If this incorrect and negative perception had gotten out—if this had been the perception fired round the world—how would Avery Dennison's customers have reacted? Certainly the confidence of its customers, which Avery Dennison had built and cultivated over the years, might have eroded seriously. If Avery Dennison was *perceived* as negligent or unable to guard its own trade secrets, how could it be expected to protect those of its valued customers? The reality was that Avery Dennison did take appropriate steps to protect its trade secrets, but remember the power of perception.

And how might Wall Street react to this type of negative perception? We were to learn all too soon how mercurial Avery Dennison's stock was, when just one negative story got out in Taiwan and circled the globe in a heartbeat.

Vendors and suppliers, too, might be expected to react badly to the dubious perception.

And what about the impact on the company's own employees? While some companies may overlook the importance of employees, Avery Dennison certainly recognized them as among its most valuable assets. As such, the company appreciated that its employees needed special handling. The last thing Avery Dennison needed was a large morale problem. These were, after all, Victor's colleagues who had worked with him (side by side in some cases) for years. Whose side would win these researchers' sympathy—their colleague Victor or the big, amorphous, parental entity that was *The Company*?

Employers need to realize that when a company takes action against one of its employees, the others will naturally put themselves into the targeted employee's shoes. The message to Avery Dennison employees, delivered in the execution of the crisis communications plan on the morning of the FBI's press conference, was purposefully blunt in its recitation of the facts of the crime. It contained the equally blunt message that Victor's actions against the company were the same as being directed against each member of the Avery Dennison family, which was true.

If all of the company's constituencies had read Victor's confession, or seen the two videotaped stings, and understood the volume of trade secrets that had gone out the door, I felt confident that sympathy would swing toward the company. This was one of the overriding reasons that the crisis communications plan intentionally provided for so many personal, one-on-one phone calls to key people.

The multiple perceptions of myriad constituencies were on my mind as time and events progressed towards the trial. By speaking openly and candidly to the news media as well as to all of Avery Dennison's constituencies, we took a big step toward ensuring that perceptions matched reality. In so doing, we were able to contain the crisis successfully and prevent a damaging escalation of problems.

Remember this reality: What happened to Avery Dennison could happen to you. While the disturbing truth is that nothing can be done to stop economic espionage outright, you can do things to stem it.

If you become a victim, you can control the message. Do not hesitate to be proactive in communicating your message to your employees, who need and deserve to hear from you first. Look at your company's mission statement and see what course of action fits with your mission goals. Allowing someone else to define the debate—such as a prosecutor or FBI agent—must be weighed carefully in terms of who can and will speak with your best interests in mind.

Kodak made the serious mistake in the Worden case of not talking to its employees before the media splashed the story all over the world. This decision was deliberate and conscious—though an unconscionable one—to allow its 30,000 local employees to read the shocking story in the next day's paper. Because, as you'll recall, some Kodak people didn't see the harm in what Worden had done and clearly needed trade secret education, this approach was wrongly conceived and harmfully executed. If anything, it throws more logs onto the fear and loathing pyre.

Here's my bottom line: If I know that employees will talk and gossip about the latest crisis with friends, relatives, neighbors, and a host of strangers in Internet chat rooms, I'd rather they rely on my client's version of the facts for accuracy and balance.

Think Big Picture

In crisis management and crisis communications terms, economic espionage is a crisis that can and should be planned for in any number of ways. When we work with clients in proactive crisis management planning, we encourage and help them to think in big picture terms rather than get bogged down in the minutiae of *who* and *what* and *why*.

For example, over the years I have reviewed previously written crisis management plans for many companies, and occasionally I see a common mistake of overplanning. The plan may cover a number of specific crises dealing with a problem at a facility, like fire, flood, earthquake, electrical outage, building collapse, terrorism, typhoon, and so on. That is largely overkill. Only a master, or big picture crisis management plan is needed—one that tells you what to do if you can't access the building, regardless of why.

While this example may be an oversimplification, the same point can be made about employee-generated economic espionage. Plan for it in a big picture way.

The Home Front

The recruiting posters during World War II shouted "Uncle Sam Needs You!" and were designed to stir the patriotism of the masses. Inside the plants, though, were different posters, such as "Loose Lips Sink Ships," designed specifically to remind all workers that security was the responsibility of each and every one of them, in real practice, every day.

In much the same way, awareness of threats of economic espionage against U.S. businesses should stir the patriotism of 21st-century American masses. But stemming the tide of economic espionage is the responsibility of every employee in real practice, each day.

The battle must be fought on the home front. And it starts with you.

The High Cost of
Economic Espionage

"A billion here, a billion there—

pretty soon you're talking real *money."*

—The late U.S. Senator Everett Dirksen

Every couple of years or so, beginning in the early 1990s, the American Society of Industrial Security (ASIS) has conducted a survey[1] to measure the depth and breadth of economic espionage throughout the nation. A survey of some 3,000 manufacturers, conducted in 1997 and released the following year, sent some significant shockwaves throughout the country—and in the country's boardrooms—when the survey revealed that economic espionage cost U.S. businesses more than $250 billion a year.

The survey was controversial and newsworthy because the dollar costs were so high. Newspapers like the *Los Angeles Times* editorialized about the staggering costs of economic espionage to U.S. businesses and what the country should do about it.

Dan Swartwood, who cowrote and analyzed that survey along with Bill Boni, explained that the hard dollar cost of economic espionage was actually closer to $50 billion, but the conventional and accepted accounting wisdom is that it takes $5 to replace every $1 stolen. Swartwood, head of security for Compaq Computer and no stranger to economic espionage, confirmed that this equation is used at Compaq and other manufacturing concerns when calculating losses of any kind.

"If you have to replace lost revenue and your profit margins are at 20 percent, it will be a five-to-one replacement ratio," agreed Boni, who is now Director of Information Protection Services for Motorola.

So, when the ASIS decided to conduct a new survey to study "Trends in Proprietary Information Loss," they brought in PricewaterhouseCoopers to crunch the numbers and give the survey more face validity. According to the accounting firm, the trend is definitely up from previous surveys. Forty-five percent of the companies that responded reported one or more incidents of trade secret theft and/or misappropriation in the previous year.

However, the most recent survey examined only the *Fortune* 1,000, and it looked exclusively at theft of trade secrets, crimes which would likely be prosecutable under the Economic Espionage Act.

The survey found that in 1999, *Fortune* 1,000 businesses sustained losses exceeding $45 billion specifically from theft of trade secrets. Nearly half of the companies that responded reported more than 1,000 incidents of theft in total. Of the reported thefts, more than half were in high technology, and one third were in service businesses.

Within the 17-month period immediately preceding the survey, the number of reported incidents of theft of trade secrets increased dramatically. The average responding company reported nearly 2.5 incidents with estimated losses of over half a million dollars per incident—the highest incident average ever in all the years ASIS has conducted the survey. This result should not be surprising, because the value of trade secrets increases each year.

Thefts of trade secrets that occurred in manufacturing businesses averaged $50 million *per incident.* This per incident statistic is up from the previous survey.

The greatest known losses are in manufacturing processes and R&D information. On-site contractor employees and original equipment manufacturers are perceived to be the greatest threat to company trade secrets and other proprietary information.

Just in terms of estimated losses to U.S. businesses from foreign economic espionage, the White House Office of Science and Technology estimated those losses at nearly $100 billion only a few years ago.[2]

It's All Subjective

When you get right down to it, what matters to you is not a national estimate of economic espionage costs in the stratosphere of $45 billion, $250 billion, or even over a trillion dollars. All that really matters is *how much did economic espionage cost you and your business?* The other figure—the total cost estimate—is a matter of interest and news value. But it may not have any direct effect on you, except that the higher the aggregate number, the more attention the government tends to pay to the problem and the harder it works to find ways and means to address the issue. For example, the high cost estimates were used to lobby congressional votes to pass the Economic Espionage Act. In that sense, the collective cost has had an indirect benefit to you and your business.

It is important not to discount or diminish your own losses as insignificant simply because they're not in the billion dollar range. Loss size doesn't make you immune to economic espionage in the long or short term.

One of the first things I tell my crisis management clients in training sessions is that a crisis is very subjective. And in a subjective view, you can measure whether an incident is, in fact, a crisis. For example, a crisis or potential crisis should be viewed as something that has a high risk of:

- Escalating in intensity
- Falling under close media and/or government scrutiny
- Interfering with the ability to do business
- Jeopardizing the positive public opinion of the company or its management
- Damaging the bottom line in any way

Notice that the criteria do not call for a specific amount of money. A crisis estimated at a total cost of $1 million may be a huge event to you, but may go virtually unnoticed at Microsoft. It's all subjective and relative.

The same holds true of economic espionage where your losses may be comparatively small. But they form a part of the $250 bil-

lion annual cost to American businesses. And no matter the absolute size of the loss caused by economic espionage to your company,
that loss is every bit as important as any other company's losses.

The 70 Percent Solution

Seventy percent or more of the market value of a typical U.S.
company resides in intellectual property. If you're like most U.S.
companies, you are probably not doing all that you should to protect your intellectual property assets.

Most companies spend lots of money protecting tangible assets,
such as property, and not enough on intangible assets, such as
trade secrets. "The importance of these assets, while often not for-
mally 'valued' by many companies, cannot be underestimated,"
according to the ASIS survey report. "In today's highly competitive
environment, it is essential for American business to recognize
that the intellectual assets of every business are highly sought-after
commodities."[3]

But let's take a closer look at the survey results—which ASIS
grouped into manufacturing, high tech, financial/insurance and
service industries—and see if any of this information can help you
lower your risks.

Where Is Your Greatest Internal Threat of Economic Espionage?

Employees used to be the biggest threat, but they have been
edged out in the most recent survey by original equipment manufacturers (OEMs) for the manufacturing and financial sectors. For
high tech and service firms, the biggest perceived threat was from
on-site contractors.

Other potential threats come from strategic business partners,
former employees, vendors, and suppliers.

Where Is Your Greatest External Threat of Economic Espionage?

High tech firms, in particular, cited the threat from foreign competition as a high potential risk area. Across all industry groups, however, domestic competition edged out foreign competition. Hacking also scored high as a threat.

What Sort of Economic Espionage Loss Would Be Most Damaging?

As you might expect, the answers depended upon which industry group responded. High tech firms, for example, think that a loss of trade secrets associated with a new, unlaunched product would be the most damaging, because that theft could give the competition critical time to beat the original product to market, underprice the rightful owner, or introduce a superior version of the product.

Financial and service firms worry about losing customer lists and other data associated with personal and confidential information entrusted to them by their customers.

Manufacturers lose sleep over possibly losing valuable R&D information.

Across all industry groups, the areas of highest concern included merger and acquisition plans and strategic business plans.

How Many Times Have You Been Hit in One Year?

The average *Fortune* 1,000 company that responded to the survey acknowledged an average of 2.45 incidents with an estimated loss of more than $500,000 per incident.

Across industry groups, slightly more than 1,000 incidents of economic espionage and theft of trade secrets were reported, but only slightly more than half were valued. So the half-million dollar per incident figure is an underestimation.

The highest dollar losses came from high tech and manufacturing, and the service industry reported the second highest number of incidents, behind high tech.

There are two noteworthy nuggets here. First is confirmation that small-sized to medium-sized businesses suffer the most significant losses. And, due to their relative size and the absence of deep pockets or deep reservoirs of good will, they have more difficulty bouncing back from such a loss.

Second, the survey confirms that theft of trade secrets and loss of proprietary information is a greater blow than any other type of security-related loss. A physical break-in is noticed at once, thefts are easily inventoried, and locks can be changed. But in cases of economic espionage, by the time you even get suspicious that your most valuable trade secrets have been seriously compromised, your competition may be crushing you in the marketplace with a close clone of your product at a fraction of your cost.

Where Were You Hurt the Most?

Respondent companies were asked to rank order the overall effects of loss of competitive advantage, loss of market share, loss of revenue, increased R&D costs, public embarrassment, increased legal costs, and increased insurance costs. On average across industry groups, embarrassment and increased legal costs were cited as the two highest consequences. But each industry group responded slightly differently.

High tech reported increased legal costs and increased R&D costs as having the biggest impact. The financial/insurance industry—an industry that has to face its customers every day—scored embarrassment as having the biggest effect. The manufacturing sector rated increased legal costs as making the biggest wave. And the services industry—which also has to face its customers and relies heavily on their confidence—scored embarrassment high and placed it in a tie for first with increased legal costs.

Also interesting across the board is the finding that increased insurance costs were not given much weight. This may be, in part, because no uniform mechanism exists to consistently value proprietary information such as a trade secret. That is not to say that you can't put a price tag on a trade secret; you can. Avery Dennison certainly had to value those trade secrets stolen by Victor. But this valuation is a flawed process.

In recent years, the AIG insurance company has begun offering a new product called Crisis Fund Insurance. This novel concept allows policyholders to immediately and without preauthorization contact and retain a preapproved crisis management firm to assist when a crisis occurs. The first $150,000 of the firm's fees are covered by the policy. So, for instance, in an economic espionage crisis where embarrassment is a high-impact concern, knowing in advance that your existing insurance policy covers a SWAT-team public relations response may also explain why increased insurance costs were not given higher concern.[4]

What Do You Fear the Most?

Across the board, things such as a loss or theft of a customer list or customer data ranked as having the greatest potential dollar loss. That number was driven by the financial/insurance sector, which understandably gave it considerable weight.

The high tech group gave its vote to unannounced product specs being swiped or made public. Manufacturing overwhelmingly picked increased R&D as being likely to have the biggest financial impact, and the services industry thought a compromised strategic plan would hurt it the most.

How Often Do You Take Stock?

If I were a shareholder in your company, here is where I would get nervous. Few of the *Fortune* 1,000 companies surveyed admit to any regular review of their intellectual property—a line item that represents some 70 percent of a company's market value. The most common answers indicated that companies rarely, if ever, take the time to value intellectual property (IP).

Often, IP valuation is not done until litigation takes place—over a stolen trade secret for example—or a merger, acquisition, or divestment occurs.

Without exception, the number one factor, hands down, across the board, considered when valuing IP is the competitive advantage it provides. Most economic espionage spies seek that very same competitive advantage when they target your company.

What I find most unsettling about this last question is how it underscores the fact that no one really knows for sure how much economic espionage costs American businesses each year. Whether you say $45 billion or $100 billion, no one blanches. Even $250 billion is an estimate that could be quantum leaps shy of the actual number.

We may not know the actual number with certainty for a long time. But we do know with certainty that those companies that continue to deny the threat and fail to take steps to reduce their risk of economic espionage are headed for trouble.

CHAPTER | **19**

STICKY FINGERS
The Media Wars Begin

Now that the big story had broken, Avery Dennison would have liked nothing better than to step aside and let the lawyers do their thing. The last thing the company wanted to do was talk to the media anymore, but you don't always get what you wish for.

Earlier, I explained that one way to classify crises is long fused versus short fused. Another distinction is based on whether you are dealing with an oppositional crisis or a nonoppositional crisis. The difference is simple but important in predicting how the media (and the public) will view you and your actions.

In a nonoppositional crisis—the more desirable of the two—you are a victim and have the public's support and sympathy. The Tylenol crisis, a textbook example in so many ways, is also a classic study in the nonoppositional crisis. I previously wrote a case study on this crisis and got to know most of the original members of the Johnson & Johnson crisis management team over the years.[1]

The public tends to have selective memory loss. It is not well remembered, for example, but in the beginning of that crisis, the public thought the likely culprit who laced the capsules with cyanide was someone on the inside of one of the Tylenol plants. This created an instant oppositional crisis that somehow made the company culpable for the deaths of seven innocent people in Chicago.

I once interviewed former Chicago Mayor Jane Byrne in conjunction with a court case in which I was an expert crisis management witness. She confirmed that during the height of the panic—yes, *panic*—she ordered all Tylenol products off the shelves of all Chicago stores, even Tylenol products that were not linked to the deaths. She was proud of her bold actions, in spite of the fact that, as she told me, she had no legal authority to order or enforce them.

Then, as the facts began to emerge and the nation learned that an outside terrorist had tampered with the product after it was on store shelves, the focal point of the story changed to a nonoppositional crisis, and J&J could speak to the media and to their constituencies without being opposed by anyone on the other side, such as a media-savvy public official with a bully pulpit and an armed police force.

In an oppositional crisis, whatever you say to a reporter, her story will almost certainly carry the conflicting and challenging comments from the other side. A responsible journalist wouldn't be doing her job if she didn't present both sides of the story. I always counsel clients in an oppositional crisis that they need to steel themselves for that reality. Oppositional crises can be very frustrating.

And Avery Dennison was definitely in an oppositional crisis.

The Wall Street Journal Story

After the sting's dust settled, I took a call from Dean Starkman, Pulitzer Prize winning reporter from *The Wall Street Journal,* who wanted to interview someone from Avery Dennison on economic espionage in general, and the Four Pillars case in particular.

By this time, the Yangs had retained legal counsel, and their lawyers had been speaking freely to the press. This was anticipated, as were most of the things they were saying to the press.

Then Starkman mentioned the "joint venture defense theme" that the Yangs' lawyers were using. That came as a surprise, and I felt that if it was not batted down, and quickly, it would put my client in a bad light. I counseled strongly that the company couldn't afford to ignore this argument and should agree to the interview. I knew that Starkman was going to write the story with or without Avery Dennison's participation, so why give Four Pillars an unchecked forum?

Even though Avery Dennison had not yet agreed to sit down for an interview with *The Wall Street Journal,* Starkman and I were still talking. I freely gave him whatever background he needed on the company.

During these conversations, as Starkman was trying to get the interview, he asked me about the joint venture discussions between Avery Dennison and Four Pillars. This question caught me by surprise. At that point, I wasn't aware of any joint venture discussions between the two adversaries. According to Starkman, however, Four Pillars was maintaining that there had been serious joint venture discussions between the two companies for more than seven years, from 1987 to 1994, and that during those discussions, Avery Dennison had freely given to Four Pillars all of the documents and other information they now stood accused of stealing through Victor. Starkman needed a response; absent a response, that explanation was going to be his lead.

(I have referred to this joint venture discussion earlier in this book, but this conversation was the moment I learned of it.)

"Dean, no business has a joint venture discussion that lasts that long," I told him. "Some of the biggest mergers in recent history happened in a matter of weeks or months. This doesn't pass the smell test."

"I know that," he replied, "but I need you or your client to tell me that on the record. Otherwise, I'm going with it."

A typical joint venture discussion between two companies lasts no more than about six months, and Avery Dennison is a typical company. Within that time frame, the companies know either they have a partner they want to work with or they don't. And if not, they move on. A seven-year joint venture discussion was hard to swallow.

But had there *ever* been a joint venture discussion between Avery Dennison and Four Pillars? I needed to know as soon as possible, then sit down with *The Wall Street Journal* once the facts were lined up. My concern was one of perception versus reality. I was able to buy some time with Starkman while I looked into the situation.

What I ultimately learned, and subsequently released to Starkman and other news media outlets whenever the question came up later, was that there had, in fact, been preliminary joint venture discussions between the two companies around late 1993/early 1994, but the talks had fizzled out after about six months, owing in part to the weak state of Four Pillars' financials.

I wondered whether Four Pillars could possibly have misinterpreted the situation to think joint venture discussions were still ongoing after they had been terminated. But I learned that was unlikely, because in early January 1994, P.Y. wrote to Avery Dennison, in part: "We are glad to know Avery is aggressively researching the Chinese market. . . ." P.Y. concluded, "Sharing our experiences of the mainland Chinese market would be mutually beneficial. Therefore, let's keep each other up to date about our activities."[2]

(It was this sort of cordial relationship card that P.Y. was playing when he got Avery Dennison to withdraw its job offer to Guo.)

Then, six months later, Alan Campbell, Vice President Pacific Basin, Avery Dennison Materials Group, confirmed to P.Y. in writing what had been told to the Four Pillars chairman verbally some months earlier, that Avery Dennison had decided to go it alone in Asia. The letter Campbell wrote said, in part, "[W]e have decided to invest in a wholly owned foreign business to be located near Shanghai. . . ." Later he explained that Avery Dennison was "in the process of obtaining land for the factory" and that the company should have "our first plant in China, which will be operational early next year," and our own "manufacturing capability in Southeast Asia within the next two years."[3]

Armed with this information, I persuaded Avery Dennison that it had everything to gain and very little to lose by speaking with *The Wall Street Journal*.

Kim Caldwell, Avery Dennison executive vice president, was the right person for the interview. He had been in charge of the Ohio-based Fasson Roll division where Victor had worked during much of the theft. And now that he had been promoted to the corporate side, he had an even broader company perspective.

From my vantage point as well as Avery Dennison's, the story that Starkman wrote was excellent, factually laying out what Victor had done and burying the joint venture accusation in the penultimate paragraph, way down on the jump page. In fact, Caldwell managed to get in one of our key talking points to refute Four Pillars' counterclaims, which Starkman used to close out this story: "For Pete's sake, Dr. Lee signed a confession."[4]

Moreover, as I predicted, other news media outlets used the presentation of the facts in *The Wall Street Journal* story as the launching pad for their own stories.

Things got easier . . . for a time.

Briefing Problems

It was a given that the news media would cover the trial if the case went that far. However, I wasn't sure a trial would actually take place. These types of cases generally seemed to settle with the defendants pleading guilty to some lesser charge, receiving probation, and paying a fine.

The truth was that the EEA was not turning out to be too much of a deterrent—at least back then. But, if the case did go to trial, it would probably be the first case to be tried under the EEA, and the media wouldn't normally overlook such a built-in news hook. Also, it was the first time that a corporation had been charged under the EEA, and that event was newsworthy, too.

Additionally, the case was somewhat "sexy," complete with foreign intrigue. Here was a foreign-born "mole" under deep cover for more than eight years, who stole the most important high-tech trade secrets from a first line American company and sold them to a foreign competitor, all caught in an FBI videotaped sting. Business news doesn't get much sexier than this.

"Taiwanese Spies Nabbed in FBI Sting," could have been a banner headline in any of the world's newspapers. Clearly, if the case went to trial, it would most likely be covered heavily by the media. But I perceived a public relations problem for my client: the case was very complex.

I was concerned at this point about how the case would play in the press. The media might dumb down the story for two reasons: One, they want their readers and viewers to be able to follow the story; two, they only have so much room in the paper or time in the broadcast, and time and/or space would not allow a lesson in the arcane features of the law, of Avery Dennison's manufacturing processes, or of adhesive formulas.

Don't get me wrong. I don't mean to imply that the media wouldn't be able to follow the story; on the contrary, I was confident that they would. But by simplifying it for their respective audiences and their respective space/time limitations, reporters or their editors might have to make certain editorial decisions or shortcuts with which I was concerned. In trying to simplify on the one hand and at the same time (at least with some media outlets) sensationalize the story, would they go overboard and blow it out of proportion?

To prevent oversensationalism or oversimplification that might make Avery Dennison appear lax with some of its customers' trade secrets in addition to its own, I concluded in early 1998 that we needed to identify in advance the likely reporters who might cover the story and invite them to spend time in Ohio to get briefed about Avery Dennison and the nonlegal aspects of the case. The more they knew in advance as background, the better our chances for accurate and less sensational reporting in the heat of a reporter's deadline.

My position was that the facts were the facts. And, while some of those facts might be embarrassing for Avery Dennison, others were not. I wanted to make sure that all reporters had all the facts early so they could digest them and ask questions. Then, when it came time to write their stories, there would be a greater chance that they would avoid the sensationalistic aspects of the basic economic espionage story. Avery Dennison agreed, and I packed my bags for Cleveland.

However, unexpected problems arose. My early recommendation had been to try to keep the story localized. Once the dust from the FBI press conference had settled and Wall Street had calmed down, nothing was to be gained by making this a corporate story. That would only raise the story's profile and run the risk of attracting more national media, as well as the wrong kind of attention from Wall Street. We might be able to better contain the story if we used local people with local media in a local story. I decided to do a dry run, pretrial briefing.

Avery Dennison had a local PR woman on its employment roster in Ohio for a number of years whom I initially thought could play a pivotal role in emphasizing the local nature of the story: *local* guy steals some secrets from *local* Painesville plant, says *local* PR spokeswoman. She was given what should have been a simple task: line up the local media for a series of individual media briefings and plant tours. But, in my opinion, she was clearly in over her head and unable to carry out the assignment with anything resembling media savvy. It didn't appear she even *knew* the local media who were supposed to be covering her company. If she had to introduce herself to each and every reporter and editor she called, we may as well have done the work ourselves from Los Angeles (which thereafter we did as the trial progressed).

At any rate, I was told that she had set a briefing schedule, but in fact she had been unable to line up the any of the major media outlets on her list. However, it was her troubling performance at the briefings that really concerned me. From the start, she became overly concerned with the quality of her black-and-white "how labels are made" presentation, fearing that it looked dull and inferior when compared to someone else's preceding presentation in color. She was rattled by this nonissue, and her nervousness was obvious to the others in the room (a reporter even mentioned it to me later). I had to steer her back on track more than once. I considered this a telltale mark of someone insecure and inexperienced. A person who is lacking ability and confidence is a potential danger, certainly not someone you want around in a crisis.

Why is this situation important to relate? Because if you have someone on your team who is in over their heads, as I felt she was, you need to find out before any serious damage is done. Also, it underscores the necessity to pay attention to details, including the all-important human resource detail.

So, while I thought my trip had been wasted, it clearly wasn't. The dry run paid off. I learned in time that I would have to make other arrangements for local media contacts if and when the case proceeded to trial. Entrusting her with this assignment would have been a mistake, in my opinion, and the general consensus was that she would be in over her head if the media wars ever kicked in.

And did they ever.

Blindsided

We entered a quiet phase that lasted a long time. I still thought this case would eventually plead out like the other EEA cases—so much so that the entire matter was off my radar screen for a while. And then we got blindsided.

Right after the new year, 1999, Four Pillars released a statement out of China announcing that it had filed a $262 million lawsuit against Avery Dennison, alleging fraud and theft of Four Pillars' trade secrets! The media had a field day, and we were bombarded with calls from all over the world.

According to the wire stories being circulated, Four Pillars claimed that Avery Dennison had fraudulently entered into joint venture discussions with the smaller Taiwanese company for seven years, but that the larger company's ulterior motive was to pick Four Pillars' brain and its trade secret pockets to gain strategic insights into the Four Pillars Asian operations.

One of the more egregious media quotes came from Sally Yang herself, who trumpeted, "We hope to put a stop to the predatory tactics of our unscrupulous competitors who use the guise 'joint ventures' to acquire trade secrets of Taiwanese companies."[5]

The media reports were everywhere, completely dominating the Asian news media and the U.S. wire services. We were on the ground scrambling. We had never even seen the wire story before those in the media reporting on events started calling for our reaction. We were caught off guard; nobody had even seen a copy of the complaint. One AP wire story quoted a new Four Pillars attorney, Nancy Luque, attempting to spin a plausible story of why a company like Avery Dennison would allegedly engage in such nefarious activity against her client, "I think the issue is entry to Asia, which is a daunting task for any company."[6]

The media respond one way when a small company is accused of stealing from a large company, but Goliath picking on David makes an even better story. The press jumped all over the story. With headlines around the world blaring things like "Avery Dennison Accused of Stealing" or "Avery Dennison Accused of Fraud," the company's stock plummeted. Trying to stop the hemorrhaging became our critical task. At the end of the day, shares had dropped $2.25 in a day of frenzied trading to a selling price that was a 30 percent discount to the S&P 400. In time, the stock rebounded, but the swift downturn on an unfounded foreign news story was unsettling.

If I had seen the lawsuit and known exactly what Avery Dennison was accused of doing, it would have been easy to fashion a prompt response. But the elusive complaint was nowhere to be found. I began to grow suspicious.

In the United States, if the media are going to quote from a complaint, they usually want to see the actual complaint with the court's stamp on it for verification of the allegations that are quoted in the news release. (As you will see, an incident happened later in this case that underscored how little trust experienced reporters have in unconfirmed press releases.) But the media in Taiwan may not have the same strict code of journalistic ethics; I frankly didn't know.

I do know that before the end of the initial news cycle, I managed to issue a statement saying that the idea of a seven-year joint venture discussion simply doesn't pass the smell test (the basic line used with *The Wall Street Journal* interview 14 months earlier). The research I had done for the earlier story paid off, because I was quickly able to provide reporters with the same joint venture background I had given to Dean Starkman.

Then, taking careful aim between their eyes, I said, "It is our contention that the lawsuit is nothing more than a blatant attempt to distract attention from Four Pillars' own criminal conduct. What they're doing is trying to put up a smoke screen, pure and simple."[7]

This quote acted like a finger in the media dyke.

I then asked reporters what to me was a fairly obvious question: Why would Four Pillars wait so long to bring their suit?

If you follow the Four Pillars chronology, the joint venture discussions ended in 1994. (It was then 1999.) I rhetorically asked numerous reporters in one-on-one interviews and background briefings: Why wait five years to bring an action like this? The reporters then seemed to view the Four Pillars claim skeptically when examined under close focus.

It is not uncommon in damage cases for the defendants to file a counterclaim for damages against the plaintiffs. Sometimes this strategy is merely to better position one company against another for settlement talks. Was that what was happening here? It was a possible ploy, to be sure.

Then, a few days later, I learned that the aggressive Four Pillars news release that seemed to emanate from China had apparently been issued by a PR firm in Washington, D.C., run by the son of failed Supreme Court nominee Robert Bork. The presence of a Washington, D.C., PR firm on the scene made my earlier decision about not involving Avery Dennison's woefully inexperienced PR woman in Ohio seem prescient. She would have been eaten alive in the type of trench warfare that was developing.

It also meant I would be going back to Ohio. For several months, I kept a packed bag in my office.

CHAPTER 20

What Is a Trade Secret?

"The world in general doesn't know
what to make of originality."

—W. Somerset Maugham

Unlike patents which are protected by Patent Law, or trademarks which are protected by Trademark Law, or copyrights which are protected by Copyright Law, until the passage of the EEA, no single, specific law on the books protected intellectual property known as trade secrets.

Let's look now at your trade secrets and what you can do to protect them and reduce your risk of economic espionage.

The EEA defines a trade secret in the broadest possible terms, which is good for you:

The term *trade secret* means all forms and types of financial, business, scientific, technical, economic, or engineering information, including patterns, plans, compilations, program devices, formulas, designs, prototypes, methods, techniques, processes, procedures, programs, or codes, whether tangible or intangible, and whether or how stored, compiled, or memorialized physically, electronically, graphically, photographically, or in writing if

- the owner thereof has taken reasonable measures to keep such information secret; and

- the information derives independent economic value, actual or potential, from not being generally known to, and not being readily ascertainable through proper means by, the public.

Unlike a patent which must be "novel," a trade secret must only contain *some* element that is not generally known and that sets it apart from that which is generally known. The critical criterion is *secrecy*. Was the trade secret generally known prior to its theft or not? For example, would it have been possible for someone to locate this trade secret on the Internet or in a library?

Did one of your scientists publish it—or some of it—in some professional journal over the years? Did anyone from your internal scientific workforce ever give a speech or a seminar or teach a class where the trade secret could have slipped out? If so, who then had access or was in attendance? Did a reporter for a technical journal sitting in the audience then write about the trade secret? Was it discussed at a trade show? Even if the trade secret was disclosed accidentally and unintentionally, any of these occurrences could void its trade secret protective status.

Was your trade secret obvious to your competitors, even to your chagrin? Just because you consider something a technical trade secret, if it is well and widely known in your industry, it will not meet the standard of a trade secret that is protected by the law.

On the other hand, not every single part of the information in question must be completely confidential to qualify for trade secret protection. A trade secret might contain a combination of elements, some of which may be in the public domain. The unique combination of the public domain portion along with the confidential information could create a legitimate trade secret. This part is covered by the part of the law that says a trade secret must contain *some element* that is not generally known that makes it novel.

You then need to take *reasonable measures* to keep it secure, such as advising, educating, and training your employees; requiring nondisclosure forms and noncompete agreements; limiting access to the trade secret on a need-to-know basis, or keeping it under lock and key. It's up to you to determine in advance what measures are reasonable to protect your trade secret. Remember though: If your trade secret is ever stolen and you find yourself in court testifying to a jury, you must be able to demonstrate satisfactorily that you took reasonable measures to protect it. For example, while an "open culture" work environment may be desirable, security measures still have to be implemented and maintained if you wish to claim protective trade secret status.

If your trade secret is disclosed in a lawsuit or in the filing of a patent, it will no longer be a protected trade secret. In the case of a patent, however, if you later modify or enhance the patent, in many circumstances the new end result may requalify as a trade secret.

Finally, the trade secret must derive independent economic benefit from not being generally known to the public. This means that the very fact that the trade secret is not well known makes it valuable. It may have value in other ways, but it must derive independent economic benefit from not being generally known.

It is perfectly legal for one of your competitors to reverse engineer your trade secret, and you would have no remedy or recourse. (Reverse engineering means taking apart a product and figuring out how it was made.) Of course, you can do the same thing to one of your competitors' trade secrets. The law specifically does not protect a trade secret owner from discovery by fair and honest means, such as independent invention, accidental disclosure, or reverse engineering.

The Bad Guys

Anybody who deprives you of your trade secrets has committed economic espionage under the terms of the Economic Espionage Act. If it happens domestically, the bad guys can be charged with a violation of Section 1832, theft of trade secrets. Section 1831 applies to theft of trade secrets by a "foreign instrumentality," which is defined as:

- any agency, bureau, ministry, component, institution, association, or any legal, commercial, or business organization, corporation, firm, or entity that is substantially owned, controlled, sponsored, commanded, managed, or dominated by a foreign government; and

- the term *foreign agent* means any officer, employee, proxy, servant, delegate, or representative of a foreign government.

But these important legal distinctions are for the FBI and the prosecutors to sort out. They matter to news headline writers, too. Let's face it, a headline that boldly screams "TAIWANESE STEAL AVERY DENNISON FORMULAS!" or "JAPANESE SCORE DNA FROM CLEVELAND CLINIC!" or "CHINESE RIP OFF LUCENT SOURCE CODE!" will be attention grabbing.

To you, though, it won't much matter who steals your trade secret except for purposes of keeping score or as a way to seek damage recovery. If you've been hit, you've been hit.

CHAPTER 21

STICKY FINGERS
The Media Wars Continue

As the time drew closer to the trial date, I learned that the case would be held in Youngstown, Ohio, rather than Cleveland, as expected. This venue had both pros and cons.

I did not expect as much media would attend the trial in Youngstown as Cleveland, which was a positive consideration for Avery Dennison. Remember, from the company's perspective, no news is good news, and little coverage is better than a lot. Recall how quickly Avery Dennison's stock tumbled in January just because of Four Pillars' news release of a countersuit charging Avery Dennison with all manner of crimes, including stealing trade secrets belonging to the Taiwanese company as a way to gain entrance in the lucrative Asian marketplace.

The bad news was that I was going to spend untold weeks in Youngstown, because the government was neither prepared nor inclined to look after Avery Dennison's corporate interests.

It was time to brief the media in preparation for the trial and to try to get a sense of how much news coverage we could expect. My purpose in the briefings was to make sure the media had a clear and unambiguous understanding of the economic espionage from

Avery Dennison's perspective. While it was clearly the government's case that was about to open, the company supported it fully.

Four Pillars lawyers were telling reporters that:

- The U.S. government should never have been brought into the case.
- The issue was a private business dispute between two companies that went awry.
- Avery Dennison was using the government to help it settle the dispute in its favor and to squash Four Pillars in the process.
- Avery Dennison had stolen Four Pillars' trade secrets as a way to break into the Asian market.

During my media briefings, I emphasized to reporters that this proceeding would be a criminal trial with charges of economic espionage brought about as a result of:

- Dr. Lee's and Four Pillars' criminal activities
- The FBI's and the DOJ's investigations
- Dr. Lee's signed confession
- P.Y. and Sally being caught and videotaped receiving Avery Dennison trade secrets in an FBI sting operation
- The Yangs' arrest and indictment

With that said, it wouldn't do to just let the Four Pillars' media claim that this was merely a "business deal gone awry" go unanswered. Precisely that sort of charge, coupled with the accusation that Avery Dennison had stolen Four Pillars' trade secrets, had led to the Chinese lawsuit debacle, the Four Pillars' news release, and the resultant decline in the Avery Dennison stock value just months earlier. I took pains to explain that no deal had gone awry, because there never was a deal on the table to begin with.

But the crippling comment, as I saw it, was simply this: If there had been a business deal in the works, what was Victor Lee's role in the discussions? With all of his activity over an eight-year time frame, what role did he play? Advisor to Avery Dennison on how to do business in Taiwan? Advisor to Four Pillars on how to do business with an American company? Obviously, the questions were rhetorical and every time I posed them to a reporter, I usually said, "If you get a reply from Four Pillars' attorneys on any of those queries, please let me know." That usually elicited a knowing smile or chuckle, as if to say, "I hear what you're saying, and I agree." That gave us an edge on credibility going into the trial.

Another reason for the briefings was that I wanted reporters to feel they could and should seek me out if they had any technical questions about any of the testimony, such as what trade secrets Victor stole. This was as much to protect Avery Dennison as it was to protect its major customers. I anticipated complex and technical courtroom testimony in the days ahead, and I knew that the government prosecutors would not talk to the press. I also anticipated (correctly) that the Four Pillars team would be actively working the media. I wanted to ensure that the reporters had someone they could turn to for clarification and accurate interpretation on a deadline.

Sticky Fingers

All in all, the briefings went well; there was a good deal of regional and national interest in the story. When I briefed John Affleck, Cleveland Bureau Chief of The Associated Press, he confirmed that the AP was going to cover the opening arguments and Victor's testimony, to be sure, but he asked for my assistance in giving the Cleveland Bureau (an hour-and-a-half from Youngstown) a heads-up if any other testimony was likely to stir interest.

Because of the business aspect of this case as well as the strong business interest in its outcome, *Bloomberg News* was very interested in the story, as I had suspected. But the day before I flew to Cleveland, I received a curious call from Jef Feely, *Bloomberg* legal affairs editor in Wilmington, Delaware. Feely told me how much they wanted to cover the trial, but that their normal reporter was unavailable. So he was sending a very young, very inexperienced stringer to the briefing. He asked me to look after the young cub—make sure he had everything he needed, didn't get lost in the pack, and so on.

The request was unusual, and I was surprised, but I told him I would do whatever I could for the young man. However, when the young reporter, Jeff Ottenbacher, showed up for the briefing, his mother was with him! Kathi Ottenbacher, the mother, was a seasoned former UPI wire service reporter. This was her son's first assignment. She was there to show him the ropes, and the two of them drove in from Cleveland to Youngstown every day without fail to cover the trial.

It was a first for me—a mother-son reporting team: *Ottenbacher mère et fils* as we took to calling them. They did a commendable job in daily reporting on the trial, but I still spoke frequently to Feely at night from my hotel room as the trial progressed. He would call to see how things were going and how young Ottenbacher was getting on.

The night I arrived in Cleveland, Melanie Payne of Akron's *The Beacon Journal* drove up and joined me at dinner. The relaxed atmosphere not only allowed me to brief her, but also gave me the opportunity to pick her brain and see what intelligence I could acquire about the opposition.

Because I knew that the Four Pillars folks—either their lawyers or their PR people—would be busy talking to the press, I was interested in getting this particular reporter's views. I had been most impressed with Payne's well-researched and well-written by-lined story in *The Beacon Journal* about the P.Y. and Sally Yang sting and arrest, and of the FBI's press conference the following day. In fact, I later learned that Payne's by-lined story earned her several journalism awards. It had been a complicated breaking story to follow and write on a fast deadline. The complexity of the case made the media briefings all the more important and would afford reporters plenty of time to learn the essential details of the story well in advance of deadline.

I was curious to know what kind of spin the Four Pillars team was putting on the story.

Payne told me she had, in fact, already spoken with Four Pillars attorney Luque, who had tried out a couple of themes on the reporter. Lawyers will occasionally do this—test the waters by laying out one or two likely themes to an experienced, cynical reporter. If the themes pass muster with the reporter, lawyers reason, they might resonate well with a jury. I asked Payne if she would share Luque's trial balloons with me. She agreed, provided we were on the record and she could take down my responses.

First, Luque had told Payne that she couldn't imagine that a jury would actually send this old man to prison.

I laughed and said, "If you can't do the time, don't do the crime," which I think was first said by TV's Baretta character years ago. Payne laughed, too, and said that she didn't think the line would find a sympathetic ear with a jury, either.

I found it interesting that Luque was apparently willing to separate her client, P.Y., from his daughter, Sally, and had said as much to Payne. If you followed Luque's logic, as I understood it, the jury might give the father a pass because of his advanced age—he was then about 71—but apparently it would be okay to convict the 39-year-old Sally, who was young enough to do prison time.

I wondered aloud if P.Y. had signed off on this strategy, but Payne didn't know. I also wondered how Sally's lawyer, Ralph Cascarella, felt about this separation of the defendants. Later, we would see Cascarella himself separate Sally from P.Y. before the jury by portraying his client as nothing more than a dutiful daughter following her aged father's wishes in the way of the centuries-old Asian culture.

Then, according to Payne, Luque also had tried to diminish the severity of the economic espionage crime itself by minimizing all of the trade secrets and millions upon millions of dollars of technology, research, and development that Victor had stolen over eight years.

"For God's sake," Luque had exhorted to Payne, "it's just glue!"

When the reporter relayed this ridiculous rhetoric to me, I replied, "Yes, but it's *our* glue, and we caught them with their sticky fingers in our glue pot!"

The Elephant in the Room

My response must have "stuck," because we never heard anyone on the Four Pillars team try that it's-only-glue theme again. Theft is theft, and for Four Pillars or their lawyers to try to downplay the crime based on perceived economic value demonstrates either their lack of knowledge about the science behind the adhesives or their lack of knowledge about the law. Personally, I don't think either is true; I think they were trying merely to spin the story and anticipate how it might resonate with a local jury.

Payne then told me that Luque's main argument—and one they tried unsuccessfully to float during the trial—was that this was nothing more than a business dispute between two industry rivals in which Avery Dennison was using a new law (the EEA) and the heavy forces of the U.S. government to crush its Asian competitor. Further, the Four Pillars lawyers tried to hold forth with the media that Avery Dennison had fraudulently engaged Four Pillars in a phony joint venture discussion for seven years while learning all about Four Pillars Asian business practices.

This gave me an opportunity to remind Payne about the facts of the failed joint venture talks, and the preposterousness of thinking that any joint venture discussions would last seven years. No U.S. reporter I met fell for that pabulum, and none thought that any jury would, either. I also asked reporters (rhetorically) if the story were true, how would Four Pillars be so gullible as to allow themselves to be engaged in spurious joint venture discussions for so extended a time? At some point, don't they bear some responsibility to question their potential partner about what's really going on? Was Four Pillars that naïve about business? The Asian company was asking the media and then, presumably, a jury to believe that their own lawyers in Taiwan would have allowed them to participate in prolonged joint venture discussions without so much as a simple confidentiality agreement or anything else in writing. If this were true, how foolish and inept would Four Pillars appear?

These scenarios were not new; we had heard them for months now, so there was little cause for concern. I shared with Payne and the other reporters the demonstrable facts that set the record straight about when and how the joint venture discussions began and ended.

All along, I had maintained with reporters that they just needed to see the FBI surveillance videotape of P.Y. in the hotel room with Victor, Sally, and the Avery Dennison trade secrets to understand the real story and to see what P.Y. and Sally did when they thought no one was watching. The proof of this blatant case was on the tape.

Luque, their PR firm, and anybody else on the Four Pillars team could try to spin their story any way they liked, I told reporters, but I wanted to know how they planned to talk their way out of the videotape. The taped sting was like a smelly, two-ton elephant sitting in the middle of the room. You can sidestep it only so long before you've got to acknowledge the obvious: You've got a big, fat, smelly elephant in the room.

And, just how are you going to talk your way out of *that* one?

CHAPTER | **22**

Protecting
Trade Secrets

"These are weighty secrets, and we must whisper them."

—Susan Coolidge

Let me lay it out for you.

Some 70 percent or more of the market value of a typical U.S. company resides in intellectual property assets, but how many of the employees who work in your company have a clue what a trade secret is?

Like many other R&D driven businesses, Avery Dennison operates in an open culture environment. This openness is designed so that its scientists can readily share their research with each other to spur creative and innovative thinking. Avery Dennison scientists handle trade secrets, pass them around internally, and help create new ones.

The open lab environment is hardly a new or revolutionary idea. *The New York Times* columnist Thomas Friedman writes about General Electric, where, "the notion of sharing ideas has been so deeply imbedded into the company's culture, that pay and promotions are based, in part, on an executive's 'boundary behavior'—his or her ability and willingness to synthesize ideas, cross-fertilize the company, and bring disparate knowledge threads together to produce value-added products."[1]

So, when Victor Lee asked for and received the entire binder of all presentations and technical research papers that had been presented at the company's 1996 technical symposium, which he had not attended, it was sent to him immediately. No one in Avery Dennison's open culture environment even thought to question Victor's request.

"When you get right down to it," said Avery Dennison's executive vice president Kim Caldwell at the time the Victor Lee thefts came to light, "you have to operate at a high level of trust."

But to properly and responsibly instill trust in employees, you need to educate them. And that, more than any other single reason, is why there is a huge gap in the area of trade secret protection. Because people—that includes management of a company—don't always know what a trade secret is, how can they know how to protect it or even that they should? Employees, top to bottom, need training and education. And, given the statistics on how rapidly economic espionage is on the rise, employers cannot address the need for education and training too soon.

Three Immediate Steps

To avoid being a victim of economic espionage, companies need to:

- Identify trade secrets
- Take reasonable measures to protect trade secrets
- Educate employees about how to protect trade secrets

Plus, *to avoid being investigated for economic espionage,* companies need to have a policies in place to make sure they are not stealing trade secrets of other companies.

This chapter alone cannot possibly tell you all that you need to know to properly protect your trade secrets, many of which also have to be valued and assessed as to risk. To begin with, each company is unique, and so are its trade secrets. What follows are guidelines to help you understand the sorts of things you should be considering. Not all of them will be right for you or your company, and some of what you should be doing may not be listed at all. But you need to start somewhere to better manage your risk.

A Trade Secret Compliance Program

The EEA has not only raised the visibility of economic espionage, it has also raised the stakes and put more of the onus on companies to protect their trade secrets. The Act tasks each business with the responsibility to take effective steps to demonstrate that it established reasonable safeguards to protect its trade secrets, prevented inadvertent misappropriation of its trade secrets, and took reasonable measures to prevent intentional theft.

Your failure to comply not only makes you an easier target for economic espionage, it also makes it harder for you to prove in court and in the media wars that you are entitled to trade secret protection. While no law or federal mandate requires that each company have a trade secret compliance program, it is a good idea because it makes you more defense oriented.

This is not a legal textbook, and you should not confuse it with one. It *is* a book on managing the risk of economic espionage. For that, we begin by consulting the United States Sentencing Commission Guidelines[2] that encourages companies to have compliance programs in place to discourage theft in general. While the compliance program does not refer specifically to theft of trade secrets, that kind of felonious theft would be covered.

It's bad enough that people are trying to commit economic espionage against your company. But if they do, and if they're caught, *you* now have to be prepared to prove that you did whatever you had to do to make the crime more difficult to commit. Therefore, if you're going to have a trade secret compliance program, due diligence requires, at a minimum, that you take the following types of steps:

- Your company's compliance standards and procedures must be reasonably capable of reducing the prospect of criminal conduct.

- The person within your company assigned to oversee compliance must be at a high level.
- Your company must use due care not to delegate substantial discretionary authority to individuals whom the company knows, or should know, have a propensity to engage in illegal activities.
- You must effectively communicate standards and procedures of the compliance program to all employees and outsiders. If your employees don't know and understand the compliance program, you might as well not have one.
- Your company must take reasonable steps to achieve compliance within its own standards.
- The standards must be consistently enforced.
- There must be an appropriate level of response following the detection of an offense—including any necessary modifications to the program.

Trade Secrets Are a Moving Target

In many companies, one of the first things to understand is that your list of trade secrets is constantly changing. So whatever you do today to identify and classify your company's trade secrets needs to be updated often and regularly.

"The life cycle of a trade secret may be finite or perpetual," according to consultant Ted Fraumann. "If the trade secret is already a product, its trade secret status will last as long as it is not discoverable through reverse engineering . . . ."[3]

You also need to know if your list has diminished. For example, if what you once thought was protected by trade secret status has been published on the Internet—regardless of how it got there—you are probably no longer entitled to trade secret protection on that particular piece of intellectual property. You need to monitor constantly what you can and what you cannot claim as protected trade secrets. Too often, companies conduct a trade secret audit and then shelve it. Audits must be updated continuously to serve a valid protective purpose.

The same tendency to shelve a key document is often true of the way companies handle their vital crisis management plans. They pay good money to have a company like mine help them create written crisis management and crisis communications plans, and they may even go through one training test and dry run session. But if they put the plans on the shelf until they need them, which could be years after their creation, the plans' usefulness may have evaporated because they haven't been continuously updated, revised, and tested anew.

The Trade Secret Audit

As with a crisis management plan, the document that is created at the conclusion of the trade secret audit should be considered a living, breathing, dynamic document as opposed to a static one. If you want to protect your trade secrets, you need to set a policy of regular audits, no less frequently than annually.

Here is a *partial* checklist that may be helpful in identifying your trade secrets, regardless of your company's industry group.[4]

Technical information, including:

- Research and development data and reports
- Proprietary technology information
- Formulas and compounds
- Computer source code
- Prototypes
- Manufacturing and R&D processes
- Laboratory notebooks
- Experiments and results
- Analytical data
- Calculations
- Drawings and diagrams

Production and process information, including:

- Cost/price/profit margin information
- Special or proprietary machinery
- Process/manufacturing technology
- Proprietary information concerning production processes

- Technical and manufacturing specifications
- Production information

Vendor/supplier information, including:

- Lists of vendors and suppliers
- Cost and pricing structures with vendors and suppliers
- Agreements with vendors and suppliers

Quality control information, including:

- Procedures
- Manuals
- Records

Sales and marketing information, including:

- Sales and marketing studies, reports, and plans
- Trend data
- Customer (current, potential, and former) lists
- Former customer lists
- Sales forecasts
- Sales promotion plans
- Competitive intelligence reports
- Customer ordering schedule

Internal financial information, including:

- Proprietary financial information
- Budgets
- Forecasts
- Product costs and margins
- Operating reports
- Profit & Loss statements

Internal administrative information, including:

- Strategic business plans
- Internal computer software
- Computer source codes
- Password/encryption information

The Trade Secret Classification and Risk Assessment

You should use this list of possible trade secrets merely as a guideline for creating your own list and adding to, or deleting from, it as your business dictates. Once done, you need to evaluate each trade secret to determine your level of risk, such as vulnerability to theft. Who has access to your trade secrets? Typically, that list would include current and former employees, contractors and contract employees, temporary workers, vendors, and partners. These people are on site (besides former employees), and their presence does not raise eyebrows. But, very real and significant risks come from outside the company—from information brokers, hackers, netspionagers, agents of foreign governments, and foreign and domestic competitive businesses.

There are six key criteria to consider after conducting a trade secret audit to help determine your level of risk. For each trade secret on your list determine:

1. *The extent to which the information is commonly known* outside *of your company.* The more people who know it, the less valuable it is, and it may not even qualify for trade secret protection.
2. *The extent to which the information is commonly known* inside *your company.* The more people who know it, the greater the risk that it is not protectable. Also, if it is not guarded within the company, it can easily be made known outside the company.
3. *The value of the information itself, both to the company and to the company's competitors.* The higher the value, to you and your competitors, the more likely that it is a protectable trade secret—and the more vulnerable it may be as a target of theft or espionage.

4. *The measures taken by the company to protect the trade secret.* If the company is lax, the trade secret may not be protectable under the law.

5. *The company's time, effort, and expenditure of resources to create the trade secret in the first place.* The more sweat that went into it, the greater the chances that your trade secret will be protected by law.

6. *The ease or difficulty others would have in uncovering the trade secret, acquiring it, or developing it in a parallel process.* If a competitor can do an Internet search and come up with your trade secret—regardless of how it got to be on the Internet; e.g., if a disgruntled employee posted it in a chat room—it may very likely be considered in the public domain and no longer a protected trade secret.

The Trade Secret Valuation

If your trade secrets are ever stolen, you need to know how much they are worth—or what their potential value is—if you want the government to charge someone with trade secret theft under the EEA and if you hope ever to recover damages from civil litigation. There are three basic and accepted ways to place a value on your trade secret: the market approach, the cost approach, and the income approach.

1. *The market approach.* This method is the most difficult to use in valuing a trade secret. It compares the sale of similar assets to what you are attempting to value. Because your trade secret is unique, by definition, finding something comparable in the marketplace is inherently difficult.

2. *The cost approach.* This technique is better suited to value trade secrets. It factors in things like the cost of replacement: How long did it take to create the trade secret? What were the costs? What will replacing it cost?

3. *The income approach.* This method looks at anticipated revenues and future economic benefits to be derived from the trade secret. Using reasonable economic models, this method

is also preferable to the market approach, which usually is filled with "blue sky" numbers.

Trade Secret Security

Even if some of your proprietary information fails to qualify for legal protection, that doesn't mean that it is not of great importance and economic value to you and should still be protected to reduce your risks.

You need to protect your trade secrets using any of a number of appropriate steps, measures, and company procedures to lower your risks and effectively stem the tide of economic espionage. The EEA says that not only must the trade secret information derive real or potential independent economic value by virtue of not being readily ascertainable, but the company must take "reasonable measures to keep such information secret."

This security step is essential both for security reasons alone and so that, if necessary, you can prove that you were careful to take reasonable measures to protect your trade secrets.

The extent to which you need such protective measures will vary according to the value of each trade secret. Following are some of the precautions that can be taken. However, keep in mind that because each company is different, not all of these measures are necessary or appropriate for every company or for all trade secrets. This list is to stimulate your thinking about what your company needs to do to reduce its risks.

- *Education.* Without question, one of the weakest links in properly protecting trade secrets is lack of education for employees. Do your employees know what a trade secret is? Do you include this information in orientation sessions for new employees? Do you periodically remind other employees? Do they understand how important a trade secret is to the welfare of the company? Do they know the dos and don'ts of properly handling trade secrets? Do they appreciate fully the criminal penalties for stealing trade secrets?

- *Training.* As with education, certain employees in certain areas of the company need specific training in the proper handling of trade secret documents. Part of a proper and thorough educational and training process includes enlightening employees and others, such as vendors or outside consultants. Don't allow employees to rationalize that "only lawyers need to understand this stuff." Often, new employees going through the human resources maze will sign a raft of papers on day one without anyone taking the time to explain their meaning and the legal implications of the employee's often mindless signature. Every employee asked to sign any company document should be able to explain its meaning.

- *Confidential and proprietary information.* Such material should be clearly and prominently stamped CONFIDENTIAL and/or PROPRIETARY.

- *Confidentiality agreements.* These should be signed by all employees at all levels, regardless of full-time or part-time status.

- *Confidentiality agreements.* These should exist with third parties, including OEM contractors, working partners, and joint venture partners.

- *Noncompete agreements with employees.* These protect you for a certain length of time if an employee should leave to work elsewhere.

- *Nondisclosure agreements.* These agreements are for both employees and outside parties.

- *Oversight policies and procedures.* These ensure that scientists and others within your organization don't publish technical articles or speak at industry conferences without someone at your company knowledgeable about trade secrets reviewing the article or speech and signing off on it. The same holds true for trade shows, media interviews, and even presentations to other employees or business partners.

- *Testimony review.* If one of your employees is required to give a deposition or testify in court on any matter that involves trade secrets, he should be well briefed by an attorney who specializes in intellectual property.

- *Controls.* Controls should be maintained on visitor access in general, and to sensitive areas in particular.

- *Background checks.* These should be performed on all employees.
- *ID badges.* Badges should have a magnetic stripe, and the card should be required to gain access to the building. The card should immediately be cancelled by security if that person is terminated.

Here are some other questions to consider.

- Are trade secrets kept under lock and key with restricted access?
- Do you have or need sign-in/sign-out procedures for access to trade secrets, including documents that leave the building or even certain areas?
- How easy is it to get from one area to another? Are keypad combinations all that is necessary to open a door at your company's site? Should magnetic cards be used that not only open the door but are programmed to limit access to certain sensitive areas? The security computers then can keep a log of who entered which areas and when.
- Are your trade secrets open to all internally, or are they controlled on a need-to-know basis?
- Is your information encrypted and/or secretly coded?
- Once a trade secret has been removed from its secure location, how easy is it for neighbors or prying eyes to see?
- Can employees freely roam about the facility, or are they required to stay within their own areas?
- What is your policy about employees who want to stay after normal work or on long weekends. What are they doing? Why do they want to stay? Are they using the photocopier after hours? Why?
- What is your policy about photocopies? Does each person have an authorization code? Is it monitored? Is anyone making copies—especially excessive copies—after normal working hours or on weekends?
- What is your policy about taking work home?
- What is your policy about equipment leaving the premises?

- What is your policy about checking briefcases and purses?
- Do you regularly shred documents that need to be destroyed, or do you toss them in the trash whole, allowing them to be recovered by dumpster divers?
- Do you admonish new employees not to impart confidential information that they learned at their previous place of employment?
- Is your plant security all that it should be?
- Do you regularly re-educate or retrain employees regarding the importance of protecting trade secrets? (This is vitally important!)
- When an employee is terminated, do you conduct an exit interview at which time that individual is reminded of her signed agreements?
- Does the exit interview attempt to disabuse the terminated employee of feeling humiliated, angry, confused, or vengeful?

Finally, are you going to do each and every item on this list? Of course not. You and I both know that. But the more important question is, do you have to? The answer here is a little trickier. Your risk reduction policies and procedures should derive from what you are trying to protect, what the trade secret's value is, and what "reasonable measures" you took to protect it.

Let me give you two examples that will illustrate these points and what your risks could be.

In the case of *IDS Life Insurance Company v. SunAmerica, Inc.,*[5] IDS sued SunAmerica, claiming that its agents were being induced to quit and go to work for SunAmerica. They were then directed to sell SunAmerica's insurance policies to the very same customers that the agents had sold to while at IDS, who charged its former agents and SunAmerica had ruined its long-term relations with thousands of its customers.

IDS claimed, and was able to demonstrate, that it had spent millions of dollars developing *confidential* customer lists and *confidential* customer information. Moreover, it could show that it had taken reasonable measures to protect the confidentiality of this information. IDS was able to demonstrate that its agents had signed and understood noncompete agreements, which specifically prohibited them from soliciting or selling competing products in the same IDS sales territories for one year after leaving IDS.

IDS won, and the court ruled that the former agents were bound by their agreements. The agents and SunAmerica had to return all of the trade secret information to IDS.

However, consider the case of *Hoffman-LaRoche, Inc. v. Frank W. Yoder.* Yoder, a former clinical investigator for pharmaceutical giant Hoffman-LaRoche, had obtained 550 pages of documents pertaining to Acutane, a medication for acne and other skin disorders. The information consisted of important clinical trial data among other things.

The drug company maintained that Yoder tried to market the information for $9.5 million, and it tried to obtain an injunction against Yoder to prevent the sale of what it claimed was "highly proprietary, confidential, and trade secret information."

But Hoffman-LaRoche lost the case when the court ruled that, while the company had taken extraordinary measures to keep the material confidential *within* the firm, it had not taken proper measures to protect its information from outside sources. For instance, the drug company never required Yoder to sign a confidentiality agreement. Moreover, of the 550 pages of data Yoder had in his possession, only three documents were marked *Confidential.* The Hoffman-LaRoche company did not have a formal policy for retrieving its testing information from the field. It lacked adequate document controls, and these particular documents were not subject to lock and key security. The final blow was the revelation that Hoffman-LaRoche had given the same information to 19 research centers nationwide, all of whom were involved in the testing of Acutane.

Some companies protect internal knowledge against possible economic espionage the way ancient kingdoms used to build moats around their castles. *The New York Times* columnist Thomas Friedman tells an interesting story of a time he went to interview someone at Sun Microsystems at their headquarters outside of Palo Alto.

Before I could get inside to see the executive I was scheduled to interview, the receptionist handed me a one-page legal form to sign entitled, "Confidential Nondisclosure Agreement." At the top of the form there were two boxes to check: "Confidential Visit" or "Unclassified Visit." Among the things I had to agree to on this document before I could enter Sun's offices was that the "Signatory agrees not to disclose the Proprietary Information to any third party. Signatory agrees to use the Proprietary Information only for purposes expressly authorized in writing by Sun and not to use it for signatory's own use." You can get into the CIA today with less paperwork.[6]

A Strong Defense Is the Best Security

Avery Dennison today publishes a ten-page booklet for employees called "Protecting Our Trade Secrets." It was distributed to all of its employees worldwide in March 1997—the same month that Victor began his confession of economic espionage.

The brochure arrived with a friendly—but stern—letter from Phil Neal, the company's president at the time, reminding employees why it's important to protect trade secrets and of the criminal and civil penalties for economic espionage.

The brochure clearly and succinctly covers what Avery Dennison considers to be a trade secret and how each operating unit is responsible for determining what constitutes a trade secret in the respective business units, and it gives examples of trade secrets under various department headings. The brochure also talks about the harm that can befall the company from disclosure of trade secrets. Importantly, it describes what *each individual employee* can do to protect the trade secrets that he comes in contact with. The last three pages are a reprint of the company's written corporate policy on the protection of confidential and proprietary information.

Avery Dennison's brochure states, "A strong defense is the best security." And this policy remains right even though its strong defense did not prevent Victor's thefts. But that was due to a weakness in Victor's and P.Y.'s character, not because of a weakness in the basic Avery Dennison organization or its ethical guidelines.

While you can never expect perfect compliance, having and enforcing policies is better than having none.

CHAPTER 23

STICKY FINGERS
The Trial Begins

Let's briefly review the bidding before we enter the hallowed courtroom of Federal Judge Peter C. Economous.

Victor Lee has confessed to massive economic espionage against Avery Dennison, naming P.Y., Sally, and Four Pillars Enterprises as the beneficiaries of his thefts. The Yangs were caught on a video-taped FBI sting receiving trade secrets. Within a matter of days, the Yangs were indicted on 21 counts including, of course, economic espionage.

Could the crimes be any clearer? Could the case be any easier? What could possibly go wrong?

If you were a betting person, you would definitely like the government's odds. Who wouldn't? The case against the Yangs seemed overwhelming—especially given the videotape. So, when the time for the trial arrived, the general questions seemed to be: Why the hell are we here? Why hasn't there been a plea bargain? What kind of defense could Four Pillars possibly mount? And was this really going to trial?

Was this going to be the *first* economic espionage case ever to go to trial?

In fact, on the eve of the trial, I hadn't even made an airline reservation, so sure was I that the case would plead out like the other EEA cases up to that point. But late one night I received a succinct message: The trial starts tomorrow. Be here.

Primitive Conditions

As you drive through downtown Youngstown, you are instantly reminded of how so many of the nation's rust belt cities were devastated by the decline of the steel industry. The town is old and depressing and doesn't have much to recommend it. If it weren't for the widespread corruption scandals, people there would have little else to talk about.

But on Market Street, across from City Hall in the heart of downtown, stands a brand new, three-story, federal courthouse, exceedingly noticeable for its freshness, spit, and polish in this otherwise decrepit urban background. It stands out because it looks too new for the neighborhood. The sturdy structure contains just two small courtrooms: a bankruptcy courtroom on the second floor and a federal courtroom on the third floor. This was the courtroom of Judge Peter C. Economous, a jurist about whom it would be said in reference to this case, was in the deep end of the pool for the first time.

For all its newness, the rules in the courthouse were draconian and the conditions there and in downtown Youngstown were technologically primitive. You were unable to bring a cellular phone into the courthouse at all. They didn't just warn you to turn off cell phones, as is customarily done in many courthouses and courtrooms; in Youngstown, the federal marshals at the entrance either confiscated your phone or sent you packing, which meant leaving your phone in your car, at least two blocks away.

To compound matters, each floor had only one pay phone, and at each break in the trial, there was a mad scramble to get to the phone. The reporters of course had the same problem, and it was worse for the wire services reporters who were on constant deadline. Even if you were lucky enough to get to a pay phone, you had no booth or privacy. The hall was small and lawyers, defendants, witnesses, jurors, and members of the press were crawling all over the place.

Because new developments were breaking constantly, I needed a more efficient communications outlet. I had to know when my clients needed to talk with me, and I needed to be able to talk with them about courtroom developments and unexpected courtroom surprises, media requests, and myriad other things. I searched around for a Kinko's or an office to sublet nearby or even a nearby hotel room to use as a base of operations. Nothing.

Then I got creative. I stumbled upon the Mill Creek Supply Company directly across the street from the courthouse. It looked like the inside of Fibber McGee's closet. At a cluttered desk in the midst of cartons strewn all over the place sat chain-smoking Karen (I never got her last name), with whom I cut a fast deal to pay to use her phone and—*glory be!*—her fax machine, too. (It was too much to expect e-mail, too.) I circulated the critical phone and fax numbers to all who needed to reach me, and I gave Karen my pager number, asking her to page me with a special code whenever there was a call for me, and a different code if there was a fax for me. The system was awkward and primitive as hell, but it worked in a pinch.

I had to leave my laptop computer back at the motel, and a few times, we needed to crank out a letter, statement, or news release on the fly. One day, when the phone was occupied on the third floor, I raced to the second floor, only to find I had been beaten there by someone else. While I was waiting, and trying not to eavesdrop on the other person's conversation, I casually wandered into the administrative offices of the bankruptcy court. There, I became friendly with a nice bunch of workers and their boss. Thereafter, on the rare occasion I had to bang out a news release on a tight deadline, I was allowed to use a personal computer and printer in bankruptcy court.

Monumental Stupidity

The dark, richly paneled courtroom was small, with hard wooden pewlike benches that grew harder and more uncomfortable each day of the month-long trial. All of the media I had briefed previously in Cleveland showed up for opening arguments, which were delayed several days due to jury selection and pretrial motions. Even so, the fireworks started almost immediately.

A young, aggressive reporter from the local Youngstown paper, *The Vindicator,* had tracked down one of the civil lawyers at his home the night before the trial began and said he wanted to ask a few questions. The lawyer gave him my name and number, as he should have, and asked him to contact me directly. Then, what the well-meaning attorney should have done was to get off the phone. The reporter kept talking, saying he had "just a couple of fast preliminary questions to help [him] better understand the issues." The attorney knew that one of my goals was to make sure the media did understand the issues, because of the case's complexity, so he thought he was being helpful—"just to clear up some of his questions"—by agreeing to talk with him briefly. But the lawyer naïvely and incorrectly assumed that the "real" interview would be with me and that nothing he said to the reporter would be quoted.

Wrong.

What actually happened is precisely why I always advise clients never to say *anything* to a reporter that you wouldn't want to see in the next morning's newspaper. Sure enough, the next morning, on the first day of the trial, the story ran large on page one right under the banner of the only paper in Youngstown—the paper read by the judge and the jury. The article was all right, except it revealed far more than the judge would like and the views presented were those of an advocate trying his case.

For example, the article quoted the lawyer saying, "It was a broad-ranging conspiracy to take about as much of the heart of Avery Dennison's technology as you can imagine," and "A lot of their [Avery Dennison's] technology was taken. It really was research and development and other areas we contend helped Four Pillars develop new products." And a final paragraph used the lawyer as a source to explain that Avery Dennison and Four Pillars had discussed a joint venture in the early 1990s, but that Avery Dennison had backed away because Four Pillars had financial troubles.

What's wrong with that?

The problem was not that the article was factually incorrect. What's wrong is that it simply is not a civil attorney's place to argue the government's case (especially in the media), and that's exactly the way the story was written (e.g., *". . . we contend. . ."*). This was not the time for Avery Dennison's civil lawyers to contend anything; it was up to the prosecutors. And the prosecutors would not talk to the press. In short, the Avery Dennison lawyer was sandbagged by this reporter.

In court that morning, the defense team, Nancy Luque, Eric Dubelier, and Ralph Cascarella went ballistic attacking the media blitz, raising nefarious motives behind it, and protesting the limited possibility of a fair trial in Youngstown. The judge merely admonished the lawyers on both sides to stop talking to the press.

This was not a good way to start with this judge.

Sitting across from me that first day of trial was a young woman with a head cold and a perennially runny nose: Patty Smith, one of Bork's junior staffers from the Washington PR firm. She was there to try to spin the Four Pillars story. Instead, she pulled a stunt in court that was so amateurish that the judge spun her instead.

The morning of opening arguments, I saw Smith carrying a sheaf of papers in her arms and asked her if she was planning to distribute a statement. She said that she was but denied my request to take a peek.

When Luque launched into her rambling opening statement to the jury, there were problems from the get-go. Several times during her remarks, after pointed objections by prosecutor Mark Zwillinger that were sustained by the judge, Luque was sharply admonished by Judge Economous for making inappropriate comments, including comments that the judge had specifically warned her earlier she would *not* be permitted to make before the jury.

Maybe these rebukes from the bench rattled Luque, which may have accounted for her verbal meanderings. By anyone's measure and for whatever the reason, the defense's opening statement was a less than stellar performance. But, finally, the agony was over.

And then I witnessed an act of monumental stupidity: Patty Smith, runny nose and all, was handing out press releases to the reporters in open court.

But the really stupid part was what the release actually said. It was all about Luque's opening statement, which had just gone down in flames moments earlier, and it was all wrong. The headline of the release: "Avery Dennison Using U.S. Government to Eliminate Asian Rival, Four Pillars Enterprise."

The astute reader will no doubt wonder how it was possible for Smith to have written a press release so quickly. The answer, of course, is that she could not, and did not. Remember, she was already carrying the releases—fully written—with her when she arrived in court that morning. The news release quoted Luque making flamboyant statements that she, in fact, had either never made at all or that she had attempted to make before being shut down by the judge. In short, the press release was full of blatant misrepresentations wrapped in quotes, attributing remarks to Luque that she either never said, or was never permitted to say by the judge. Whatever the intentions when the release was written, to distribute it after the fact is knowingly to dispense a packet of lies.

The final nail in the stupidity coffin was that Smith was attempting to peddle the news release to seasoned reporters who knew better and had just witnessed the event themselves.

In phony broadside after phony broadside in the two-page release, Smith quoted Luque as having said such things in her opening statement as the prosecution of P.Y. was "an outrageous attempt, bought and paid for by Avery Dennison, to use the U.S. government to eliminate its chief Asian rival, Four Pillars Enterprises," and, "The evidence will show that Avery Dennison bought off the only government witness in its case against Four Pillars," and that, "The Economic Espionage Act was designed to help stop the flow of America's intellectual property to other governments—not to be used as a tool to aid an American company seeking to eliminate its chief competitor in the glue market." Not only was this never said, it also misstates the law.

This is not to say that Luque didn't try mightily to get these comments and more past the judge, but to no avail.

Out in the hallway, I asked John Affleck of The Associated Press if I could take a look at the release, and I couldn't believe it as I read it. Neither could Affleck. On his copy, he had drawn a line through the page with a big *NO* written on it. We looked at each other in amazement. Melanie Payne of *The Beacon Journal* gave me her copy because she was never going to use it, and she also was dumbfounded at the release. Another reporter crumpled the release and said, "This isn't spinning; this is out-and-out lying!"

Let me take a moment to put the full egregiousness of Smith's actions into context and perspective. A Four Pillars press representative had just been caught red-handed trying to mislead the media by passing off as *real quotes* statements that were nothing of the sort. Even the general gist of the story was wrong, because the message Luque had tried to convey in the opening statement never got across, although the news release being hawked by Smith said that it did.

At that time, I got an urgent coded message on my pager from Karen at Mill Creek Supply. I dashed across the street to learn that *Bloomberg News* had moved at least one of the damaging quotes—*"an outrageous attempt by Avery Dennison to use the U.S. government to eliminate its chief Asian rival"*—in a wire story. I thought I had contained it on the third floor of the federal courthouse. Now it was out worldwide.

When I got back to the courthouse, I had a blunt conversation with the Ottenbachers, *mère et fils,* the local *Bloomberg News* reporters on scene, asking them how they could move that story if they were sitting in court and heard and saw what happened? A wire service reporter covering breaking news generally telephones in a story to a rewrite desk, which is what the Ottenbachers did. They told me that they didn't include those quotes in their story, but I showed them the wire copy that had been faxed to me at the Mill Creek Supply office. It had young Jeff Ottenbacher's by-line on the story, and when I had seen that my first thought was his youthful inexperience might explain the mistake.

They quickly called their editor to raise hell and reported back to me that they had clean hands in this debacle. They learned that Bork's office in Washington also moved the same release over PR Newswire. A *Bloomberg* editor, liking the Luque quotes, dropped them into the Ottenbacher story without bothering to check with the reporters on the scene. These sorts of miscues can happen under deadline pressure.

Within minutes, Judge Economous got wind of the situation and summoned all the lawyers into his chambers, whereupon he ordered Luque to retract the inaccurate release immediately and gave his OK for a court-approved release correcting the error.

Within 30 minutes, we had crafted a news release, approved by the judge, whose headline read: "Four Pillars Distributes Inaccurate News Release in Violation of the Court's Admonition." The release explained that the earlier release contained "lengthy, inaccurate quotations from" Luque's opening statement that could improperly influence the jury, and that it was "distributed in violation of the admonition" of the judge. It made a point of stating that Luque "was repeatedly admonished by Judge Economous for making improper arguments during her opening statement."[1]

All of this served to make both Luque and Smith appear foolish to the media on the scene.

Upon demand, a Bork staffer faxed me her activity log, showing that the initial inaccurate press release was faxed to approximately 50 reporters at 11:22 AM on April 1st and moved on PR Newswire exactly one minute later. At 1:35 PM, she issued a retraction on PR Newswire, and four minutes later she distributed the same embarrassing retraction to those same 50 reporters. But, in a global and wired world, a lot of damage can be done in two short hours.

My concern was on several levels, not the least of which was what might happen to Avery Dennison's stock price given how closely the *Bloomberg Wire* is followed by the financial community. Fortunately, this time we were able to catch the story in time, and no harm was done on Wall Street.

I wanted to know who those 50 reporters were and made sure I got the full distribution list of Four Pillars'/Bork's "key writers and editors." So I now knew who the defense team was talking to at which papers, and thereafter, anytime we had a statement to issue, we made sure we rolled that distribution list into our own.

Smith then beat it out of Dodge. Sometime later, the judge must have reread the original news release and got his dander up. Although Smith wasn't planning to be back in that courtroom anytime soon, through Luque the judge ordered her to be in his chambers at 8 AM the following Monday morning. Smith did show up as ordered, with her own lawyer, and the judge let her off with a warning. It wouldn't be the last light sentence he handed down in this case.

This had not been a good day for the Four Pillars team, nor for Smith in particular. And the trial had barely begun.

What puzzled me was this: Even though Smith had the press release with her, didn't she hear what was going on in court during Luque's opening statement? Didn't she realize that the news release she was clutching was rendered grossly inaccurate by the judge's admonishments to Luque? Or was Smith's head cold clogging her hearing? Smith should have stuffed those press releases back into her bag and never let them see the light of day.

Worse, knowing that her office in Washington was planning on disseminating the release via the wire, why didn't she at least telephone her office to explain what had happened in court and fashion a new and correct release on the spot?

At the same time, I must question the Bork office itself. In this case, opening arguments had already been delayed about three days, and they might have been delayed again. How could Bork have known when to move the release unless Smith (or someone else) called from the courthouse and gave the green light? If we assume Smith called her office, does this means that she withheld the critical information that the release was a lie and let her boss and the company go on the hook for distributing the misleading story? Or would the Bork office issue a release it knew was inaccurate, or without getting a green light from someone in the field?

I have no explanations for what Smith or Bork did, but their actions made my job a lot easier in the weeks ahead. The crisis was still oppositional, but the opposition was badly wounded—with a self-inflicted gunshot wound.

"This Is a Case about Stealing"

Before Luque stumbled through her opening statement, the government first presented its opening statement to the jury. Stepping up to the plate was young Mark Zwillinger, trying his very first case. In fact, his parents had flown in from New York to hear him make his first opening argument. But, because there were a number of procedural delays and a longer than anticipated time to select a jury, Zwillinger's folks had to hang around in the back of the courtroom for three days before he finally got a chance to strut his stuff.

Zwillinger turned out to be the one bright light on the prosecution side of the aisle. When he approached the jury, he said in a clear, unambiguous voice: "This is a case about stealing." He then succinctly and articulately set forth what the government intended to prove when it put on its case—that Dr. Lee was paid by the defendants to steal Avery Dennison's trade secrets for eight years.

Zwillinger kept it simple, and that was a good thing. Many on the jury panel looked like they were having a hard time following the trial, starting with the *voire dire* (jury selection) process.

For example, during *voire dire,* the defense wanted to know from prospective jurors if they could consider the defendants innocent unless proven guilty even if the defendants didn't take the stand in their own defense, thus tipping off what their actual defense strategy was going to be. Some prospective panelists said sure, they could keep an open mind, but they still wanted to hear what the defendents had to say. In other words, yeah, I can be objective but what are they hiding?

Jury selection took so long that at one point, they actually ran out of prospective jurors and had to make some phone calls to round up a fresh batch. Finally a jury was seated, and Zwillinger got to his feet at last.

Over the next four weeks, Zwillinger's opening statement would remain the high point of what was to come from a wholly ineffectual prosecution.

CHAPTER 24

Do You Want Fries with That Secret?

"What a piece of work is a man!"

—William Shakespeare

Jim Bodine, who served as president and CEO of the former First Pennsylvania Bank, once revealed to me that the one thing that used to give him nightmares was the disturbing realization that his customers' first impression of his bank was made by the lowest-paid employees: the tellers. He was right to worry. Whether it's the low-paid bank teller, the highly educated scientist, or the kid taking orders at the fast food drive-through, employees have always been a potential cause for headaches and nightmares.

Even though I refer to Victor by his first name in this book, during the Avery Dennison/Four Pillars spy case, I made certain that all public references to him were as Dr. Lee. We went out of our way constantly to remind news reporters and readers of news stories that Victor was not a low-level employee who found Avery Dennison trade secrets sitting around unprotected or by dumpster diving for discarded formulas. Nor did we want the media to misrepresent Avery Dennison as having been sloppy in its handling and protection of trade secrets. No, we wanted people to know that one of the reasons Victor was able to perpetrate the thefts and get away with them for so long was precisely because he was Tenhong "Victor"

Lee, Ph.D., distinguished senior research associate at Avery Dennison, with access to the company's most important trade secrets and a beneficiary of the company's trust. Avery Dennison referred to him as "hard-working, bright, and meticulous" in various court papers. It was precisely because of his high position that he was trusted, and it was that trust that he violated.

As stated earlier, more than 80 percent of trade secret theft is carried out by employees and on-site contractors. This is true whether the theft is engineered by a rogue employee on her own, perhaps hoping to go into business against her employer, or by a competitor—foreign or domestic—or a foreign power that pays an employee to steal.

In addition to illustrating that the greatest risks of economic espionage are right under a company's nose, the stories in this chapter also demonstrate that *all* types of companies are at risk. It's not just the high tech defense contractors, it's *everybody*. No exceptions.

And remember: Not all economic espionage is carried out by highly placed and trusted employees like Victor. Sometimes the thief is the minimum-wage kid who serves you lunch, and that's scary.

MasterCard: Charging a Costly Lunch

As unlikely as this seems, a food service worker for a New York City catering company was arrested by the FBI and charged with stealing valuable trade secret documents belonging to MasterCard International. One document in question outlined MasterCard's top secret plan to enter into a $1 billion alliance with the Disney Corporation. The suspect, Fausto Estrada, who worked as a waiter and sometime bartender at the MasterCard corporate dining room at the company's Purchase, New York, headquarters, was accused of trying to sell the pilfered plan to MasterCard's arch competitor, Visa, using a crude cover letter addressed to Visa's CEO that read: "An Offer to Think About." Visa thought about it and promptly notified MasterCard, who notified the FBI.

Estrada, a native of the Dominican Republic but living in the Bronx, was arrested and charged with stealing reams of confidential documents, CD-ROMs filled with confidential corporate data, binders, and other confidential information from the dining room and nearby areas in MasterCard's headquarters, according to Federal complaints and published reports. It appears the absentminded MasterCard officials—entrusted with the company's most sensitive and strategic plans—routinely left them lying about in the dining room.

Using the code name Cagliostro (possibly for the 18th–century European Count Cagliostro, but more likely for the children's comic book character), because he considered himself a master of deception, Estrada was more a master of incompetence. He used his own return address on almost every one of his letters and envelopes when corresponding with Visa, and with the FBI when the Feds posed as a Visa company executive. Later, he told an FBI undercover agent to call him on a cell phone number that was registered to his wife, according to charges.

The waiter allegedly offered to sell not only the MasterCard/Disney plans, but also additional information from the years 1999-2001. Because he worked in the dining room, it wasn't as though he was making photocopies of the material and returning the originals. (One report had him pulling original faxes off of the fax machine.) Estrada would have to be walking off with the original documents, which only begs this question: How much material could go missing from the dining room without MasterCard wising up?

But, waiter or master criminal, he apparently knew the value of his haul, which he tried to sell for $200,000. According to the criminal complaint, Estrada told Visa it would have "almost direct contact with your competitor without the competitor realizing the fact." He even told Visa he could videotape MasterCard executives in the dining room without their knowledge, provided Visa ponied up the money necessary to buy special recording equipment. And he offered Visa "very unique" budget and profit margin information from MasterCard. He also insisted he be paid in cash, "because I don't pay any taxes."[1]

Estrada was only a temporary employee. When the FBI lured him to a New York hotel for what he thought was going to be a big pay day, he was carrying three—*three!*—milk crates of confidential MasterCard material.

In a fit of wishful thinking, MasterCard spokeswoman Sharon Gamsin said, "We think our security system and procedures are solid."[2]

Estrada was charged under the EEA for theft of trade secrets. MasterCard was charged with leaving the dining room without cleaning up after itself.

(Here and below, remember the right of presumed innocence.)

What Fools These Mortals Be

Estrada's use of his home address on envelopes sent to Visa, while certainly dim-witted, is not that unique in the chronicles of what laughingly passes for the criminal mind.

I recall a story about a young woman accused of stealing articles of clothing, who showed up in court wearing a stolen jacket with the victim's name embroidered on the inside.

Here's one even Chief Inspector Clouseau could have solved. An *imbécile* walked into a bank with a gun in Bordeaux, France, and demanded 12,700 francs. When the teller said she didn't have that much money on hand, he lowered his demand to 6,800 FF. When she refused, he asked if he could withdraw money from his own account. She said, "*Mais, oui,*" and he dutifully filled out a withdrawal slip using his own account number, which was promptly turned over to the gendarmes who arrested the fool in his home.

And then there were some geniuses who tried a gold heist by posing as security employees of Pasadena's famed Jet Propulsion Laboratory. The would-be thieves set up an office in a strip mall and sent a fax to the gold supplier using a Mail Boxes USA fax machine. That name was emblazoned as an ID line across the top of the fax when the "purchase order" arrived at the supplier. Then, misspelling Sergeant as "Sargent," the "purchase order" directed the supplier not to deliver to the regular JPL address, but to be sure to use the strip mall address instead. The FBI delivered the package and arrested those nonrocket scientists, who were all sitting around just waiting for their package to arrive.

My favorite involved a youthful-looking armed robber who held up a liquor store. After emptying the cash register he demanded a bottle of gin. The store owner refused, saying the robber looked underage and he'd lose his license if he gave liquor to a minor. When the robber insisted he was over 21, the clerk asked for ID. The robber handed over his driver's license and . . . oh, you can figure out the rest.

The annals of economic espionage has its own pantheon of all-stars, and I encourage you to meet them all. Unfortunately, the space limitations of book publishing do not allow room for them all. So what follows is a thumbnail sketch of a handful of economic espionage cases involving employees of dubious criminal skills. The full story on each, including how the perpetrators were nabbed and what they were charged with, can be found on my Web site <www.crisismanagement.com>, under the Economic Espionage link, or directly on <www.economicespionage.com>. When you read the full stories, you may be amazed at what people think they can get away with—and what often happens when otherwise average employees go bad.

IDEXX Labs: Animals and Spies—Large, Small, and Dumb

IDEXX Laboratories, Inc. makes and sells diagnostic tests and kits for the animal health industry. Via the Internet, one of IDEXX's former technical service representatives, Caryn L. Camp, met Stephen R. Martin, a fast-talking California veterinarian and purported owner of several businesses in the western United States that competed with IDEXX.

Before the sun had set on the first day of their e-mail relationship, he was offering her a job, and she started sending him every trade secret she could get her hands on—a blatant theft-of-trade secret spree that lasted for many months. How were they caught? On her last day at work, she foolishly sent an incriminating e-mail meant for her conspirator to one of her IDEXX coworkers.[3]

Deloitte & Touche: "Fastrack" to Prison for Espionage "SAPS"

Mayra Trujilo-Cohen was terminated as a consultant for ICS, Deloitte & Touche. As a parting present, she helped herself to two software programs from her employer: "4FRONT for SAP" and "FASTRACK for SAP"–proprietary SAP Implementation Methodology considered trade secrets. She removed the Deloitte name from the program and tried to sell it as her own. In her first and only attempted sale she asked for–and fully expected to receive–$7 million.

While she was in a larcenous frame of mind, she used an insurance company's bank account to pay her American Express credit card bill through wire transfers, buying such big ticket items as a Rover sport utility vehicle, several Rolex watches, some furniture, and jewelry.[4]

The *Atlanta Journal-Constitution:* Stop the Presses

In September 1997, the *Atlanta Journal-Constitution* was involved in litigation with its smaller rival, the *Gwinnett Daily Post,* over the right to publish county legal notices. Looking to make a fast buck, Caroll Lee Campbell, circulation manager for the *Gwinnett Daily Post,* contacted the *Atlanta Journal-Constitution* and offered to sell it proprietary financial and business information from the *Daily Post* for $150,000.

Using the code name *Athena,* Campbell directed the recipients of his offer to place an ad in the personals section of the Atlanta paper if they were interested in doing business. The FBI was brought in, placed a "Message to Athena" ad in the paper, and began negotiations that led to arrests.[5]

Intel and Cyrix: Meet Dumb and Dumber

Two computer-literate thieves, Steven Hallstead and Brian Pringle, contacted Cyrix Corp. and offered to sell it five "Slot II" computers that had been stolen from Intel, Inc. in April 1998. Intel placed the value of the various trade secrets contained within the prototype computers at $10 million, had a competitor been able to get its hands on the information before Intel released the computers to the public the following month.

Without realizing the jig was up before it ever began, Hallstead offered to sell the computers to undercover FBI agents for $75,000.[6]

R.P. Scherer: Paintballs and Dumbbells

R.P. Scherer, Inc. is a leading international developer and manufacturer of many things, including recreational paintballs. A former employee, Jolene Rector, obtained numerous R.P. Scherer formulas and other information she knew was proprietary and confidential and much of it trade secrets. She planned to use the information in her new job with an RPS competitor, Soft Gelcaps West. But, when she was fired there, she tried to sell RPS's trade secrets to another RPS competitor, Nelson Paint Ball, Inc., for $50,000.

She openly admitted that she had obtained the formulas while working at RPS, thinking that would enhance the value of the trade secrets. It didn't take long for Nelson Paint Ball to contact RPS, who contacted the FBI, which set up a classic videotaped sting to nab Rector and her accomplices.[7]

Solar Turbine: The Caterpillar's Crawl

What is noteworthy about this last case is that it demonstrates how stolen trade secrets are often used to benefit a competitor, or for someone to go into business against his or her former employer. Not all spies and thieves are caught, and not all victims want the publicity that going public will likely bring. The Solar Turbine case might never have come to light had it not been for a couple of twists of fate and patriotic fervor.

Jack Shearer was terminated from Solar Turbines, Inc., of San Diego after 26 years. Solar, with 5,100 employees, is a wholly owned subsidiary of Caterpillar, Inc. The company designs and manufactures industrial gas turbine engines and turbo machinery systems

254 SECTION TWO / Loose Lips Sink Ships!

for the production and transmission of crude oil, petroleum products, and natural gas all over the world.

After his termination, Jack Shearer used trade secret information from his former employer to start and build a successful $8 million business to compete with Solar—a business to overhaul and refurbish and service Solar's own turbines and compressors.

Using at least two accomplices working for Solar, Shearer obtained Solar's drawings, plans, and schematics that included confidential specifications of Solar parts from 1993 through 1999, valued at millions of dollars. He then manufactured counterfeit Solar parts using third party manufacturers and sold the parts—along with completely bogus "Certificates of Compliance" as proof that these were genuine Solar parts—to unsuspecting Solar customers.

Here's where it gets interesting.

One of Shearer's primary and lucrative customers was an Iranian businessman who operated an oil and gas parts broker business in Sweden. The orders he placed were designed for oil field applications, but the parts were all painted desert beige. Some of Shearer's employees became suspicious that the machinery and parts that were ordered by this Iranian businessman were going to prohibited countries, such as Iran, to be used in Iran's oil fields in direct violation of U.S. policy.

Consider this. On the one hand, Shearer doesn't think twice about committing economic espionage against his former employer. But now, he and his employees are confronted with the sticky ethical problem of whether or not to fill the Iranian's order, because they are now suspicious that doing so might violate U.S. national policy against providing goods and services to a prohibited country.

Other things began to unravel, including suspicion from some of the third party manufacturers, who began to notice Solar's name on some of the specifications. They started to refuse Shearer's orders. It was only a mater of time before Solar got wise and brought in the FBI. Shearer and his crew all pled guilty to conspiracy to steal trade secrets under the Economic Espionage Act and received one of the longest sentences ever imposed in an economic espionage case.[8]

Are You Next?

Just think about the wide diversity of the companies mentioned here. Economic espionage happened to them, and it can happen to you. The biggest mistake a company can make is to think it's immune. Remember: 80 percent of economic espionage comes from employees and other insiders. As I said before, the only thing necessary for economic espionage to flourish is a business with at least one employee or at least one competitor.

And the IQ of the employee doesn't seem to matter.

CHAPTER 25

STICKY FINGERS
The Three Amigos

Let me make one personal observation up front: Some of our tax dollars need to be redirected toward better training of our government lawyers, especially courtroom training.

The Three Amigos versus the Three City Slickers

Sharing the prosecutors' table with young Mark Zwillinger were two senior DOJ prosecutors: David Green, the principal deputy chief of the Computer Crime and Intellectual Property Section of the U.S. Justice Department, and Rudolfo ("Rudy") Orjales. Green was in charge. Orjales had only one crucial assignment: taking Victor through his testimony.

It seemed to me that the government prosecutors had the far better case but needlessly shot themselves in the foot with alarming frequency. It was not so much that the prosecutors were outmatched at many turns by the Four Pillars lawyers; rather, the government failed to capitalize on far too many missed opportunities. In my opinion, in the hands of more experienced prosecutors—specifically meaning more experienced in actually getting on their feet in front of a jury—I believe this case would have had a very different outcome.

The best way to describe David Green, the government's lead prosecutor on the case, is to say that he looks like a nonmanic version of *Life Is Beautiful* star Roberto Benigni but reminded me, too, of Woody Allen, with his stilted movements and halting speech pattern. He seemed tentative almost every time he spoke, as though he wasn't sure where any sentence he began was going to end, or perhaps what else he was going to say, or how it would be received. Many times I found myself gripping the arm of the courtroom bench, white-knuckling my way though his examination of a witness or oral arguments on a motion before the judge. His courtroom skills can best be compared to a flight in a small plane where the single engine periodically sputters and you think you're going down, only to pull out of a nose dive at the last minute. But make no mistake: Green is one of DOJ's top lawyers and played a role in the writing of the government's *Prosecuting Intellectual Property Crimes* handbook for prosecutors. Whatever his intellectual legal abilities, however, what I personally observed of his skills as a courtroom prosecutor are sorely wanting: he never connected with the jury at all. In arguing motions before the judge, standing alongside the defense attorneys, Green looked like a junior high freshman in a debate with high school seniors, who overpowered him with verbal jujitsu and demeanor. Of slight build, he looked like he might get blown away by Eric Dubelier's verbal attacks.

Dubelier, who along with Nancy Luque represented P.Y. Yang and the Four Pillars company, has sort of a bulging, bug-eyed look when he gets excited, which happened regularly during this trial. He came across in a belligerent way, and the first time I saw him bulldog his way across the courtroom, I thought I saw some jurors in the front row flinch backwards as though he might leap over the railing and attack. Someone on his team must have muzzled him, though, because after a time he toned down. But his temper still seemed to lurk just beneath the surface of his thin skin.

Young Zwillinger made up in enthusiasm what he lacked in experience. As stated earlier, he was articulate and quick on his feet.

When he physically moved from point A to point B in the courtroom, he looked like he knew where he was going and why. That was definitely not the case with Green.

Zwillinger got into many a heated exchange with Nancy Luque, who was dubbed the "Ice Maiden" by many who sat on my side of the aisle, including one or two reporters. She made the previously described disastrous opening statement and then sat down. She never examined or cross-examined a single witness.

Ralph Cascarella represented Sally only. Of the six lawyers in the well of the courtroom arguing this case, I believe he and Zwillinger probably made the best impressions on the jury. Cascarella seemed to be able to remain calm and cool throughout, and when he cross-examined a government witness, he did so in a nonbelligerent, professional way and in a well-modulated voice that came across as more respectful of the witnesses than Dubelier was. That approach seemed to play well to this jury, even if he didn't seem to have a fingertip grasp of the technical points of the case. In front of the jury, he never raised his voice. His tactics, though, were transparent. It was his job to save *his* client, so he set about to separate Sally from P.Y. whenever and however he could. If Sally was in the hotel room with P.Y. while P.Y. was committing economic espionage, Cascarella's position was that she was there only as a dutiful daughter acquiescing to her father's demands, just the way a compliant Asian daughter is supposed to do. She was not there, he would continue to spin his tale to the jury, because she was an officer of Four Pillars at the time and therefore actively engaged in an economic espionage conspiracy.

Finally, there was Rudy Orjales, the designated government hitter whose sole job was to take Victor through his testimony so that the jury would have a clear and unmistakable understanding of what Victor did, and what Four Pillars, P.Y., and Sally did with Victor under the heading of economic espionage. This should have been relatively easy; it wasn't.

The first problem was that Victor was not a good witness. He speaks with a heavy accent so some of his words are hard to understand. But Victor's attitude was a greater impediment than his accent. For obvious reasons, Victor wasn't particularly happy about his present circumstances. Look where he was, and why. He had come up—*way up*—from a life of poverty on the streets of Taipei to a position of respect and esteem in the United States and with a leading company, and even as an honored "consultant" in Taiwan. Now his once good life was ruined; the American dream he had once lived was now a nightmare. He had stolen trade secrets from an employer that had been very good to him and trusted him. And now he sat in the witness box having to explain to a judge, a jury, and a room full of strangers why he had committed economic espionage for eight years. While testifying to his crimes in exchange for immunity, he was forced to face the very people he was accusing—P.Y. and Sally—the old man who had been like a father to him and the woman he had tried to impress. The last time he had seen them was when they shared blueberry bagels at a Holiday Inn outside of Cleveland. Victor's bad attitude was understandable.

And his attitude was sorely aggravated by Orjales's astonishingly inept bumbling while taking Victor though his testimony. The more Orjales mishandled the questioning, the testier Victor seemed to get. And bulldog Dubelier only made things worse.

Rattled

I've taken you through the nuts and bolts of what Victor stole, the how and why, and the money. I've also covered how he was recruited—where and when and why and by whom. Victor testified to all of that, so I don't need to repeat it again here. What follows is a very painful look at how the government dropped the ball at so many key turns in Victor's testimony.

To begin with, Orjales had difficulty phrasing his questions properly and, therefore, had trouble eliciting the information from Victor and making a clear record of evidence. What Orjales's phrasing problems did elicit was a plethora of objections from the defense lawyers, many of which were sustained by the judge, and all of which interrupted and derailed the flow of Victor's testimony. The disruptions seemed to badly rattle Orjales, who would often stumble verbally, try to recast the question, only to be challenged again by the defense to the point of distraction. This pattern was repeated over and over.

It got so problematic that in several instances, the judge actually tried to help Orjales rephrase the question, perhaps fearing that Orjales's difficulties might prejudice the jury. For example, Orjales asked Victor a leading question (leading a witness to answer a question a certain way), a procedure that is not allowed:

Orjales: When you gave this document to the defendants—

Judge [instructing Orjales]: To *whom* did you give this document?

And that wasn't the worst of it. At times, after an objection was lodged and sustained to one of his questions, Orjales still could not properly rephrase the question without subjecting himself to further objections by the defense lawyers and criticism from the judge. In sheer frustration, Orjales would sometimes then give up—dropping the line of questioning altogether. Far too many times, Orjales abandoned important lines of inquiry completely because he simply couldn't get the *form* of the question right.

This was an unexpected coup for the defense. Whereas they previously might have worried about how to keep damaging documents out of evidence, it now seemed all they had to do was shake Orjales's cage a couple of times with objections and he'd stop trying to get particular documents into evidence altogether.

The jury might have had difficulty following some of the technical aspects of the case, but they seemed to have no trouble seeing what was happening to Orjales. Remember how important perception is.

And the more trouble Orjales had, the testier Victor became. He had come to testify but was being prevented from doing so for lack of proper questions.

Part of Orjales's job was to help get Victor ready for cross-examination by going through the sorts of questions that defense attorneys might ask him and to make sure how he would respond. But the answer to one of the first cross-examination questions was a shocker.

Paraphrasing, the defense asked: Did P.Y. ever ask you to send him Avery Dennison confidential or proprietary material? And Victor's answer: P.Y. never asked me to do anything.

Pardon me?

The prosecutors appeared dumbstruck. I was incredulous. It seemed to me that people in the courtroom on the government's side of the aisle started coughing up their breakfasts. Even the defense table seemed stunned. What was Victor up to? Was he suddenly recanting his confession? Was he trying to be cute?

P.Y. never asked Victor to do anything?

How could Victor say this? And why didn't the prosecutors know he would say this? Hadn't this come up in pretrial preparation? Hadn't the FBI covered this in their investigation? What had Orjales been doing for all those months?

It turned out that, despite his extensive confession, Victor still tried to protect P.Y. and Sally as much as he could, and that answer was one example.

Quite a few other little bombshells dropped. Example: Victor had testified that he had stolen from Avery Dennison and for eight years sent confidential material to Four Pillars. But when the defense asked: Did you know what you were doing was wrong? Victor waffled and said that he didn't think so. How was the jury reacting to this news?

Finding the Switch

Other problems that may seem minor had big cumulative effects on perception.

For example, a couple of pieces of electronic equipment were in the courtroom, one of which was a slightly elaborate overhead projector. Orjales couldn't figure out how to operate the thing—he literally couldn't find the on/off switch—and almost gave up on introducing a key piece of evidence due to his own frustration and technical ineptitude. Just as he turned to walk away, Zwillinger stepped up and easily found the switch that had eluded Orjales. In an effort to help his colleague recover some lost ground, Zwillinger stood on his feet and operated the machine for Orjales. How can an experienced prosecutor—anyone who makes presentations for that matter—not bother to check out the equipment in advance? It seems so basic. Was Orjales so anxious or nervous or cocky that his attitude clouded his thinking or his ability to turn on a switch? It's simply hard to fathom.

By contrast, whenever the defense team had to use any audio/ visual equipment, they knew exactly what they were doing. Their computer software was easier for the jury to follow, too, such as when they wanted to highlight certain key phrases in a written document so the jury could see it easily.

Now, the dynamics of a courtroom are easily as important as the record of testimony and/or evidence. When an attorney appears bumbling, it can turn off the jury. When testimony drags on because an attorney seemingly can't follow the rules of evidence or ask questions in the right form, a jury can get frustrated, annoyed, bored, and vengeful. Problems with the questions can rather easily rub off on jurors and become problems, in their minds, with the answers. If the attorney doesn't stick with the questioning and drops it, the importance of that evidence—and other evidence from the same witness—can be diminished in the jurors' minds.

Ultimately, cases have been won and lost because of the disposition a jury has toward a defendant or plaintiff because they either really like or really dislike one or more of the lawyers.

This was turning out to be one of those cases.

CHAPTER 26

Greatest Economic Espionage Risks

"But boundless risk must pay for boundless gain."

—William Morris

Because you can't cover all of your bases to be 100 percent protected against risk of economic espionage, you have to look to probabilities based on past occurrences—the greatest predictor of future events.

The Classic Fraud Triangle

The classic fraud triangle is *means, motive, and opportunity.* Given the rampant fear and loathing in the workplace and in the world against American companies, as previously discussed, Motorola's Bill Boni feels that motive might better be replaced with *rationalization.*

Michael Mee, supervisory special agent and program manager of the FBI's intellectual property rights initiative, told me that about 80 percent of all trade secret theft is an inside job, a statistic supported by many other sources, including Ted Fraumann who used to have Mee's job at the FBI.[1] Inside jobs, though, do not just include full-time employees. Many of today's businesses outsource services to contract employees, so an insider is anyone who has ready access to your company.

The ASIS survey of *Fortune* 1,000 companies breaks down likely trade secret thieves as follows:

- 30 percent are employees.
- 28 percent are former employees.
- 22 percent are vendors, contract employees, OEM employees, consultants, etc. In other words, outsiders with an insider's access and privileges.
- 20 percent are domestic and foreign competitors, foreign governments, or agents working for these entities.

What Are They After?

In no particular order, the most targeted trade secrets across the board are:

- Customer lists
- Pricing information
- R&D information
- Sales information
- Manufacturing information
- Strategic plans
- Cost information

Who Are They After?

The specific industries targeted most for economic espionage are:

- Pharmaceutical
- Chemical
- Food
- Computer software
- Aerospace
- Automobile

Generally, though, high-profile targets of economic espionage are companies that have or work with:

- Formulas
- Patterns
- Programs
- Devices
- Methods
- Techniques
- Proprietary processes

Military Critical Technologies List

In addition to the above, the Department of Defense maintains a Military Critical Technologies List of industries essential to helping the United States maintain its military superiority. As you will quickly observe, the majority of the technologies on the MCTL are dual-use technologies, which means they can be used for both military and civilian applications.

Also, if you are a supplier to any of these industries, your risk just increased by virtue of doing business with them.

If you work in any of the major technology categories or industries in the following MCTL, you are at a higher than average risk for economic espionage:

- Aeronautics systems
- Armaments and energetic materials
- Chemical and biological systems
- Directed and kinetic energy systems
- Electronics
- Ground systems
- Guidance, navigation, and vehicle control
- Information systems
- Information warfare
- Manufacturing and fabrication
- Marine systems
- Materials

- Nuclear systems
- Power systems
- Sensors and lasers
- Signature control
- Space systems
- Weapons effects and countermeasures

What's Most Attractive to Steal?

Anything that is already in, or can easily be converted to, digital format is most desirable to steal because of the ease with which proprietary information and trade secrets can be stored, copied, and transported. The use of digital forms to commit economic espionage is the single biggest risk companies face.

Why Do They Do It?

Greed.

Revenge is up there, too, but greed (or envy) is really the driving force. You've got something and somebody else wants or needs it. If a competitor has stolen from you, taking your information simply saves them money.

If the bad guy is an employee with a misguided sense of entitlement who wants to strike an entrepreneurial pose, he may feel entitled to take what he worked on while in your employ. He may think it's an easy way to start out in a new business venture.

And revenge is a secondary factor. If you laid off thousands of workers, you have created thousands of potential trade secret leaks.

What Should You Do?

First, make trade secret protection a priority in words as well as action. Don't just pay it lip service. On your own or with an outside consultant, begin to take the steps necessary to:

- Identify and audit your trade secrets
- Value your trade secrets

- Educate and train your employees, top to bottom
- Assess all of the risks you face in protecting your trade secrets
- Provide the reasonable measures necessary to protect your trade secrets
- Start all over again next year

A companywide education and training program should not be a one-time event. It must be ongoing and should be driven by senior management. But it is equally important that the entire company go through the process, and senior management should lead by example. If the case studies in this book have demonstrated anything, it is that economic espionage happens at all levels within a company, so the entire company needs to become more aware.

Trade secret protection should include employees at all levels, and your trade secret protection program is only as good as your employees make it. There are three typical controls: physical, technical, and social. Physical controls, such as locking doors and files, are meaningless if people don't use the locks. Technical controls won't work if people give out or don't protect their passwords. Social controls—educating and training employees—are essential.

What Tools Do You Need?

According to Boni, two things are essential to fighting economic espionage:

1. *Counterintelligence mind-set.* It's not pleasant to say, especially to companies that like to operate in an open culture environment, but everyone is not your friend. Lots of people want what you've got and are prepared to steal it. Assume someone is after your goods and take the counterintelligence steps necessary to protect yourself.

2. *Content monitoring software toolkit.* No one questions that hacking and netspionage are enormous economic espionage problems, but remember that 80 percent of economic espionage is done by insiders. They don't have to hack their way into your

systems; they're already there. So all the money you spend on firewalls and other Internet security procedures are still missing 80 percent of the potential risk.

Vulnerabilities by Categories

Security consultant Ira Winkler says there are four broad categories of vulnerabilities within a company: operations, physical, personnel, and technical.[2] The laundry list is very long, but here are just a few examples of where you should be paying attention to risks.

Operations vulnerabilities include:

- Social engineering
- Unchecked Internet usage
- Carrying work around (such as taking work home or on trips)

Physical vulnerabilities include:

- Easy building access
- Open or poor storage of information
- Lack of computer passwords

Personnel vulnerabilities include:

- No background checks on new hires
- Susceptibility to crime
- Personal situations causing stress or financial hardships

Technical vulnerabilities include:

- Known bugs in the system
- Easily broken passwords

ANSIR

What do you do if you suspect you are the victim of economic espionage, and how do you stay informed in advance?

When Bill Boni was running security at Amgen, and he was informed that the Nippon Television folks wanted to videotape and conduct interviews, he first contacted the FBI to see if they had any information on this crew.

"The FBI called me back immediately," Boni told me, "and told me to watch out for these guys. The Bureau had received a number of complaints from other biotech companies where they had taped interviews previously."

But whom did Boni call? ANSIR—the FBI's Awareness of National Security Issues and Response Program. The Feds consider ANSIR the public voice of the FBI for espionage, counterintelligence, counterterrorism, economic espionage, cyber and physical infrastructure protection, and all national security issues.

One of the program's purposes is to provide unclassified national security threat and warning information to U.S. corporate security directors and executives, law enforcement, and other government agencies. Any legitimate business presumably can become a member of ANSIR and receive notifications of known threats. More information on ANSIR is available on its Web site, listed in the Appendix.

Globalization Risks

Multinational companies with facilities in foreign countries have two additional elements for heightened economic espionage risk:

1. *Opportunity.* If you have a facility in a country where economic espionage is high, you are just too convenient an opportunity for spies in that country to pass up. Because you will be hiring locals, a foreign competitor or a foreign power will find it easier to recruit one of your workers to spy for them. Assume you are a target of economic espionage.
2. *Recovery.* But, what do you do if you have been targeted or victimized in a foreign country? Whom do you contact? What are the chances of recovery? And what are the laws in that country that protect your trade secrets?

Many countries have some form of trade secret laws (which naturally vary widely from country to country and may change frequently) and some means of redress. Know your risks. In some instances, the EEA affords the FBI broad territorial reach that could aid you if you are an economic espionage victim abroad.

CHAPTER 27

STICKY FINGERS
The Trial Winds Down

Fundamentally, the biggest problem with the government's case was the introduction of evidence.

Victor was a scientist and was used to keeping meticulous notes in a lab book. He did the same for the eight years he was shipping Avery Dennison's trade secrets off to Four Pillars. His notes should have been a prosecutor's dream come true. Victor not only could testify that he sent something to Four Pillars, he could presumably provide the documentation in his notebook. So meticulous was Victor, that he had also kept receipts from the post office which matched the dates in his notebook exactly. He had kept the receipts to get reimbursed from Four Pillars. All prosecutor Orjales had to do was introduce the material into evidence.

In their deliberations, a jury cannot review a document if it hasn't been introduced into evidence. It may be discussed in court during witnesses' testimony, but if the judge hasn't ruled that it may be admitted into evidence, the jury can't examine it in the deliberation room. Therefore, this element of Orjales's mission was critical: the introduction into evidence of everything that Victor had shipped off to Four Pillars.

But there were numerous, important documents that Orjales just couldn't manage to get introduced into evidence. At this point, the case wasn't so much one of economic espionage as a basic documents case. Introducing documents into evidence is taught in law school. It's basic.

The saddest part was that Orjales seemed to know how poorly the trial was going for him. At one point during a break in the proceedings, I was standing in the hallway with several people when Orjales walked by, and the following quick exchange took place without his breaking stride on his way back to the courtroom:

Orjales: Are any of you guys Catholic?

Bystander: Yes, I am.

Orjales: Could you say a couple of Hail Marys?

J. Edgar Hoover Is Spinning in His Grave

One reason why many documents in this case didn't get introduced was because of bad investigative work and sloppy document handling on the part of the government, starting with the FBI. The FBI, you may recall, came under intense fire in May 2001 for mishandling some 3,500 documents in the case of convicted Oklahoma City bomber Timothy McVeigh. On the heels of that fiasco came the revelation that the Bureau had lost hundreds of weapons and laptop computers, at least one of which contained top secret data.

Careless document handling happened in the Four Pillars case, too.

In many cases, one of the key witnesses for the government is the cop—the guy who can whip out his notebook and tell the jury chapter and verse how a document was obtained and how it has been carefully maintained in custody until the trial.

FBI Special Agent Mike Bartholomew—who was *the* cop in this story—was never called as a witness by the government. Why?

Remember, after P.Y. cut up Avery Dennison's patent application to remove company logos and CONFIDENTIAL warnings, he instructed Victor not to leave those scraps lying around the hotel room, that he had better take them home and dispose of them there. Victor took them home, but he never disposed of them. He kept them as he had been instructed to do by the FBI. And he kept them. And he kept them . . .

And he kept them . . .

And he kept them . . . .

According to Victor's courtroom testimony, he kept them with his other Four Pillars material in his basement for about two weeks before the FBI got around to asking him for them.

In legal parlance, the phrase *chain of custody* is important, because when that cop is on the witness stand, he will undoubtedly be asked about the chain of custody involving a key piece of evidence. Who had the evidence at any given time, and was it under proper care from the time it was seized until right now?

Neither Bartholomew nor anyone from the FBI could testify about the chain of custody while the scraps were in Victor's unsupervised possession for several weeks. And the defense exploited this problem to the hilt, when it blindsided Orjales during cross-examination.

It became painfully obvious that the DOJ and the FBI had dropped the ball when it came time to understand exactly what Victor sent to Four Pillars, notwithstanding the scientist's lab book. Victor had kept copies of everything he sent, but it did not appear that anyone from the FBI or the DOJ had ever asked Victor during his months of confession if what he retained was always a true copy of what he sent. That question apparently never was asked until the defense lawyers asked him on cross-examination.

If the defense could demonstrate that Victor had sent documents that were not exact copies of what he retained in his possession and the government didn't know it, this would become a serious problem of Victor's and the government's credibility. Just plant the seed of doubt, and everything else, by association, becomes suspect. Example (showing a document to Victor on the witness stand):

Defense Question: This document says "Confidential." Did the document you sent to Four Pillars say "Confidential"?

Victor: No, I removed the label before I sent it. . . .

Q: So was there any way for Four Pillars to know it was confidential?

A: No.

Or, at different times, Victor would have kept a document that had the names of Avery Dennison personnel on it but would have removed those identifying names before sending the document. Apparently, when the Feds collected evidence from Victor, they never asked if what they were picking up was an exact copy of what Victor had sent to Four Pillars, and this lapse caused serious problems for Orjales in court.

At other times, Orjales tried to introduce into evidence a letter that Victor said he had sent to P.Y. and Sally and several other people. But the defense asked the questions that Orjales didn't think to ask, such as: How many envelopes did you use? Did you send each person their own copy, or did you put all of the copies into one envelope (which he did many times), and if so, how do you know who actually received copies? If you sent three copies of a document—one to P.Y., one to Sally, and one to C.K. Kao—and you put them all in one envelope addressed to Sally, how do you know P.Y. ever got a copy?

Answer: I don't know.

Or they asked Victor a question such as: If you sent one lengthy document, say a report, and you didn't make copies but you wanted several people at Four Pillars to see the document, how do you know the document was copied at Four Pillars or circulated to the people on your distribution list?

Answer: I don't know.

Or they asked Victor whether, if he sent a letter with the *cc:* notation next to various people's names, did he send copies in the same envelope as the one addressed to P.Y.?

Answer: Sometimes.

Q: If a letter has the cc: notation and the letter has an attachment, did you copy the attachment for everybody?

A: Sometimes (or I don't remember).

See the problem? You can almost see the seeds of doubt and uncertainty being sprinkled in the jurors' minds by the defense's questions. With enough ambiguity, it isn't difficult to sow confusion and ultimately even reap the harvest of a not guilty verdict.

Bear in mind, the questions weren't asked exactly this way. This is to give you an idea of the relatively easy job the defense had in raising doubt in the jurors' minds and blocking certain key documents from ever being introduced into evidence for lack of foundation. Orjales was unable to elicit from Victor the proper foundation that what he sent to P.Y. was received by P.Y., or that P.Y. would necessarily know that what he was receiving was confidential, proprietary, or a trade secret. This doesn't mean P.Y. didn't do what he was accused of doing, but remember my admonition that a defendant is presumed innocent until proved guilty. The burden was on the government to prove P.Y., Sally, and Four Pillars guilty beyond a reasonable doubt, and the defense was starting to inject troubling doubt into the jury's mind.

This was heavy lifting, and Rudolfo ("Rudy") Orjales was ill prepared to carry the load.

X-Ray Vision Required

Another embarrassing problem had to do with the overhead transparencies Victor used in Taiwan for his technical seminars to the Four Pillars scientists.

Orjales held up some transparencies and had Victor identify them as the actual Avery Dennison transparencies he had used in Taipei. Avery Dennison, as you might expect, is big on labels, and right on the face of the transparency, in a corner but still prominent, was an oblong Avery Dennison CONFIDENTIAL sticker, white lettering against a blue background. Orjales proudly displayed the transparencies to the jury.

Oh, but wait. Ralph Cascarella had a little something to contribute on cross-examination. When you use an overhead transparency on a projector, the only part of a label that can be seen by the audience is the black, completely solid, oblong shape of the sticker. The light doesn't shine through the label and the word CONFIDENTIAL on the front of the label cannot be seen at all. The defense made sure the jurors knew that there was no way for anyone from Four Pillars sitting in Victor's seminar audience in Taipei to know that the transparencies they were looking at were trade secrets or in any way confidential or proprietary to Avery Dennison. Such elementary logic had eluded Orjales and the FBI.

This was painful to watch.

Let's Go to the Tape

The one thing the jury and the assembled reporters understood more clearly than anything else was the videotape. That capper was saved for the dramatic end of the government's case.

All along, the one question asked by reporters and others was whether or not the Yangs were going to take the stand. I confidently predicted that they would not, and I was right. How could they? The videotape was too compelling.

The jury was mesmerized as the lights in the courtroom dimmed and the video screens jumped to life.

I have described the videotape to you earlier and in detail so I will not repeat that here. When you recall what is on the tape, think about how P.Y. could possibly explain to a jury what he was doing in that hotel room in a way that could possibly exonerate him. There he was, clearly shown on videotape pawing a confidential Avery Dennison document; telling Victor that all they had to do was "modify" a product and that they had the research talent to do that; taking a knife and scissors from his pants pocket and excising Avery Dennison company logos and CONFIDENTIAL and PROPERTY OF AVERY DENNISON messages from the purloined patent application; taping the pieces back together into one document again; boasting, *"Often times, all of a sudden, sometimes I cannot remember which company it came from;"* telling Victor to dispose of the scraps at home, not wanting him to leave any evidence behind in a hotel room; bragging about how careful he was.

The jury saw it all with unblinking eyes and an understanding look on their faces that was largely absent during most of the trial. If a picture is worth a thousand words, a videotape is worth millions.

How can anyone take the stand and put up a plausible defense against that kind of evidence? You can't—not when you're caught with your sticky fingers in somebody else's glue pot.

The surprise was that the Four Pillars lawyers mounted no defense at all. They rested without ever calling a witness. In their opinion, presumably, the government had just failed to prove its case. The burden of proof is on the government to prove guilt beyond a reasonable doubt.

The only time the defense ever addressed the damning videotape was in their cross-examination of Victor, trying to pick apart whatever they could of Victor's actions and complicity in trapping the Yangs in the sting. Here, Cascarella tried again to separate his client, Sally, from the deeds of her father.

Cascarella got Victor to talk about the differences between American culture and the more patriarchal Asian culture. Victor opened up about father-daughter relationships in Asia, explaining to the jury the way it was with Asian daughters of strong Asian fathers, and how it was inculcated in the women from the time they are girls to follow their father's every wish and command. Wasn't it possible, Cascarella suggested more to the jury than to Victor, that Sally accompanied her father to that hotel room not as a coconspirator but as a devoted daughter following her father's wishes?

Perhaps Victor was reminded of the father who died when he was three, whom he barely remembered, or maybe it was the way he thought of P.Y. as the father he never had. Whatever buttons Cascarella pushed, it was at this point that Victor, after withstanding days of assault from the bumbling Orjales and the hostile defense team, broke down and cried on the witness stand.

It was unexpected, and there was an eerie silence in the courtroom, broken only by the muffled sound of Dr. Tenhong "Victor" Lee, confessed spy, broken man, sobbing into his hands.

Falling Leaves

Frankly, the government's case started to collapse even without the debacles in court. At the outset, there was a 21-count indictment against P.Y. Yang, Sally Yang, and Four Pillars Enterprises. But another review at the end of the trial shows that 18 of the 21 original counts had been dismissed by the judge.

Eighteen of 21! No wonder the Four Pillars lawyers didn't mount a defense. It almost seemed that if they held out just a little longer the judge would toss out the government's whole case.

How could so many charges be dropped by the judge? There are several possible explanations depending who you ask. Either the government piled on—meaning that they added more counts than were warranted to make the magnitude of the case seem larger (think "trophy case")—the prosecutors were out-lawyered in pretrial motions and arguments by the Four Pillars city slickers, or maybe the judge believed Four Pillars when it accused Avery Dennison of using the government to squash a competitor and used that as a reason to throw out some indictments.

Another possibility was that preparation and investigative work by the government was worse than what I've described. For example, it came out months later during the civil trial that Victor had actually lied to the government during the criminal phase about how much he had actually stolen from Avery Dennison. In trying to protect P.Y. and Sally as much as he could, Victor had withheld information from the prosecutors and the FBI about 10,000 additional documents that he had sent to Four Pillars, many of which were highly confidential and were labeled as such. In all, he had sent and Four Pillars had received some 20,000 pages of some 12,000 separate documents, 71 adhesive formulas, including trade secret information on 37 specialty adhesive tapes, as well as trade secret information on 20 label primers.

The government never tried to subpoena these documents from Four Pillars because they believed them to be in Taiwan. However, the documents had been already brought to the United States by Four Pillars in preparation for the civil trial. Had the prosecutors issued a subpoena, presumably the documents would have been turned over to them in time to be used at the criminal trial.

It also came out during the civil trial that at one point Victor had sent Sally a six-page letter. Victor showed the letter to the government—all but the last two pages. Instead he had just signed his name to the bottom of page four and duped the FBI and the Three Amigos into thinking that this was just a four-page letter. The last two pages were very incriminating. And numerous other examples of this type of deceit and chicanery surfaced.

Whatever the explanation or excuses, the bottom line was that carelessness by the government caused those counts to come unglued and to drop and drop and drop.

And Then There Were Three

The case that finally went to the jury had been reduced from 21 original counts to just three: P.Y. and Sally as individuals, and the Four Pillars corporation, were each charged with two counts of economic espionage and one count of mail fraud.

If the Yangs were acquitted on the criminal charges, it would be anybody's guess what would happen to the civil trial—the trial where Avery Dennison had a chance to recover some of its losses. If the Yangs walked, they'd be back in Taiwan, and who would Avery Dennison have left to sue? True, Avery Dennison could try to get a default judgment against Four Pillars, but then they'd have the logistical problem of collection in Taiwan.

Still worse, the countersuit that Four Pillars had leveled against Avery Dennison just five months earlier would undoubtedly pick up steam, just as Avery Dennison's stock might lose some steam in the face of a verdict that went in Four Pillars' favor in the criminal phase.

"Hard Science, Simple Crime"

When it was time for closing arguments, Zwillinger put on his best game face and reminded the jury that, "Everything you need to know is on the videotape."

Knowing that the jury had had a difficult time following this very long and complex case, he tried to simplify it by telling them that this is a case about "hard science, but simple crime." He wanted them to put aside the hard science complexity of the case and focus exclusively on the simple crime of what Victor, P.Y., and Sally had done, which had been captured for posterity in a grainy black-and-white FBI videotape.

All the defense had to do is raise a reasonable doubt in the jury's mind, so Dubelier's closing asked the jury, "Is there too much doubt in this case? I would respectfully suggest to you that there is."

And then, after a month-long trial in a case that began years earlier, the first economic espionage case ever to go to trial since the passage of the Economic Espionage Act was finally sent to a weary jury for their deliberations.

And so we waited for a verdict . . .

And waited . . .

And waited . . . .

CHAPTER 28

Reducing Economic Espionage Risks

"It has been known for quite some time that economic espionage takes place. But only now people are starting to talk about it. The real question is what to do about it?"

—Richard Helms, former CIA director

"Kodak's proprietary and trade secret information are the life-blood of the company," said Gary P. Van Graafeiland, the company's general counsel after Harold Worden was sentenced for stealing the company's trade secrets. He could have been talking about any company in any industry group.

Given how valuable trade secrets are, you would think that companies would bend over backwards to protect them, especially because some 70 percent of a company's valuation is based on intellectual property. But that is not the case.

Think how tough it sometimes is just to get into some buildings as a visitor. At some of my client locations, I have to sign in and be issued a badge. At some locations, visitors have to be escorted in certain sensitive areas. You need to know and then punch in on a keypad special door combinations or have card keys to open doors or have elevators stop at specific floors. Security guards greet and watch you when you arrive in the lobby or walk around or enter or leave the parking lot. Closed circuit TV cameras are mounted in ceilings or some other inconspicuous locations keeping an eye on you.

In most cases, what is actually being protected is physical property from outsiders, not trade secrets from insiders. Typical security people in office buildings are concerned with guarding against thieves walking off with a computer; they wouldn't know a trade secret if their lives depended on it.

Given that some 80 percent of trade secret theft is perpetrated by employees or other insiders, the focus on reducing risk of trade secret theft should be on education and ethics, not physical security. In eight out of ten times, the bad guys have already gotten past security and are in the building because they work there.

So, in companies where 70 percent of the company's assets are in trade secrets, what you have is an out-of-balance equation. The majority of money spent on protecting a company's assets is spent on protecting the 30 percent that represents the physical assets, and it is spent largely to protect the company from only 20 percent of the risk—from outsiders.

Most companies simply do not properly address the issue of protecting trade secrets. This lapse only increases a company's risk that an employee, ex-employee, or some other insider will walk off with a valuable trade secret, whether intentionally or not. A trade secret that gets out into the marketplace accidentally can cause every bit as much harm as those that are pilfered by true spies.

You would think companies would be motivated by their own enlightened self-interest to be sure that their trade secrets are properly protected to reduce their risk.

Attitudes and Precautions

The ASIS survey of the *Fortune* 1,000 companies that we looked at before also addressed certain attitudinal questions. One interesting bit of information had to do with the frequency with which a company took certain precautions to prevent the loss of proprietary information. The survey looked at three categories of precautions: *administrative steps, physical steps,* and *information systems security.* It then asked how often companies take precautions to prevent information loss: *always, sometimes, rarely,* and *never.*

On average, all industry groups surveyed answered "Sometimes."
Why?

If you looked at your trade secrets as Kodak claims it does—"the
lifeblood of the company"—does it make sense to check your life-
blood just "sometimes"? Is that often enough to reduce your risks?

Is it worth having the Economic Espionage Act on the books to
help you protect what you only go to the trouble to protect "sometimes"? Maybe educating management is as needed as addressing
the rank and file employee. People may be unaware just due to lack
of education and training.

Here's why. Not one of the four industry groups said they
"strongly agreed" when asked if information security was a priority
within their company. How could that be? If you were to recast the
question like this—*Is it important for you to protect certain information
that, were it to be stolen, copied, or compromised in any way could run the
risk of putting you out of business?*—what do you think the response
would be then? Pretty high, I'd wager.

Understand that the respondents are not saying that they feel the
issue is not one of importance; they are saying that the management
of their companies doesn't place as high a premium on information
security as they do and that management support is weak. Additionally, the majority of *Fortune* 1,000 companies surveyed felt that company management does not take the necessary precautions to
prevent intellectual property loss. With this kind of attitude, economic espionage will continue to thrive, EEA or no EEA.

Globalization

Globalization also adds to the complexity. More than one-fifth of
the employees of the companies in the survey work outside the
United States. One common reason cited for why written guidelines about safeguarding and protecting trade secrets are sometimes not followed has to with cross-cultural and cross-sociological
problems inherent with globalization.

All groups recognize and strongly agree that the Internet has created significant new threats to their ability to safeguard proprietary
information.

The high tech industry, more than the others, identified the largest risk of economic espionage from foreign government intelligence or business intelligence agencies. The perceived risk from the
Fortune 1,000 is still consistent in that the largest percentage of economic espionage—even economic espionage sponsored by a foreign
business—is most often perpetrated by an insider.

Education and Awareness Are Crucial

So it appears that many companies have a head-in-the-sand attitude about economic espionage. As long as it's not happening to
them, the problem doesn't exist—much like the proverbial tree falling in the forest. So what's the Philosophy 101 query when applied
to economic espionage? If I am not aware that I've been robbed,
does economic espionage not exist?

Periodically, I'll be involved in a high-profile crisis such as the
Alaskan oil spill, and about ten big oil companies will suddenly contact me to discuss crisis management and crisis communications
planning. A few years ago, when I was involved with the Jack in the
Box hamburger crisis, suddenly four or five well-known fast food
chains contacted me about crisis management assistance in case
something like what happened to Jack in the Box should befall them.

It may take a really high-profile economic espionage case to make
companies more vigilant about being proactive to reduce their own
risk. I can tell you that I was contacted by a number of companies
after the Dr. Wen Ho Lee case broke—the Chinese-born, Los Alamos scientist who was accused of stealing nuclear weapons secrets
and passing them along to the Chinese. The case of this Dr. Lee—
no relation to Dr. Victor Lee—was certainly high profile enough to
cause many companies to look deep inside and ask themselves if
they were at risk.

That internal reflection is a critical first step to reducing risk in
the long run.

CHAPTER | 29

STICKY FINGERS
The Verdicts

The jury deliberated for three days. Ultimately, on April 28, 1999, they returned with a mixed and disappointing verdict.

P.Y. and Sally, as well as the Four Pillars corporation, were found guilty on two counts each of violations of the Economic Espionage Act: theft of trade secrets.

However, they were all acquitted on the other remaining count, mail fraud. The mail fraud charge dealt with what Victor had sent to Four Pillars and what ineffectual prosecutor Rudy Orjales was unable to introduce successfully into evidence.

Louis Freeh directed the FBI to issue a statement, in which he said, "This investigation and conviction clearly demonstrate the importance and value of law enforcement and industry working in partnership under the Economic Espionage Act to combat the theft of American trade secrets and jobs by foreign business interests. It is essential that this partnership continue to adequately combat a crime which has such an impact on the economic well-being of this nation."

Avery Dennison issued only a very terse statement from Phil Neal, its new president and CEO, saying the company "is not surprised by the guilty verdicts reached today. There was never any doubt in our mind that the evidence of illegal activity by Four Pillars was overwhelming." The media didn't report about the 19 counts that got away (18 dropped counts plus one acquittal); they focused on the *news,* which was the convictions in the first economic espionage case to go to trial since the passage of the EEA. That was the way I had presented the story to the news media; Four Pillars put its own spin on the outcome, but the media essentially ignored it.

A few days later, I attended the Avery Dennison annual meeting in Pasadena, where someone asked what I thought of it all.

I said it gives new meaning to the phrase, *Close enough for government work.*

Sentencing Guidelines

Under Section 1831 (which did not apply in the Four Pillars case), a defendant convicted of committing economic espionage can be imprisoned for up to 15 years and fined $500,000, or both. Corporations and other entities can be fined up to $10 million,

Under Section 1832 (the section under which P.Y., Sally, and the Four Pillars corporation were convicted), a defendant convicted of committing economic espionage can be imprisoned up to 10 years and fined $500,000, or both. Corporations and other entities can be fined no more than $5 million.

So, while fines can be levied by judges hearing criminal cases, keep in mind that the primary purpose of a criminal case is to mete out punishment, not recover damages on behalf of the victim. Avery Dennison and the Three Amigos eagerly awaited what they expected to be stiff sentences for the Yangs, who had just been convicted of the first case of economic espionage to go to trial. They had another disappointment coming.

The Sentences

On January 6, 2000, Judge Economous sentenced P.Y. to six months of home confinement and fined him $250,000.

Sally was fined $5,000 and was put on probation for one year. She left the country immediately.

The Four Pillars corporation received the maximum fine of $5 million.

David Green, who had worked so long and hard on prosecuting this case, was outraged by Economous's light sentences. "Is the message," Green railed, "if you steal information from your competitor, you'll be given a probationary term?"

Co-prosecutor Mark Zwillinger, who left the DOJ at the end of his first case to practice law in Washington, D.C., as though he were flung from a revolving door, said, "The judge's downward departure from the sentencing guidelines was inappropriate." Economous departed from the guidelines' recommended sentencing by 14 levels to render such a light slap on the wrist. Zwillinger believes this was Economous's way of "taking Avery Dennison to task for what the judge called inappropriate conduct in using the government's case as a dry run for its upcoming civil case."[1]

Trying to put the best face on it, one assistant U.S. attorney general, Jim Robinson, said, "The imposition of the statutory maximum fine of $5 million should make it perfectly clear that corporate espionage is unlawful and will be aggressively investigated, prosecuted, and punished."

Unlawful? Yes. Investigated? Often. Prosecuted? Sometimes. Punished? Lightly.

When he was sentenced, P.Y. said, "I'm deeply sorry for what I've done." At one point, in trying lamely to explain his actions in the sting, he actually said that when he saw the Avery Dennison patent application he recognized it as stolen Four Pillars technology, which caused him to temporarily lose his mind. (So, naturally, the thing to do is cut off the portions of the document that would prove where it came from.) Plus, if you recall my description of the sting, there wasn't a fast heartbeat in the room.

Victor, who had cut a deal with the government to plead guilty to one count of wire fraud in exchange for immunity on all other possible counts, was sentenced to six months in a federal halfway house in Youngstown, where he could leave during the day but had to return at night for lockdown. Following that, he was placed under house arrest at his home outside of Cleveland for another six months, then put on probation for three years and ordered to repay Avery Dennison the $160,000 he had received from Four Pillars.

But there was worse to come.

Tale of the Tape

If you want to fully appreciate how the government squandered what should have been a slam dunk case and eked out the slimmest of victories by the skin of its teeth, consider this telling statistic: Of the original 21-count criminal indictment lodged against P.Y., Sally, and Four Pillars, the only two on which they were actually convicted in criminal court were the two that specifically occurred in the hotel room sting with Victor. In other words, the government was unable to get a single conviction on anything that occurred during any of the eight years during which Victor had *confessed* that he was providing the Yangs and Four Pillars with more than 12,000 research and development documents, 71 adhesive formulas, including trade secret information on 37 adhesive tapes, and trade secret information on 20 label primers. By sharp and distinctive contrast, you need look no further than the civil case to see the difference in the results with much the same evidence.

Just a few days after the criminal phase sentencing in Youngstown, the civil trial started in Cleveland on essentially similar charges: misappropriation of trade secrets, conversion, and violations of civil RICO (Racketeer Influenced Corrupt Organizations Act). By that I mean, what the Three Amigos tried—and largely failed—to prove in Youngstown, Avery Dennison's own gang of legal gun slingers from Thomson Hine and Quinn, Emanuel, Urquhart & Oliver achieved overwhelmingly in Cleveland. They were particularly successful in getting documents introduced into evidence.

Note: In fairness, there is also a different burden of proof in a civil trial, where you need to establish a preponderance of guilt as opposed to guilt beyond a reasonable doubt required in a criminal prosecution.

In the civil judgment in February 2000, P.Y., Sally, Four Pillars—and Victor—were found liable for $80.16 million. The exact breakdown of the award on behalf of Avery Dennison was $10 million each on the RICO charge, misappropriation of trade secrets, and conversion; plus $30.16 million in punitive damages. The $10 million RICO award was trebled by U.S. District Judge Donald C. Nugent.

Avery Dennison immediately filed a creditor's suit against Four Pillars' biggest U.S. customer, Manco, to try to collect its judgment. Four Pillars could continue to sell its products to Manco, estimated to be about $15 million per year, except that Manco would have to pay Avery Dennison instead of Four Pillars.

If the civil appeal fails, Avery Dennison can execute the judgment in Taiwan, too.

As of this writing, Avery Dennison has received no money from its judgment.

Because Victor had lied during the criminal trial, Avery Dennison voided its agreement with him, in which the company had earlier promised to limit his damages to the $160,000 he had received from Four Pillars in exchange for his cooperation and truthful testimony. Instead, Avery Dennison sent him a letter telling him it was holding him liable for his share of the $80 million judgment.

Today, Victor lives a quiet existence of his own making in his home outside of Cleveland.

He is unemployed.

EEA
Bear Trap or
Mouse Trap?

Has the Economic Espionage Act succeeded?

The EEA was passed primarily to halt the economic espionage activities of foreign powers against U.S. businesses. The FBI director at the time was adamant that some two dozen countries were trying to commit economic espionage against U.S. companies. He called economic espionage the greatest threat to our national security since the Cold War. We had to fight back.

If that is the only yardstick used, then the EEA has been a dismal failure—more of a mouse trap than a bear trap. The EEA has not been much of a deterrent, indeed, perhaps not a deterrent at all. As of this writing, five years after the Act's passage, only one Section 1831 indictment—foreign economic espionage—has been handed down.

"If you're looking at it from a strictly international view, I don't think the Economic Espionage Act has succeeded," said Richard J. Heffernan, a private information security consultant, who testified in Congress in support of the bill's passage. "It hasn't really deterred the Chinese or the Japanese. The problem hasn't gotten better at all."[1]

In short, the EEA has not diminished your company's global risk of economic espionage.

Another relative yardstick has been the punishments meted out. To date, if you have looked to the EEA as a means to punish those who steal trade secrets, you would have been disappointed, too. The sentences have been anemic and don't appear significant enough to provide any credible deterrence. To that extent, therefore, your company's global risk of economic espionage has not diminished, either.

What this all means, of course, is that, now more than ever, you need to be your own first line of defense in the war to manage your risks of global economic espionage.

As you might expect, though, the FBI's Michael Mee thinks that other numbers tell a different story, on the domestic side.

When I spoke with Mee in March 2001, he told me that on that date there were 140 open and active cases of economic espionage. "Since the passage of the Economic Espionage Act, there has been a marked increase in complaints, in reported thefts, in indictments, and in civil lawsuits," said Mee. "And we're batting a thousand in convictions." At the time of our conversation, that meant 23 convictions for 23 indictments under the EEA. However, the FBI and the DOJ have been accused of cherry picking the cases they think they can win. While 23 out of 23 is impressive, another 800 or so potential cases go crying in the wilderness, on top of the 140 that are open and active.

Part of the reason for the increase is the spotlight the EEA has put on the whole subject of economic espionage. Companies are becoming more aware of their risk and are stepping up to the plate to deal with their vulnerabilities in larger numbers. And to that extent, I would have to say the EEA has been more successful.

Additionally, because of the increased visibility of the overall topic of economic espionage, forward-thinking businesses have an easier time going into court and persuading a judge and jury that a particular stolen item is, in fact, a protected trade secret.

To the extent the EEA specifically protects trade secrets—filling a huge void in the law—there is no question the EEA has been successful.

Mee spends part of his time spreading the gospel among U.S. businesses as he travels the country, telling them what the FBI and the EEA can do for them. "I urge them to be more proactive in reporting crimes of trade secret theft." He pointed out that economic espionage, and other intellectual property crimes, is the fastest growing white collar crime in the nation.

"Economic espionage in particular is occurring at a very rapid pace," said Mee. "It most definitely is."

However, he pointed out that many companies are still reluctant to come forward due to fear of bad publicity, although that, too, is changing. By being properly prepared to go public—talking to the media, employees, shareholders, customers, and other key constituencies—companies are seeing that they can control their message in a way that tells the story without making the company look foolish or suffer from bad press.

Companies should not fear going public. A company's communications program when facing any crisis—and economic espionage is a crisis that needs to be managed as such—should be strong and proactive. If you have decided to file suit or bring in the FBI, you need to take charge of your communications strategy, get control of the message, and let the world know you are still in charge. Such a strategy most assuredly helped Avery Dennison when it was faced with near humiliation in Youngstown.

Which brings up a critical point: Should you call in the FBI if your company has been targeted or victimized by economic espionage?

To try to answer that question for a mass audience, recently the FBI persuaded Avery Dennison to cooperate in the production of a videotape, called "Insider Betrayal: Protecting Industry Trade Secrets," recreating how the company was victimized by economic espionage and how Avery Dennison turned to the FBI for help. It's a slickly produced piece that completely overlooks the realities as presented in this book. It's an amusing bit of fluff at best, and I would view it with a grain of salt. It will not help you intelligently weigh your risk about whether or not to call in the Feds.

I wish I had a blanket answer about whether companies should call in the FBI in economic espionage situations, but there isn't one. Every case is different. In the abstract, there are definite advantages in having the FBI on your side. The biggest downside is that you lose control.

One of Avery Dennison's biggest problems in the Victor Lee/ Four Pillars case was a lack of experience and/or competence in the people from the government.

That's just not acceptable.

Acts of terror notwithstanding, economic espionage remains one of the most serious threats to our national security since the Cold War. Therefore, we ought to have seasoned generals leading, and weathered soldiers fighting, the good battles that need to be fought. If our government is going to engage our nation's enemies in whatever form they take, we ought to have the very best people on the front lines. And, while the quality and experience of the federal agents and prosecutors working economic espionage cases were certainly improving as this book was being completed, if you do decide to call in the Feds because you suspect you've been victimized by economic espionage, keep your fingers crossed that you'll still be able to get their attention.

Because as a direct result of the terrorist acts of September 11, 2001, and beyond, the FBI announced one month later that it was completely reorganizing itself and its goals to focus most of its attention on counterterrorism measures. (I support that decision, by the way.) But until the Bureau fully gears up, other FBI activities will either fall by the wayside or receive short shrift due to the effects of thinly stretched resources. On top of which, is it such a far leap for the type of cybercrimes detailed earlier in this book to turn into more malevolent cyberterrorism, turning economic espionage into economic terrorism?

All of which means that you *still* need to be your own best defense against economic espionage with proper internal education, training, and procedures.

So, if you do call in the Feds, hope for the best. But, under no circumstances, delegate the crisis management work for your company to the government. It is too important.

For here is the ultimate reality: America is still the world's leader in research, development, new technology, products, and trade secrets. Nobody does it the way we do, and nobody does it better.

While that's good, it also makes us a high-profile target. With or without the EEA—with or without terrorism—economic espionage spies are still going to come after our companies. And that only increases your risk global risk of economic espionage. It is the classic double-edged sword.

In the final analysis, though, I'd rather have them coming after us because they covet what we've got, than ignoring us because we don't have anything worth stealing.

Knowing that, govern yourself accordingly.

ACKNOWLEDGMENTS

Many people were generous with their time and comments in the writing of this book, and I am grateful to them all.

Despite Avery Dennison's historical penchant for hiding its light under a bushel, the company's cooperative spirit during my writing of certain portions of this book is appreciatively acknowledged. In particular, Jim Robenalt, of Thompson Hine in Cleveland and one of Avery Dennison's attorneys in the landmark Four Pillars civil case, was exceedingly patient and helpful in reviewing and offering comments on relevant sections of this manuscript. His navigational skills through some land mines were invaluable. Dominic Surprenant of Quinn, Emanuel in Los Angeles and co-counsel in the civil case against Four Pillars, provided an additional helpful voice, as did Terry Szmagala, the company's divisional counsel at its Painesville operation where Victor Lee worked.

Bill Boni of Motorola and Dan Swartwood of Compaq were most giving of time and spirit in discussing their considerable labors on past and present surveys of the American Society of Industrial Security and other economic espionage-related matters. Ted Fraumann, who formerly headed up trade secret theft at the FBI and is now a private security consultant, was very helpful in providing background from the FBI's perspective, as was Steve Argubright of the National Counterintelligence Executive. In addition, several FBI agents provided considerable information on a variety of counterintelligence issues, as well as background into the fight for passage of the Economic Espionage Act, but asked not to be identified by name.

I am very grateful to Sheryl Sandberg, former Chief of Staff at the Treasury Department, for opening some key doors in Washington, D.C., and providing introductions that proved extremely beneficial. Neal Wolin, who furnished some valuable insights into the CIA and the National Security operations that deal with economic espionage issues, was very helpful and patient in discussing the ins and outs of the 13-member Intelligence Community. Thanks also to Catherine Bridge for introducing me to her Latham & Watkins colleague, David Schindler, a former U.S. Attorney whose observations about cybercrime were significant and illuminating. And Maya Gorman, Thomas Friedman's able assistant at *The New York Times,* was able with one phone call to turn up an important bit of research that had me stymied.

Thanks also to my editor, Jean Iversen, and the people at Dearborn Trade who understood (or at least gritted their teeth and tolerated it) when urgent client matters translated into writing delays.

A large thanks to my agent, Alice Martell, for her encouragement and support of this project.

Finally, my everlasting love and appreciation for three family members who, when I finally got up from the computer, still recognized and welcomed me back into the fold: my wife, who is my first and most important editor on this manuscript as well as in the daily text of my life; my daughter, who now gets Dad back for bedtime reading adventures and weekend softball; and my golden retriever, who faithfully patrolled the outer door to my study, patiently waiting to go for long morning walks again.

Useful Web Sites

The following Web sites, some of which were referenced in the book, may be useful in providing additional information on how to guard against the global risk of economic espionage and what to do if you should become a victim.

At the time of publication, all sites listed below were up and operating.

Author's Web sites:

Crisis management <www.crisismanagement.com>
Economic espionage <www.economicespionage.com>
The Economic Espionage Act <www.economicespionage.com/ EEA.html>

Association Web sites:

American Society of Industrial Security <www.asisonline.org>
Computer Security Institute <www.gocsi.com>
Intellectual Property Owners Association <www.ipo.org>

Government Web sites:

Department of Justice <www.cybercrime.gov>
Embassy Page <www.embpage.org>
FBI's ANSIR <www.fbi.gov/hq/nsd/ansir/ansir.htm>
National Counterintelligence Center <www.nacic.gov>
National Counterintelligence Executive <www.ncix.gov>
National Infrastructure Protection Center <www.nipc.gov>

National Security Institute <www.nsi.org>
Overseas Security Advisory Council <www.ds-osac.org>
Travel Warnings and Consular Information Sheets
    <www.travel.state.gov>
U.S. Department of State <www.state.gov>
U.S. Intelligence Community <www.cia.gov/ic/index.html>

ENDNOTES

Introduction

1. Del Jones, "FBI: Spies Cost U.S. Firms $2B a Month," *USA Today,* February 10, 1999.

SECTION ONE

Chapter 1

1. Many Asian names have more than one Americanized spelling. The spelling that I use of *Tenhong*—sometimes seen in court documents and news articles as *Ten Hong*—is taken from Dr. Lee's own handwriting on his signed confession. I will use this spelling, except where I am citing a court document that has it as two words.

2. As with Dr. Lee, P.Y.'s full name also has several iterations. He used to Americanize his last name and travel in the United States as *Young* but still use the name *Yang* in Taiwan. His first name also has some variations. The U.S. government used the name *Pin Yen Yang* when they charged him, and I will use that convention, unless I am quoting a written source with a different variation of his first or last name.

Chapter 2

1. American Society for Industrial Security (ASIS) surveys (1997, 1999). Dan Swartwood, interviewed by the author, March 2001; Swartwood is the manager of corporate information security for Compaq Computer Corporation, a member of ASIS, and one of the key authors of both surveys. The 1997 survey of 3,000 companies took direct costs of some $50 billion and added $200 billion in estimated indirect costs. The 1999 survey of just the *Fortune* 1,000, conducted by PricewaterhouseCoopers for ASIS, posted similar direct costs but stopped short of publicly adding the indirect costs to avoid the level of controversy that had swirled around the 1997 survey. However, Swartwood believes the extrapolation is accurate and points to the known direct and indirect costs calculated by Compaq Computers in such situations. "It costs us an additional $4 to replace every $1 that is stolen, and that's just to

break even," said Swartwood. The survey and the economic espionage cost to U.S. businesses is discussed in detail in Chapter 18.

2. ASIS survey.

3. Senate Select Committee on Intelligence; Senate Committee on the Judiciary–Subcommittee on Terrorism, Technology, and Government Information, *Hearing on Economic Espionage,* 104th Cong., 2nd sess., February 28, 1996.

4. Del Jones, Ibid.

5. *Risky Business: The Threat from Economic Espionage,* National Counterintelligence Center videotape, Washington, D.C., 1997.

6. John J. Fialka, *War by Other Means: Economic Espionage in America* (New York: W.W. Norton & Co., 1997).

7. Ibid.

8. For a fuller account, see David J. Jeremy, *Transatlantic Industrial Revolution: The Diffusion of Textile Technologies between Britain and America, 1790-1830* (Cambridge, MA: MIT Press, 1981).

9. Thomas L. Friedman, *The Lexus and the Olive Tree: Understanding Globalization* (New York: Anchor Books, a division of Random House, Inc., 2000), 139-140.

10. Ibid, 8.

11. Ibid, 9.

12. Del Jones, Ibid.

13. Senate Select Committee on Intelligence; Senate Committee on the Judiciary, Ibid.

14. James Chandler, "Economic Espionage and the Economic Espionage Act of 1996," White Paper, March 1999.

15. Ibid.

16. Presidential Commission on Competitiveness.

17. James Chandler, Ibid.

18. Thomas L. Friedman, Ibid.

Chapter 3

1. *United States v. Four Pillars* (1997), testimony of FBI Special Agent Michael Bartholomew.

2. Ibid.

3. Affidavit of FBI Special Agent Michael Bartholomew.

4. *United States v. Four Pillars* (1997), testimony of FBI Special Agent Bartholomew.

5. Ibid, signed confession of Dr. Lee, testimony of Dr. Lee and FBI Special Agent Michael Bartholomew, and court documents.

6. Ibid, signed confession of Dr. Lee, testimony of Dr. Lee, and court documents.

7. Ibid.

8. Ibid. Also, as with the earlier explanation of Asian names, Sally's first name is alternately reported in court documents and news reports as *Hwei Chin* or *Huen-Chan,* and perhaps some others. Where the name Sally came from is anybody's guess, and the same could be said for Tenhong choosing the name Victor for himself. For ease of the narrative and to avoid confusion, I will refer to her as *Sally* unless citing specific court documents.

9. Ibid.

10. Ibid.

11. Ibid.

12. Ibid.

13. *United States v. Four Pillars* (1997), testimony of FBI Special Agent Michael Bartholomew.

14. Dr. Victor Lee, correspondence to Mr. Pin Yen Yang, July 31, 1989; cited in *Avery Dennison Corporation v. Four Pillars Enterprise Co., Ltd., P.Y. Yang, Huen-Chan (Sally) Yang, and Tenhong (Victor) Lee* (1998), court documents.

15. Ibid, August 2, 1989.

16. Ibid, August 6, 1989.

17. Both Four Pillars and Avery Dennison sometimes refer to Dr. Jong S. Guo as *Dr. Chung-Hsin Kuo.* However, he is referred to in English as *Dr. Jong S. Guo,* and that is the name I will use for this narrative, unless otherwise indicated.

18. Dr. Guo and Dr. Krish, correspondence; courtroom testimony; relevant court documents.

19. P.Y. Yang, correspondence to Alan M. Campbell and Kim A. Caldwell, June 6, 1996; relevant court documents.

20. Alan M. Campbell, correspondence to P.Y. Yang, June 20, 1996; relevant court documents.

21. P.Y. Yang, correspondence to Alan M. Campbell and Kim A. Caldwell, June 25, 1996; relevant court documents.

22. Ibid.

23. Alan M. Campbell, correspondence to P.Y. Yang, July 18, 1996; relevant court documents.

24. *United States v. Four Pillars* (1997), affidavit of FBI Special Agent Michael Bartholomew; courtroom testimony; relevant court documents.

25. Ibid.

26. Ibid.

27. Victor Lee, FBI surveillance video, confession, and affidavit; Michael Bartholomew affidavit.

Chapter 4

1. Stephen E. Ambrose, *Ike's Spies: Eisenhower and the Espionage Establishment* (New York: Doubleday, 1981).

2. "Industry-Government Cooperation Essential in Countering Theft of U.S. Intellectual Property," *Focus* (Ann Arbor, MI: National Center for Manufacturing Sciences, February 1995), 5.

3. *Risky Business: The Threat from Economic Espionage*, National Counterintelligence Center videotape, Washington, D.C., 1997.

4. Edwin Fraumann, "Economic Espionage: Security Mission Redefined," *Public Administration Review* (July/August 1997): 303.

5. Federal Bureau of Investigation, "Economic Espionage and Protection of Proprietary Economic Information Act of 1996," a proposal, December 4, 1995.

6. The Associated Press, "Economic Spies Took $300 Billion Toll on U.S. Companies in 1997," January 12, 1998.

7. Edwin Fraumann, Ibid., 308.

8. Neal Wolin, interviewed by the author, May 2, 2001.

9. J. Michael Waller, interviewed by the author, March 20, 2001.

10. J. Michael Waller, "These Spies Steal American Jobs," *Readers Digest* (February 1996): 168.

11. Peter Schweitzer, "The Growth of Economic Espionage," *Foreign Affairs* (January/February 1996).

12. Ibid.

13. Ibid.

14. Douglas Pasternak and Gordon Witkin, "The Lure of the Steal: America's Allies Are Grabbing U.S. Technology," *U.S. News and World Report* (March 4, 1996): 45-48.

15. Wan-fang Ting, *United Daily News*, September 7, 1997.

16. Pasternak and Witkin, Ibid.

17. William Boni, interviewed by the author, May 18, 2001.

18. J. Michael Waller, Ibid.

19. "Industry-Government Cooperation Essential . . .," Ibid.

20. UPI, "Europe in a Fury over U.S. Spy Reports," February 24, 2000.

21. Ibid.

22. "French Minister Sees U.S. Business Spying," *Reuters*, February 23, 2000.

23. William Drozdiak, "A Suspicious Eye on U.S. 'Big Ears,'" *Washington Post* Foreign Service, July 24, 2000.

Chapter 5

1. Avery Dennison Annual Report (2000); <www.averydennison.com>.
2. <www.averydennison.com>
3. P.Y. Yang, in a message; public documents
4. <www.fourpillars.com.tw>
5. The other three were C.C. Young, C.Y. Cheng, and Y.T. Hsieh.
6. S.Y. Wang, T. Chou, and C.B. Wan.
7. <www.fourpillars.com.tw>
8. Ho-ming Lin and Chen-wei Chang, "Patent Suit Made Pen-yen a Celebrity," *United Daily News,* September 7, 1997.
9. Ibid.

Chapter 6

1. Neal Wolin, Ibid.
2. Peter Schweitzer, *Friendly Spies: How America's Allies Are Using Economic Espionage to Steal Our Secrets* (New York: Atlantic Monthly Press, 1993).
3. *Risky Business: The Threat from Economic Espionage,* Ibid.
4. Senate Select Committee on Intelligence; Senate Committee on the Judiciary, Ibid.
5. *Congressional Record,* 104th Cong., 2nd sess., October 2, 1996.
6. Ibid.
7. Charles Piller, "High Tech's Distrust of FBI Could Impede Hacking Probe," *Los Angeles Times,* February 11, 2000.
8. Ibid.
9. Neil A. Lewis, "Internet Executives Are Reassured after White House Meeting," *The New York Times,* February 16, 2000.

Chapter 7

1. Annette Haddad and Scott Doggett, "In Industrial Spy Cases, It's Those Americans That You Have to Watch," *Los Angeles Times,* October 25, 1999.
2. *United States v. Hsu,* relevant court documents; *The Corporate Counselor* (November 1997).
3. *United States v. Pin Yeng [sic] Yang, Hwei Chen Yang* (1997), testimony of Michael Bartholomew.
4. The voluminous list that follows is taken from a combination of sources, including the confession and affidavit of Tenhong "Victor" Lee, Ph.D., the affidavit of FBI Special Agent Michael Bartholomew, relevant court documents, and the courtroom testimony of Dr. Lee. All

of the documents agree on the essentials of what Dr. Lee confessed to having stolen and sent to Four Pillars during the time indicated. To facilitate the flow of the narrative in this section, I have borrowed liberally from the public documents cited, going back and forth from one document to another, without specific citations. All of the references and allegations as to who at Four Pillars received specific documents or attended specific meetings, as well as how the company used and/ or benefitted from the material Dr. Lee confessed to having sent, is based on Dr. Lee's confession, various Avery Dennison civil litigation papers, Justice Department documents and courtroom presentation during the criminal phase of the proceedings, and the courtroom testimony of Dr. Lee.

5. Tenhong Lee, affidavit.

6. Lawrence C. Mitchell, Ph.D., affidavit.

7. *Avery Dennison Corporation v. Four Pillars, et al* (1998), court documents.

8. The full list of what Victor stole is, by its very nature, highly technical, and I have attempted to simplify it as much as possible for the lay reader. I have tried to show, where relevant and where not otherwise obvious, how a proficient competitor could benefit from the trade secrets Victor stole from Avery Dennison. If I have oversimplified, it is for the sake of readability, and I ask the technically proficient readers for their tolerance.

Chapter 8

1. Karen Kaplan, "A Bad Day for Tech: 31,000 Jobs Slashed," *Los Angeles Times,* July 27, 2001.

2. Evelyn Iritani, "In Global Economy, U.S. Job Gains, Losses Know No Borders," *Los Angeles Times,* April 6, 2001.

3. U.S. Department of Labor, Bureau of Labor Statistics report, April 6, 2001.

4. Alex Berenson, "Questions of Firing and Severance at Computer Associates," *The New York Times,* March 20, 2001.

5. Maureen Dowd, "The Asbestos President," *The New York Times,* April 1, 2001.

6. Carol J. Williams, "Anger Erupts over U.S. Move to Controls on Emissions," *Los Angeles Times,* March 31, 2001.

7. Ibid.

8. Editorial, "A Dirty Business: Mr. Bush Has Put U.S. Credibility on the Line," *The Guardian,* March 30, 2001.

9. Polly Toynbee, "America the Horrible Is Now Turning into a Pariah," *The Guardian,* April 4, 2001.

10. Editorial, "Environmental Rollbacks," *The New York Times*, April 8, 2001.

11. Editorial, "Revolt at the U.N.," *The New York Times*, May 5, 2001.

12. Editorial, "Snub at the U.N.," *Los Angeles Times*, May 6, 2001.

13. The Associated Press, "China Press Revels in U.S. Loss," May 5, 2001.

14. Robin Wright, "U.S. Has Lost Not 1 but 2 Seats on Key U.N. Panels," *Los Angeles Times*, May 8, 2001.

15. Ibid.

16. "Snub at the U.N.," Ibid.

Chapter 9

1. An extensive list of Avery Dennison's major customers and partners is available on the company's Web site <www.averydennison.com> as well as in its annual reports.

Chapter 10

1. The Associated Press, "Welsh Credit Card Hacker Sentenced," July 6, 2001.

2. Kevin Mitnick, interviewed by Ed Bradley, *60 Minutes*, January 2000.

3. Ibid.

4. Thomas L. Friedman, "Digital Defense," *The New York Times*, July 27, 2001.

5. David Schindler, interviewed by the author, May 24, 2001.

6. Computer Science Institute and the San Francisco FBI Computer Intrusion Squad, sixth annual survey (March 2001).

7. Janet Reno, speech before a national conference of technology executives and law enforcement authorities (Herndon, VA: June 19, 2000).

8. Louis Freeh, statement at the InfraGard rollout announcement, January 5, 2001.

9. Don Ulsch, interviewed by the author, April 13, 2001.

10. Rachel Konrad, "Leaks and Geeks: International Espionage Goes High-Tech," CNET News.com, June 29, 2000.

11. The Associated Press, "Noted Hacker Speaks before Senate Panel," March 2, 2000.

12. Kevin Mitnick, interviewed by Ed Bradley, *60 Minutes*, January 2000.

13. The Associated Press, Ibid.

14. Ashley Dunn and Charles Piller, "Hacker Tapped into Microsoft for 3 Months," *Los Angeles Times,* October 28, 2000.

15. John Markoff and John Schwartz, "Microsoft Says Online Break-In Lasted 6 Weeks," *The New York Times,* October 28, 2000.

Chapter 11

1. Charles D. Miller, letter to Avery Dennison employees, September 5, 1997.

Chapter 12

1. Brian O'Connor, interviewed by the author, May 4, 2001, provided or verified much of the information in this chapter.

2. Eric Herman, "Kodak Undercover," *Corporate Counsel Magazine* (December 1997) is an excellent recap of this case from a legal perspective. Herman makes the point that, "Georgia law generally permits the videotaping of unknowing subjects during meetings of two or more people, when the participants have given up their expectation of privacy." Of two sting meetings, only the Atlanta meeting was recorded.

Chapter 13

1. Judge Economous, in a confusing decision during the trial, ultimately ruled the patent application had no value as a trade secret. That ruling in large measure formed the basis for an appeal by the Yangs before the Sixth Circuit Court of Appeals in June 2001. The government vigorously argued the precedent set in the Third Circuit Court of Appeals in the Taxol case, but each Circuit forms its own decisions.

Chapter 14

1. Uri Landesman, chief investment officer of AFA Management Parnters, as quoted in "Lucent CFO Resigns after 1 Year on Job," *Los Angeles Times,* May 7, 2001.

2. Simon Romero, "3 Charged with Giving Lucent Secrets to China," *The New York Times,* May 4, 2001.

3. Bill Price, interviewed by the author, May 8, 2001.

Chapter 15

1. Avery Dennison news release confirming economic espionage activities and filing of the civil suit.

Chapter 16

1. *United States v. Takashi Okamoto and Hiroaki Serizawa* (2001).

2. Press release, "First Foreign Economic Espionage Indictment; Defendents Steal Trade Secrets from Cleveland Clinic Foundation." U.S. Dept. of Justice, U.S. Attorney, Northern District of Ohio, May 8, 2001.

3. Robert Wallace, interviewed by the author, May 18, 2001.

SECTION TWO

Chapter 18

1. ASIS and Pricewaterhouse Coopers survey, "Trends in Proprietary Information Loss" (taken in 1999, released in 2001). My comments reflect only a summary of several relevant aspects that the survey touched on. For a complete copy of the survey, visit the ASIS Web site <www.asisonline.org>.

2. *Law and Policy International Business,* January 1995.

3. ASIS and Pricewaterhouse Coopers survey, Ibid.

4. Full disclosure: My firm, Lexicon Communications, originated the concept of crisis insurance and presented it to AIG many years ago. Today, we are one of about a half-dozen other firms who are on the pre-approved panel.

Chapter 19

1. Steven Fink, *Crisis Management: Planning for the Inevitable* (New York: AMACOM–1986, iUniverse–2000), 203-218.

2. P.Y. Yang, correspondence to Alan Campbell, January 4, 1994.

3. Alan Campbell, correspondence to P.Y. Yang, June 14, 1994.

4. Dean Starkman, "Secrets and Lies: the Dual Career of a Corporate Spy," *The Wall Street Journal,* October 23, 1997.

5. Widely quoted in many news stories, including "Avery Dennison Sued over Aborted Asian Joint Venture," *Bloomberg News,* January 5, 1999.

6. The Associated Press, "Avery Dennison Accused of Stealing," January 5, 1999.

7. Ibid.

Chapter 22

1. Thomas L. Friedman, Ibid., 221.

2. Federal Sentencing Guidelines, <www.ussc.gov/1998guid/98chap 8.htm>, May 24, 2001.

3. Dr. Ted Fraumann, interviewed by the author, March 22, 2001; Edwin Fraumann and Joseph Koletar, "Trade Secret Safeguards," *Security Management* (March 1999).

4. There are many places to turn for these sorts of checklists, and a competent intellectual property attorney is one. Another excellent resource, from which a portion of this list emanated, is the Web site of intellectual property lawyer R. Mark Halligan <www.execpc.com/~m hallign>.

5. Fraumann and Koletar, Ibid.

6. Thomas L. Friedman, Ibid., 222.

Chapter 23

1. Avery Dennison news release, "Four Pillars Distributes Inaccurate News Release in Violation of the Court's Admonition," April 1, 1999.

Chapter 24

1. *United States v. Estrada;* William K. Rashbaum, "Food Worker Is Accused of Corporate Espionage," *The New York Times,* March 22, 2001.

2. Larry Neumesiter, "Credit Worker Accused of Espionage," The Associated Press, March 22, 2001.

3. *United States v. Caryn L. Camp and Stephen R. Martin,* grand jury indictment (1998); Donan Deady, IDEXX general counsel, interviewed by the author, May 11, 2001.

4. Department of Justice sources and Web site <www.usdoj.gov>; Chris Carr, Jack Morton, and Jerry Furniss, "The Economic Espionage Act: Bear Trap or Mousetrap," *The Texas Intellectual Property Law Journal* (winter 2000): 185; FBI personnel, interviewed by the author.

5. Department of Justice sources and Web site <www.usdoj.gov>; Carr, Morton, and Furniss, Ibid., 185-186.

6. Department of Justice sources and Web site <www.usdoj.gov>; Carr, Morton, and Furniss, Ibid., 190.

7. Department of Justice sources, grand jury presentment, Web site, and news release.

8. Ibid.; Carr, Morton, and Furniss, Ibid., 195; Halligan Web site <www.execpc.com/~mhallign>.

Chapter 26

1. Michael Mee, FBI special agent, interviewed by the author, March 30, 2001; Dr. Edwin Fraumann, interviewed by the author, March 22, 2001.

2. Ira Winkler, *Corporate Espionage* (Rocklin, CA: Prima Publishing, 1997).

Chapter 29

1. Mark Zwillinger, interviewed by the author, July 10, and July 12, 2001.

Afterword

1. Richard J. Heffernan, interviewed by the author, May 24, 2001.

INDEX

A

Acutane, 235
Adhesives, 61, 62–63
Adirondack Workbooks, 70
Administrative information, 229
Administrative precautions, 284–85
Advisories, 40–41
Affleck, John, 217, 242–43
Agfa, 141, 143
AIG, 199
Airbus, 53
Albright, Madeleine, 110
Alcatel, 172
Allen, Thomas E., 31–32
Alzheimer's disease research, 180–83
Amazon, 75, 126
Ambrose, Stephen, 35, 36
American Foreign Policy Council, 44, 50
American Safety Razor, 82
American Society of Industrial Security (ASIS)
    economic espionage costs, 7, 193
    foreign risk, 51
    proprietary information loss trends, 194, 196–200, 284–85
    trade secret thieves, 266
Amgen, 49–50, 271
Analysis paralysis, 134
Animal health industry, 251
ANSIR. *See* Awareness of National Security Issues and Response
AOL Time Warner, 102
Arlon, 28, 29
Asia Pacific Resources, 145
ASIS. *See* American Society of Industrial Security
Associated Press, 109, 217, 242

AT&T, 130, 165
Atlanta Journal-Constitution, 252
Attitudes, 284–85
Audit, 227–29
Avery, R. Stanton, 57–58, 60–61
Avery Dennison
    Annual Technical Symposium, 92, 93, 98
    Aquarius Project, 98
    betrayal, xviii–xix
    civil suit, 290–91
    communication plan, 135–39, 173–78, 188–90
    company history, 57–61
    competitive benchmarking reports, 95
    consumer goods products, 114
    corporate manufacturing clients, 114
    creditor's suit, 291
    crisis management, 113–18
    customers, 176
    employee notification, 137–38
    employment issues, 26–31
    emulsion adhesives, 88
    espionage cost to, 176
    Fasson Roll Division, 24, 31, 89, 91, 98, 204
    FBI sting, 155–64
    high-speed release technology, 90, 91, 94, 95
    hotmelt technology, 89, 93
    industry use of products, 59–60
    joint venture discussions, 26, 66–67, 96, 202–4, 208–10
    label, 61–64
    lawsuit against, 208–10
    litigation difficulties, 16
    mastercurves, 24, 87–89
    Materials Group, 27, 204

315

STICKY FINGERS

For special discounts on 20 or more copies of *Sticky Fingers: Managing the Global Risk of Economic Espionage,* please call Dearborn Trade Special Sales at 800-621-9621, extension 4410.

Dearborn™
Trade Publishing
A **Kaplan Professional** Company